Students' Mental Health Needs

Students' Mental Health Needs

Problems and Responses

Edited by Nicky Stanley and Jill Manthorpe

Foreword by Barbara Waters

Jessica Kinglsey Publishers
London and Philadelphia

First published in the United Kingdom in 2002
by Jessica Kingsley Publishers Ltd
116 Pentonville Road
London N1 9JB, England
and
325 Chestnut Street
Philadelphia, PA 19106, USA

www.jkp.com

Copyright © Jessica Kingsley Publishers 2002

Library of Congress Cataloging in Publication Data

Students' mental health needs / edited by Nicky Stanley and Jill Manthorpe; foreword by Barbara Waters.
    p. cm.
  Includes bibliographical references and index.
  ISBN 1-85302-983-1 (pbk : alk. paper)
  1. College students--Mental health. 2. College students--Mental health services
 3. Students--Mental health services. 4. Crisis intervention (Mental health services) I.
Stanley, Nicky, 1955- II. Manthorpe, Jill, 1955-

RC451.4.S7 S78 2002
378.1'9713--dc21
                                                                                    2001054526
British Library Cataloguing in Publication Data
A CIP catalogue record for this book is available from the British Library

ISBN 1 85302 983 1

Printed and Bound in Great Britain
by Athenaeum Press, Gateshead, Tyne and Wear

Contents

Part Three: Identifying Effective Responses

List of Tables

List of Figures

Foreword

The opportunity to engage with learning throughout life is a necessity in our rapidly changing world. Lifelong learning both increases our skills and knowledge and helps us deal with the demands of everyday life. Providing opportunities for students with all kinds of disabilities to continue their studies beyond school is central to Skill's mission; that is why I am delighted to introduce this book. It gives much needed insight into the complexities of providing support to individuals and to planning and delivering education that is flexible and inclusive for learners who have experienced mental health problems. It deals with subjects we all find uncomfortable at times, and debunks many commonly held misconceptions about mental ill health.

It is becoming better recognised that students with hidden disabilities may require support that is less easy to quantify than physical adaptations to meet the needs of students with physical and sensory impairments. Institutions need to concentrate on raising awareness, across both teaching and non-teaching departments, to change the environment to one within which students can bring forward their problems and express their needs. The work undertaken by Nicky Stanley and Jill Manthorpe and other Higher Education Funding Council for England funded projects has created greater awareness of the involvement of educational professionals in student well-being and improved recognition of the existence of discrimination. In the case of students with mental health problems this discrimination has its roots in the portrayal of mental illness as scary, out of control and ultimately violent. Many studies have shown that the greatest danger posed by someone with a mental health problem is to themselves. (The much-needed chapters on student suicide will be helpful to all those who have to deal with this most distressing human act.)

The introduction of the Human Rights Act 1998 and the inclusion of education in Part IV of the Disability Discrimination Act 1995 clearly make discrimination unlawful. The latter puts a much clearer responsibility on education institutions not to discriminate against students with disabilities and to avoid their unlawful exclusion. Particularly welcome is the requirement under the Disability Discrimination Act for education institutions to anticipate the needs of disabled students in all areas of planning and delivery of education. This represents a welcome and much-needed shift from the medical model of disability where the problems are seen to be located in the individual, to a more responsible social model, which is explored in this book.

The Tomlinson (FEFC 1996) report, *Inclusive Learning*, looked at the needs of students with disabilities and learning difficulties in further education in England, and described the need to 'focus on the capacity of the educational institution to understand and respond to the individual learner's requirement' (p. 4). This report identified a clear difference between 'offering courses of education and training and then giving some students additional human or physical aids to gain access', and 'redesigning the very processes of learning, assessment and organisation so as to fit the objectives and learning styles of the students' (p. 4). The report argued that only this second approach was truly inclusive. Within higher education there is now more recognition that a similar approach is needed, and work is going on throughout the UK to make subject areas more accessible. Recent initiatives to improve quality, for example, the Quality Assurance Agency code of practice for students with disabilities and the Further Education Funding Council's quality initiative, have raised the profile of disabled students' support needs.

This emphasis on the student at the centre of the process enables us to listen more clearly to the student voice. For those with mental health problems the opportunity to explain their difficulties and identify how support can be most appropriately given will contribute to their ability to continue their studies. Working in partnership with families, community health services and voluntary sector support groups will enable the development of a network of responses through which flexibility can be negotiated and practical difficulties resolved. For example, an advocate from a voluntary organisation can act on behalf of the student to assist in agreeing and supporting work timetables. A housing association providing somewhere stable to live and good information on local support could make all the difference or alternatively could offer support to hall of residence staff so that the student does not have to leave familiar surroundings at the point when they are most vulnerable. Higher education institutions themselves should be aware of the regulations with regard to welfare benefits and be willing to use their discretion to provide financial support from hardship funds.

These actions are complex and harder to achieve because they require co-operation from those who would not naturally be part of the same team. They constitute a fundamental shift towards removing barriers that prevent disabled people from using their skills and abilities. Working in this way will contribute to the holistic approach that the anticipatory requirements of Part IV (education) of the Disability Discrimination Act are designed to promote.

In his report, *Implementing Inclusiveness* (1999), Robert Beattie identified the transition for young people with disabilities in Scotland as 'not a straight line from school to education, training and subsequently to work. By the very nature of their problems they live uncertain lives' (p.iii). Dealing with this uncertainty is at the very heart of this book. Readers will find it helpful and informative. I hope they will develop from it action plans for their own situation that will provide the support and guidance needed by students with mental health problems and those who work with them.

Barbara Waters
Chief Executive
Skill: National Bureau for Students with Disabilities
2001

References

Beattie, R. (1999) *Implementing Inclusiveness: Realising Potential.* Edinburgh: Scottish Executive.

Further Education Funding Council (1996) *Inclusive Learning Principles and Recommendations: A Summary of the Findings of the Learning Difficulties and / or Disabilities Committee.* Coventry: FEFC.

*This book is dedicated to the memory of David Brandon,
an inspiring teacher and campaigner,
who died in 2001 after a short illness.*

Chapter 1

Introduction

Constructing the Framework

Jill Manthorpe and Nicky Stanley

Introduction

A high proportion of those studying or working in higher education will encounter students with mental health problems. This book is explicitly addressed to those employed in higher education institutions (HEIs) but argues that these include academic, administrative and student support staff as well as those working in traditional welfare roles within higher education, such as counselling or chaplaincy services. We take this broad approach because we consider the needs of students with mental health difficulties to be relevant to their participation in student life as a whole. Moreover, for those students who develop mental health problems while studying, an institution-wide approach to their support helps to create an effective and co-ordinated response.

This book aims to both examine the needs of students with mental health problems and to offer ideas and examples of effective responses. Mental health emerged during the 1990s as a key element of the UK government's initiative to improve the health of the nation. In parallel, policies and services have stressed the importance of including people with disabilities (including mental health problems) in education and employment. Social inclusion theories, government policies and anti-discriminatory legislation have provided a means of widening the debate about disability beyond an individualised model which stresses treatment and segregated provision of support and services.

Much has been made of the need for higher education to address issues of class and gender, and to improve access for groups who have traditionally been excluded from participation. Disabled students have pointed to the very real barriers constructed by HEIs which make the physical environment inaccessible and reinforce the negative attitudes which impede the development of appropriate support and flexible learning methods. Students who have acquired disability while attending HEIs, particularly mental health problems, may feel that they have been treated unfairly and discriminated against. This book provides a range of experiences which can stimulate thinking and planning within HEIs to attract and sustain those who wish to learn as students, with long-term, recent or current mental health needs.

This introductory chapter sets the scene for the book. It starts with an overview of the challenges which the contributors have identified and provides a context for their discussion. It identifies a key series of policy initiatives which have arisen in response to criticisms launched against higher education in the UK. Such criticisms have focused on the failure to fully embrace comments on the opportunities and challenges arising from a major expansion of and rethinking about the role of higher education. They have come from campaigning organisations outside the sector, such as Skill (the National Bureau for Students with Disabilities) but also from within. The influential Dearing Report (1997) drew the attention of government to the under-representation of a range of groups, including disabled people, within higher education.

This chapter then outlines findings from a research study undertaken by the authors that explores responses to students' mental health needs, and directs attention to the way HEI staff are combining pastoral and academic roles. It draws out specific points relevant to international students, those engaged in professional education and academic staff's communication within their own HEI and beyond. We also consider the implications for staff support, and for non-academic as well as teaching staff. Many of these themes are taken up in the book by other contributors and, while each chapter may be read on its own, there are many useful cross-references which relate to the variety of responses available.

Promoting diversity

Higher education's ability and willingness to open its doors to students with disabilities have been radically altered by policies that locate access to higher education within a legal framework. From September 2002, the Disability Discrimination Act 1995 is extended to higher education, with provision relating to additional aids and physical adaptations being implemented in 2003 and 2005. However, funding councils already had a duty to have regard to the needs of disabled students (DfEE 1999, p.61) HEIs have had their duties explicitly framed in a code of practice issued by the Quality Assurance Agency for Higher Education (1999) together with a guidance document on base-level provision for disabled students (HEFCE 1999).

Both documents incorporated the needs of students with mental health problems within overall provision for disabled students. The HEFCE report noted a 'patchy' picture and variable progress in measures to support disabled students (paras. 16–17). Nonetheless, it acknowledged a growth in numbers, with increases ranging from 10 per cent to 105 per cent and ascribed these to:

- policy changes and a higher profile for disability
- improved access and support services
- the impact of the Disabled Students Allowance
- increases in staff support and expertise
- better relationships between HEIs and other education providers
- the recognition of dyslexia
- 'word of mouth' encouragement.

(para. 24)

This combination of push and pull factors paints a picture of demand from disabled students and a recognition by the higher education sector that it must respond to this in conjunction with pressures from central government. The HEFCE guidance also noted that many HEIs report expanding numbers of students with mental health problems. These, it argued, should be responded to by a level of services which, at their minimum or base-line, should include: encouragement to students to air their problems, help to find appropriate support, and the possible involvement of mental health specialists in assessment. Practically and administratively, students with mental health problems were seen to require flexibility and adjustment. It suggested, however, that their needs may encompass more than responses from learning support, 'since behaviour affects all aspects of an institution' (HEFCE 1999 para.37(d)). Interestingly, in contrast to the sections on physical disability, no mention is made of staff receiving training in this area, nor the creative responses identified in published work.

While these documents have incorporated students' mental health needs into the definition of student disability, two further publications have sought to draw attention to mental health problems in HEIs as an issue requiring a specific response. The publication of *Degrees of Disturbance: The New Agenda* (Rana *et al.* 1999), a report from the heads of university counselling services, was the outcome of increasingly high levels of emotional and behavioural disturbance recorded in the annual reports of counselling services in the 1990s. The report identified the pressures on students, noted the decline of the personal tutorial system and called for a full acknowledgement of the resource implications of mental health problems in the student population.

This report was followed in 2000 by the CVCP's (Committee of Vice-Chancellors and Principals, now renamed as Universities UK) *Guidelines on Student Mental Health Policies and Procedures for Higher Education*. The significance of these guidelines resides largely in their formal recognition of students' mental health needs as an area where HEIs should acknowledge ownership and be proactive in developing responsive systems. The guidelines focus heavily on the concept of 'duty of care', which is defined as constituting part of the contract between the student and the institution. This is located in a legal rather than a welfare framework, with many references to the HEI's potential liability in relation to students with mental health problems. These guidelines highlighted the need for training to ensure that a wide range of relevant staff were made aware of clearly defined procedures for supporting and referring students with mental health problems. While an emphasis on the legal implications of failing to provide adequate standards of support clearly aimed to promote a response from HEIs (Universities UK has no authority to enforce these guidelines), this publication, coming from within the HEI sector, stressed the institution's liability rather than the student's rights.

Responding to the challenge of mental health

For many of those working in higher education, the experience of academic life is changing. The expansion of student numbers and the move to university status for many institutions within higher education (chronicled by the Dearing Report 1997) has resulted in a diverse student population, comprising:

- traditional A/AS and higher level entrants, aged 18+

- mature students

- part-time students

- those living at home

- international students – for short or long-term periods of study

- those on professional programmes.

This population is heterogeneous and fragmented. It includes many who are first-generation entrants to higher education.

In terms of the capacity of higher education, such expansion in student numbers has not been accompanied by commensurate increases in staffing or resources. A growth in modular programmes and a decline in staff:student contact have been exacerbated by pressures on academic staff to be research 'active', to generate income and to respond to a plethora of quality assurance demands. Such changes within HEIs make it difficult for the organisation to rely on individuals' 'goodwill' to deliver an effective and consistent response to disability. Resource issues are also relevant to students, and the issue of student financial hardship is particularly addressed by Roberts and Zelenyanszki in Chapter 6. As they demonstrate, financial hardship may contribute to stress and health problems. Such pressures may also compel students to choose programmes of study which are short or part-time, or situated in areas close to home or to other sources of financial or practical support. We have yet to discover the full impact of funding issues on those who have been discouraged from entering higher education.

Despite these difficulties, it is important to outline the very real advantages of higher education. As a passport to success, as well as for its inherent academic and personal opportunities, higher education remains a valued prize. It provides opportunities for creativity, reflection, socialisation and development. For those who have had earlier problems with health or learning, it can offer a fresh start or a chance to develop confidence and self-esteem.

Disabled students, therefore, are the focus of policies in respect of education and employment as well as disability and social inclusion. To achieve student status is significant in terms of rehabilitation, but also in relation to their engagement with or reintegration into the world of work and self-sufficiency. Both debates can draw on the discourse of social inclusion to provide a value-base and legitimacy for action and expenditure.

At the level of policy implementation, HEIs have generally been seen as repositories of expertise around higher education, and have been relatively closed systems. Disability has compelled them to seek partnerships with other sources of expertise. As the contributors to this book argue, one of the indications of a successful approach to meeting the needs of students with mental health problems is the ability of the HEI to forge alliances with experts, informal groupings and the health and welfare sectors. In the next section, we report on a research project undertaken at the University of Hull which explored this theme in relation to the role of the personal tutor or supervisor. This project, which is described more fully elsewhere (Stanley *et al.* 2000), provided the genesis for this book and identified a number of the themes fully explored in the chapters that follow.

Researching student mental health needs

A number of projects funded under the Special Initiative to Encourage High Quality Provision for Students with Learning Difficulties and Disabilities (funded by HEFCE from 1996 to 1999) chose to direct their attention to mental health. The work of these projects is summarised in an appendix to the CVCP guidelines. At the University of Hull, this focus derived from the project team's own experiences as academics who had worked with a number of students with declared or suspected mental health problems. When allied to an academic interest in community services for people with mental health problems, these two elements suggested the need to make sense of anecdotal experience. As the HEFCE report had indicated, there was a general feeling that more students were showing evidence of mental health problems. Reports from HEI counselling services (Phippen 1995) were also indicating that increased numbers of students with severe mental health problems were being identified. The research was conceived as a means of exploring academic staff's perceptions of the extent and type of difficulties, but also to examine what seemed to constitute an effective institutional response. The first stage of the project involved the design and distribution of a survey to all academic staff at the University of Hull (response rate 76% n = 429).

Over a third (35%) of respondents reported their experience of supervising students with a mental health problem in the previous five years. They were asked to categorise the problems they had come across according to the degree of severity, and to exclude those that involved only drug or alcohol misuse. Sixty per cent of problems encountered were classified as minor mental health problems, while 28 per cent were described as 'severe' or 'life threatening'. Although such figures are the product of lay judgements rather than clinical diagnosis, they serve to communicate the extent to which academic staff experienced students' behaviour as distressing and anxiety provoking.

While these figures were drawn from one HEI, feedback from focus group participants and from staff at other HEIs where the project's training programme was later delivered, indicated that the experience of staff surveyed at the University of Hull was not significantly different from that of staff in other institutions. Many of the difficulties encountered by personal supervisors at Hull were familiar to those elsewhere. The research was considered valuable by staff in other HEIs in that it opened up an area for discussion which, although a source of considerable concern, was rarely addressed outside the context of individual students' problems.

The range of groups and individuals with whom supervisors had had contact in the course of their attempts to support students with mental health problems indicated that the University's on-campus counselling service played a significant role in supporting students, but that other key contacts were students' friends, family, hall wardens and GPs (see Table 1.1). It was evident that, despite concerns about confidentiality and students' status as independent adults, there was a significant degree of contact with students' families. Friends and flatmates also emerged as significant sources of information and support; one supervisor commenting: 'Friends gave me a better picture of the circumstances than anyone else and gave the most valuable picture of the student, especially in the most serious case…' Such evidence suggests the importance of targeting awareness-raising initiatives in the field of mental health at the student population as a whole, rather than focusing on 'vulnerable students'.

Table 1.1. Supervisors' contact with agencies and individuals

Individual / organisation	Supervisors reporting contact
University counselling service	105
Other counselling service	21
Students' friends/flatmates	66
Students' family	51
Hall warden/tutor	47
GP	55
Psychiatrist	21
Community psychiatric nurse	12

Supervisors were asked to identify what had proved helpful to them in attempting to support students with mental health problems (see Table 1.2).

Table 1.2. Helpful factors identified by supervisors	
	% of respondents
Accessibility of university counselling service	30%
Supervisor's personal skills/experience	30%
Support from colleagues	18%
Time to talk to student	16%
Access to specialist/medical help	16%
Students' friends or family	13%
Nothing	9%

The responses highlighted the accessibility of the university counselling service. Academics were clearly relieved to be able to refer students to someone with expertise:

> I was told by the student that the counselling service was very helpful. I appreciated the fact that when I phoned from my office with him present they gave him an immediate appointment. (Personal Supervisor)

There were also examples of the counselling service being used in a consultative capacity by the academic staff:

> The student counselling service was very helpful and suggested a specific approach. Their suggestion that I should give a very difficult student a specific time in which to come and discuss problems with me proved invaluable. (Personal Supervisor)

Supervisors had acquired their personal skills and experience from a variety of sources. Academics teaching in the fields of psychology, social work and nursing were particularly well represented in this group of respondents, and identified their professional training as relevant to the task of personal supervision: 'My nursing background in communication skills and also an awareness of my own limitations, i.e., when to involve another agency'. (Lecturer in Nursing) However, a number of those academics who felt confident about their skills and experience had acquired this confidence 'on the job', as a personal supervisor:

> I was aware that talking to someone and being listened to was often useful in its own right and I always made it clear that I could not solve their problems for them. (Personal Supervisor)

This lecturer appeared to have a good understanding of both the need for sympathetic listening and of the boundaries to the role of personal supervisor. The training programme for HEI staff developed by the project aimed to communicate both that the task of personal supervision did not entail specialist counselling, but encompassed skills which staff were already using, as well as a clear understanding of the limitations of their roles and a knowledge of referral routes.

Table 1.3. Difficulties identified by supervisors	
	% of respondents
Student unable to see problem/accept help/inaccessible	27%
Supervisor's lack of personal knowledge/skills/experience	26%
Problems with confidentiality	22%
Lack of support from colleagues/others	11%
Lack of time	10%
Role confusion	10%

However, it was clear from the difficulties identified by personal supervisors (see Table 1.3 above) that many lacked confidence in their ability to respond effectively to students with mental health problems:

A total lack of professional ability to deal with the case. I think I handled it quite well, on the basis of common sense, but I lacked the confidence that I was doing the right thing. (Personal Supervisor)

The difficulty most frequently experienced by supervisors was students' inability to acknowledge their problems or to accept help. The stigma conferred by mental health problems was seen as contributing to such problems:

The students were extremely reticent about using the university counselling service, saw it as having a stigma attached as well as the very public entrance to the offices. Also one student did not want me to contact professionals, he wanted it kept within his family. (Personal Supervisor)

The stigma attached to using formal services provides a strong argument for protecting the role and function of the academic supervisor or tutor who provides a front-line, non-stigmatised form of support for all students. Academics also acknowledged that mental health problems might impact on an individual's capacity to communicate their distress:

Student reluctance to accept the need for psychiatric help of any sort. It is often difficult to get in contact with, for example, severely depressed students as they do not respond to initiatives. (Personal Supervisor)

Problems with confidentiality have been identified as a major issue in the effective delivery of community mental health services. In the HEI setting, personal supervisors found that confidentiality codes blocked communication and that they often failed to receive feedback following a referral: 'The counselling service was very reluctant to discuss cases, even in confidence. The GP was not really responsive either.' (Personal Supervisor) However, supervisors were also uncertain as to how they should protect students' rights to confidentiality: 'It's sometimes difficult to help a student by pleading mitigating circumstances in the academic context and to maintain confidentiality.' (Personal Supervisor)

It was clear from the survey that academics frequently felt unsupported in their roles as personal supervisors. Some lacked time to do the job adequately and were confused about conflicting demands placed upon them; some described difficulties in accessing help both from within and from outside the HEI:

> Getting effective help, in the more serious cases, from some outside agencies. Despite obvious and serious deterioration in one student's mental health, there seemed to be a reluctance to take effective action until a serious and life-threatening incident had actually occurred. One felt isolated and left to get on with it oneself. (Personal Supervisor)

A local response to the findings of this survey has been the appointment of a disabilities co-ordinator with responsibility for mental health at the University of Hull. The co-ordinator is able to offer individual members of staff support and advice in responding to students with mental health problems, in addition to working directly with students. She also has a brief to improve and develop communication with community mental health services.

One of the characteristics of mental health problems is that they are negatively perceived. A climate of concern about 'madness' has been fuelled in the UK by media and policy focus on rare instances of homicide by people with a mental health problem and the failings of judicial and support systems to provide safe care in the community. HEIs are not immune to such public fears and debates, and a key aspect of the mental health co-ordinator's role is to challenge stereotypes and raise awareness on campus of mental health needs. Events and campaigns have been targeted at the full range of staff and students.

This research aimed to explore a variety of perspectives other than that of academic supervisors. In considering the HEI as a system, it was evident that secretarial and administrative staff could play a major role as they were often the public and most accessible face of the institution. While not having formal pastoral responsibilities, they could take on an important mediating role in delivering messages and communicating concerns to staff. In a focus group composed of secretaries and administrative staff, they identified a need to know more about referral routes and to receive training. Their role in supporting students was undervalued in their view and rarely recognised. At times however, it could be stressful. As Chapter 13 on student suicide explores later, their position may be overlooked, and offers to help them may not be thought of as relevant.

This research also considered the perspective of international students through a focus group that offered them the opportunity to share ideas

with academic and student support staff. Work on cross-cultural awareness and counselling suggested that the staff-student relationship might
be more prone to misperception between people from different cultural
backgrounds, with different first languages, divergent approaches to
learning and teaching, and different perceptions of the academic supervisory relationship. Twelve focus group participants considered that reluctance to seek help with mental health problems could be compounded by
cultural differences. Some academics felt that, in the cases involving international students, they had not handled cultural issues well and that
cultural misinterpretations and differing communication styles had
affected their judgement of the severity of the mental health problem. One
respondent reflected that when international students showed signs of
mental distress he was worried about: '...the extent to which cultural
norms might influence behaviour and definitions of the "usual".' (Personal
Supervisor)

All students participating in the research voiced similar concerns
regarding the types of pressures that might contribute to the development
of mental health problems. They cited relationship problems, feelings of
isolation, academic pressures, financial difficulties and problems with
accommodation (these issues are discussed in more depth in later chapters
by Roberts and Zelenyanszki and by Jacobson). Some problems were
specific to international students; for example, many felt excluded from
relationships with 'home' students. Their perception was that relationships
rarely progressed beyond the superficial stage. Although they were many
months into their time at university, they felt that personal relationships
had not developed. 'It is difficult to know who is a friend', reflected one
student. Shared living space was frequently cited as an area which led to
considerable pressure. The predominance of alcohol in student culture
could lead international students to feel marginalised. Different learning
and teaching styles could also contribute to negative experiences. Vulnerability appeared heightened when there were political unrest and uncertainty at home. One international student said: 'It's about feeling out of
control and this can lead to mental health problems.'

Both groups of students wanted clear statements from the HEIs concerning the help on offer. Many international students preferred to receive

information verbally and for it to be repeated at regular intervals in face-to-face contact. Some international students were unimpressed by the formal welcome and receptions. They were viewed as lacking in substance, particularly if there was little follow-through after the event. One student described it thus: 'A red carpet was rolled out during induction and orientation week, but then put away and it was business as usual.' International students thought that HEIs could offer more tangible support. For example, they were concerned that there were no facilities on campus where they could go if they were mentally ill and needed something akin to an asylum. They also thought that accommodation should be planned in order to help redress feelings of loneliness, of being set apart from the main body of students. International students were unanimous in their view that HEIs should provide cultural awareness training for academic staff, since when it came to mental health issues, they thought that staff were likely to misread signs and potentially aggravate the situation. Such training is increasingly provided in a number of HEIs, but there is as yet little evidence that it succeeds in drawing on the range of programmes that have been developed in mental health services to address race issues and transcultural communication. If HEIs seek to develop a multicultural identity, the mental health needs of international students merit sustained attention.

Key themes arising from the research

Training

Throughout this project, the need for staff support was identified as central to their support of students with mental health problems. Staff identified their anxieties, the competing pressures on their time, and their worries about doing the 'right thing'. Their training and support needs have to be taken into account in developing support services for students. As this research indicates, joint training programmes for HEI staff with student support personnel can be one way of raising awareness and improving communication. In the training programmes commissioned following this research, for example, it was clear that many academics and student support staff were unknown to each other, communicated infrequently, and then only at times of difficulty or crisis.

Confidentiality

Barriers to communication were expressed by a range of participants in the research study outlined above, and appeared to parallel those experienced in mental health services in the community. The issue of confidentiality, for example, is problematic in seeking to defend or define the rights of individuals where communication between agencies and professionals is seen as beneficial. The duty of confidentiality to users of mental health services derives from the doctor–patient relationship and the recognition by the medical profession that assurances of confidentiality will be the bedrock of a trusting relationship. Such trust enables patients to fully disclose the extent and nature of their problems.

Similarly, student and supervisor relationships have an expectation of confidentiality; the student will expect discussions to be handled with discretion and that personal information will be treated with respect and not form the subject of gossip. However, just as medical confidentiality does not preclude a doctor from sharing information with the clinical team, so academics work in teams or departments. Students may find that information is scrutinised in a variety of forums. Some HEIs have tried to reduce the number of staff who are made aware of personal details by establishing sub-committees of examination boards, for example, or permitting general categories to indicate the basis for the mitigation claimed.

Issues of confidentiality are also exposed when there is fear that a person may cause harm to him/herself or to others. Principles in HEI counselling and medical services are similar to those operating in mental health services for adults. Good practice in respect of sharing of information between professionals and agencies and their co-operation in constructing and delivering care plans can make it difficult to uphold confidentiality (Szmukler and Holloway 2001). Academic staff may find it useful to discuss a student's circumstances with a colleague or member of the HEI's support services in order to assess whether there is cause for concern, or to identify particular needs for support.

The moral panic around mental health issues, however, has added a further dimension to this picture of constructive assistance. Students who have mental health problems may evoke fear among academic staff; fear of the unknown and fear linked to the spectre of mental illness conveyed by public and media presentations of those with mental health problems as out of control and potentially dangerous. Despite its structured informality, HEIs can be an environment with unspoken rules and expectations about conformity. Staff may seek to allay their own anxieties by treating matters as confidential to the staff group, or even the whole institution. Students may be unaware of the definition of confidentiality operating in their programmes, with broad variations according to staff culture and personal inclination.

Professional suitability and fitness

Institutional obligations and individual responsibility to students with mental health problems may be further complicated by programmes of study that contain or lead to professional qualifications. The Hull research pointed to the issue of professional suitability as a grey area in which a whole range of concerns about fitness to practise, professional competence and mental health were assuming significance in the efforts of academics to support students with problems (for a fuller discussion, see Manthorpe and Stanley 1999). These were particularly identified by those preparing students for the 'caring professions', such as nursing and social work, but also included those in the fields of teaching and law. Academics could feel a tension between their role as 'gate-keepers' to the profession and their desire to support students. Many have recognised the importance of encouraging those with mental health problems to enter work in the welfare field in order to provide positive role models and in the belief that their experiences and ability to critically evaluate professional services would contribute to the delivery and development of such support (Rooke-Matthews and Lindow 1998).

Some elements of broad discretion leading to confusion were identified in this research, and suggest that systems and procedures need to be clarified within professional circles and in conjunction with the higher education sector. Such systems need to cover matters of confidentiality and data protection, personal and professional accountability and in the area of information exchange, issues around references. While students with mental health problems are often seen in the context of their current studies, there are important issues in respect of what is conveyed by references, particularly as time passes. The influence of the Allitt report (Clothier 1994) has been to raise levels of anxiety regarding the content of references, since this report made a number of general but pointed criticisms of those that did not accurately reflect student mental health problems. Given the significance of references, it might be helpful for the sector to address staff responsibilities regarding entry to the professions, particularly for those in professional education. Questions of suitability and fitness also arise in the context of admission and selection procedures. Decision making in relation to disability in these areas has generally been conceived as a two-way conversation: student needs are communicated to the institution and a process of negotiation ensues. Mental health problems, however, as the HEFCE report observed, may be 'temporary, episodic and chronic conditions' (para. 37 (d)). Explicit material for those considering professional programmes of study might usefully take up the issue of mental health problems. Such developments need to involve professional training bodies and regulatory organisations. They need also to engage with the concerns from mental health service users that employment is one major area of social exclusion. Research from MIND, for example, showed that expectations of discrimination are high among people with mental health problems, with one study reporting that 69 per cent had been put off applying for jobs for fear of unfair treatment (Read and Baker 1996).

Hard-to-engage students

This research noted that those students who were 'hard to engage' often caused anxiety for staff. Staff felt that they were at times placed in a position where it was difficult to determine whether or not the student had problems. Cases where academic staff considered that there were problems, but students were not able to acknowledge this or accept help, were particularly worrying. Such situations caused staff to question whether disciplinary measures were appropriate or justified. Mental health services themselves have developed proactive strategies to engage with individuals who are assessed as needing contact with mental health professionals. Indeed, new proposals to amend mental health legislation in England and Wales will sanction greater powers for professionals to maintain contact and increase their powers of access to individuals (Department of Health 2000). This reduction in individual autonomy is significant but it is designed to apply to those at high risk of deterioration of health and to those who pose a risk of harm to themselves or to others. In higher education, a different environment, students have a relationship close to that of a consumer who is valued by the HEI and for whom mutual obligations are defined.

However, when there is evidence to suggest mental health problems, but students refuse help, staff are left with few options. In these situations academic staff may benefit from the advice and support of specialist student support staff such as counsellors or the disability co-ordinator for mental health. One outcome of the HEFCE-funded projects which addressed mental health and of the CVCP guidelines has been the development of policies on students' mental health needs in a number of HEIs. This process has produced some useful attempts to address the position of 'hard to engage' students, and these need to be evaluated.

About this book

Students' mental health problems are properly the concern of higher education systems. The HEI has a role in prevention, providing support and in offering a range of opportunities to enable students to participate in higher education. This issue is not restricted to individual problems and responses; nor should higher education institutions feel they are the only agencies with responsibility or functions. This book is firmly based upon a social model of disability which draws attention to rights rather than help or care (Shakespeare 2001) and emphasises the value of peer support and helping relationships. It is grounded in a systems perspective, encompassing the multiple agencies and roles involved in providing support for students and also seeing key themes such as blame, stigma and account-ability as relevant to the matter of disability support.

Part One of this book describes the experiences of students and their families. These are central to any debate; the 'user voice' perspective is now widely accepted as important in the design and delivery of all services. In Chapter 2, David Brandon and Jo Payne present experiences covering several decades and offer the opportunity to explore the perspectives of individuals. Their first-hand accounts are followed by James Wade, who uses students' own accounts to illustrate some of the important peer-support systems and relates the issue to students' own welfare provi-sion. In Chapter 4, Margaret Harvey brings together a number of accounts from parents whose children have taken their own lives while they were studying at university or further education college. Parents' perspectives offer the opportunity to consider the potential for families to provide support and to explore the changes in family relationships as children move away from the parental home to adult status.

Part Two of this book moves to examine mental health problems among students and contributory factors. Recent research from the Uni-versity of Leicester outlines the extent and nature of mental health problems, and is compared to American data. This report from one of the largest surveys of students in the UK provides extensive data to inform service provision. In Chapter 5, Annie Grant sets out some of the develop-ments at Leicester that occurred in response to the study. Chapter 6 follows with research data on students' financial position and the relationship of this to health problems, particularly alcohol use. Ron Roberts and Christiane Zelenyanszki have made critical developments in our under-standing of the pressures of student life and their wider structural and economic causes. Chapter 7 continues the health theme by exploring the primary care identification of students with mental health problems. Lionel Jacobson sets these in the context of primary care encounters with young people and the challenges posed by student mobility. In the final chapter of this section, Colin Lago explores the pattern of communication between higher education counselling services and mental health services in the community. Rather than seeing these as discrete systems, Lago identifies a number of channels of communication and also draws in family relationships as potentially important contributors to student support.

Part Three of this book provides a clear focus on effective responses to the difficulties presented and analysed. In Chapter 9, Barbara Rickinson and Jean Turner describe the systems and strategies identified as relevant in one university and the work of student services that have developed direct strategies in their support of students over time and in crisis. From the further education context, in Chapter 10 Kathryn James outlines an innovative support service that enables users of mental health services to participate in further education and alerts education providers to their own responsibilities in promoting access and mainstream support services. In Chapter 11, Graeme Whitfield and Chris Williams present further effective responses in the form of self-help material for students used in the context of a community mental health service. This chapter outlines the theory and rationale for self-help and behavioural approaches, particularly relevant to students with anxiety problems. Chapter 12 explores the influence of belief and spirituality on students' mental health with a contribution from a former university chaplain, Reverend Angela Bailey. The final chapter moves to consider responses to student suicide, since the potential for this often lies behind the fear of staff and, when it does occur, may bring the issue of student mental health into the public arena. Two case studies are used to identify responses at the individual and institutional level, and these are contrasted as to their sensitivity, support and learning potential.

This collection has brought together a wide variety of contributors whose experience and insight give grounds for optimism that mental health problems are being increasingly addressed within higher education. It is published in the context of heightened attention to social inclusion agendas and is firmly rooted in the view that higher education provides unique opportunities for people with mental health problems to acquire a valued status, marketable and personal skills, activity and inclusion, and to construct their own identity. Less rarely spelt out are the advantages accruing to higher education from students with mental health problems who promote inclusive communities, contribute to the variety of student life and offer important role models for other students and staff in communicating that difficulties and disabilities can be overcome, and experiences positively built upon.

References

Bradley, G. (2000) 'Responding Effectively to the Mental Health Needs of International Students.' *Higher Education 39*, 417–433.

Clothier, C. (1994) *The Allitt Inquiry: Independent inquiry relating to the deaths and injuries on the children's ward at Grantham and Kesteven General Hospital during the period February to April 1991.* London: HMSO.

CVCP (Committee of Vice-Chancellors and Principals, now renamed Universities UK) (2000) *Guidelines on Student Mental Health Policies and Procedures for Higher Education.* London: CVCP.

Dearing, R. (1997) *Higher Education in the Learning Society: Report of the national inquiry into higher education.* London: HMSO.

Department of Health (2000) *Reforming the Mental Health Act.* London: Department of Health. Cm. 5016–1.

Higher Education Funding Council for England (1999) *Guidance on base-level provision for disabled students in higher education institutions.* London: HEFCE.

Manthorpe, J. and Stanley, N. (1999) 'Dilemmas in Professional Education: Responding Effectively to Students with Mental Health Problems.' *Journal of Interprofessional Care 13*, 355–365.

Phippen, M. (1995) 'The 1993/4 Survey of Counselling Services in Further and Higher Education.' *Newsletter, Association for Student Counselling*, November, 25–36.

Quality Assurance Agency (1999) *Code of Practice for Assurance of Academic Quality and Standards in Higher Education: Students with Disabilities.* Gloucester: Quality Assurance Agency.

Rana, R., Smith, E. and Walkling, J. (1999) *Degrees of Disturbance: The New Agenda.* Rugby: British Association of Counselling.

Read, J. and Baker, S. (1996) *Not Just Sticks and Stones; A Survey of the Stigma, Taboos and Discrimination Experienced by People with Mental Health Problems.* London: Mind Publications.

Rooke-Matthews, S. and Lindow, V. (1998) *A Survivor's Guide to Working in Mental Health Services.* London: Mind Publications.

Shakespeare, T. (2001) *Help.* Birmingham: Venture Press.

Stanley, N., Manthorpe, J. and Bradley, G. (2000) *Responding Effectively to Student Problems: Project Report.* Hull: University of Hull.

Szmukler, G. and Holloway, F. (2001) 'Confidentiality In Community Psychiatry.' In C. Cordess (ed) *Confidentiality and Mental Health.* London: Jessica Kingsley pp.53–70.

PART ONE

The Experiences of Students and their Families

Chapter 2

Breakdown

David Brandon and Jo Payne

This chapter contains two personal accounts of psychiatric breakdown while studying at university. David Brandon was a student first at the University of Hull and later undertook a social work course at the London School of Economics (LSE). While at the LSE he had a 'breakdown', but still qualified and later became Professor of Community Care at Anglia Polytechnic University (APU) and a Chair of the British Association of Social Workers. Jo Payne was a student at Durham University studying Philosophy and Politics; she later became a social work student at APU in Cambridge, where David Brandon supervised her second placement. She qualified in 1998 and has mainly worked as a researcher. The chapter ends with some conclusions about responses, treatment and recovery.

David Brandon

Going to Hull University in 1960, as a young social studies student, was an immense challenge. I came from a poor home in Sunderland – itself a town of poverty. My dad was in and out of mental hospital, with a track record of erratic behaviour and regularly beating up my mother and myself. I'd already spent some time living on the streets of London and carried the shadows of many beatings from the age of two years onwards. Attending the university was an alien and unsupportive experience. Sitting at the long tables in the halls of residence, the public school, para-military culture seemed a very long way from growing up on a council housing estate just off the Durham Road. We were learning about the sociology of poverty in various lectures and seminars, but in a distant and abstract way. Both the academics and their books were a long way from the daily reality of living on national assistance; their suburban Cottingham homes far from the bare feet and torn trousers of the 'bairns' I'd known back home in Sunderland.

When I returned home from university at the first Christmas, my family was homeless again. It wasn't the poverty of the sociology text-books but the experience of a chill North Sea wind on inadequate clothing, and insufficient to eat and drink. Dad had a new girlfriend, got the locks changed, and sent us back out onto the windy streets. We stayed in my uncle Lewis' house on two easy chairs in the lounge. The contrast with the comforts of university was enormous. At the end of the first academic year I came close to leaving but had nothing to go back to.

The next two years were much better. I made friends for the first time and grew accustomed to the bourgeois lifestyle. I also met Althea, a zoology student, and fell in love. I concentrated on the societies: became secretary of the Student Christian Movement, got involved with social service volunteering and marched with the Campaign for Nuclear Disarmament. The academic side seemed pretty irrelevant.

After graduation, Althea and I got married and I spent some years working in homelessness in London. My involvement with the famous TV programme *Cathy Come Home* (I was a consultant and did a voice-over for the programme) resulted in being forced out of my job and London because of the huge publicity it generated. I escaped to the South coast and worked in the mental health service. In 1968, I began training as a psychiatric social worker at the LSE. The pressures were enormous and the days interminably long. I got up each morning before 6am at my home in Shoreham-by-Sea and travelled by train to London – sometimes to the LSE, on other days to the Royal Free Hospital, often returning well after 10pm.

The mental health course was immensely disappointing. I was vastly under-nourished by what I saw as the desiccated hands-off, stale psychodynamic tradition, mainly taught by tutors who knew little of current practice. I'd made considerable sacrifices – selling our bungalow and getting leave from work – yet the intellectual rewards were meagre. I felt there was no vision in the teaching, nothing much that could enrich my practice based at a local health centre. It seemed to me that the training of psychiatric social workers encouraged dry pomposity; sitting in stuffy lectures listening to long hours of pontificating and dissecting verbal corpses. We spent much time flying over distressed people in a theoretical 'helicopter', so noisy that what they said and felt could not be heard.

The intellectual message was oppressive: that people in poverty, the mentally ill and homeless, were often irretrievably damaged. In our practice we weren't allowed to visit our clients at home (outside the hospital clinics) as if we might become infected. The explanation for this apartheid was that our objectivity would be compromised. My argument was that we couldn't understand their situation sitting in a comfortable clinic. My protests were viewed as primarily pathological. I was viewed, very benevolently, as having 'some authority problems' and 'not using supervision effectively'.

At home, our marriage was in shreds. We had moved back with my in-laws because we had so little money to cover the costs of training and travel. My employing authority, West Sussex, had refused to sponsor me. My beloved mother-in-law was slowly and painfully dying of cancer. She was so obviously suffering, yet we had been instructed by the family doctor, who I thought was a complete half-wit, never to discuss her illness. In those days, patients and relatives obeyed their medical advisors almost unthinkingly. Both Althea and I struggled with her mother's slow and gradual demise.

In nearby Brighton, my nanna was also dying. At 92 years, that seemingly unconquerable spirit was flickering. I visited her every weekend to take some shopping and to resume our long quarrels. It was difficult but necessary to make contact with dad again. Every time I talked with him I recalled his violence against us as kids, which was agonisingly painful. We were both on the edge of great fury; long-buried events were constantly and injuriously recalled.

I was simply disintegrating, falling into ten thousand fragments. I couldn't concentrate on the vast quantities of largely irrelevant reading or attend to my clients with their various psychiatric problems. I couldn't write the stupid essays, demands for which came with oppressive regularity. I related hardly at all to Althea and our small sons. I went out for long, lonely walks on the beach at weekends and at home spoke hardly at all. Althea got even more depressed and desperate.

In weekly tutorials with my academic tutor, whom I respected a great deal, I didn't talk much but sobbed a lot. Tears seeped through every part of me, full of guilt and shame. Harsh voices filled my head, mostly about personal failure. So many people demanded so much – the family, nanna, the social work course and the Royal Free patients – but I felt empty and shrivelled. My mind had become an instrument for punishment, from which there was no escape. I couldn't sleep, couldn't eat, and couldn't concentrate. I was dimly aware I had become a subject for discussion in the course meetings; there was 'a concern' about me. I was losing contact with the other students. I was burning with fury so much of the time, it was hard for them to relate to me. Anyway, I despised most of them.

Then finally my tutor said it, came out brutally with it. It was a late winter's afternoon in the middle of an hour-long tutorial. I was crying bitterly, and he spoke quietly as usual, 'I'm going to suggest that you see a psychiatrist'. That dreadful word 'psychiatrist' echoed and re-echoed, rolled roughly around inside my head. There was a long silence and more tears, and then he asked me the standard social worker question: 'How do you feel about that?' How did I feel? Did I feel at all? might have been a better question. My tutor had echoed the response of the academic at Sussex University almost a year previously, when I'd applied to do their social work course: 'If we accepted you, with your family background, we'd have to seek psychiatric help for you.' It was horrifying. I was to become a patient, an official crazy working with crazy people.

Obviously this was a decision made after long discussion by the relevant academic staff. I had asked too many difficult questions and was by now refusing to go to the stupid social work seminars. A course on lunacy couldn't deal with a single, relatively harmless, mad student. The staff felt I was falling off the far edge and so psychoanalysis was suddenly jettisoned and the boys with velvet straitjackets called in. When the chips were down, they went for the psychiatrist, the knockout drugs and the cold baths rather than the comfortable couch.

I felt betrayed, sad and angry. Somehow the course and staff had taken my experiences of everyday life on a north-east council housing estate and turned it into something inherently pathological. From what I knew, it was relatively normal. Most kids got the leather belt and worse on my estate. I'd never seen it any other way until the admissions interview at Sussex University. The LSE ran an inadequate professional course and I was made the scapegoat for its irrelevance, its Madame Tussaud's quality. But I was also relieved. Things were really bad and my own resources were woefully inadequate and stretched. I had reached the far edge of something. I couldn't cope – the great coper couldn't manage any more.

So I was formally referred to a psychiatrist. The academic team seemed omnipotent. What was the alternative? I became a depressed package in the mail. Seven days later I sat outside the psychiatrist's office, feeling humiliated, numb and nervous. I thumbed through the ageing magazines in the comfortable waiting room. This elderly man with greying hair greeted me warmly and ushered me in to the office with his professional diplomas framed on the wall, very American in style. He seemed warm and reasonably inoffensive.

He had a short referral note from my social work tutor, but really wanted to hear my account. I went through a brief social history without a tear. He began to explore our marriage. 'After all that love and affection why do you think your relationship with Althea has deteriorated so badly? Why so little support for one another when you both need it most?' Good question, but I didn't have much energy to explore it. I was such a huge ball of pain and anger. Then something extraordinary happened. I don't know whether he was a fool or genius but I incline to the former. He talked incessantly about himself. 'I live in north London. My wife and I have a difficult relationship. We are on reasonably polite terms but the essential spark of our marriage has long gone. We don't share anything important in our lives any more. We live separately on an emotional plane. What do you think could be done to change that?' The tables were turned. Suddenly I became the professional and he the patient. I slipped smoothly into the role with consummate ease, not missing a single stride. Sorting other people out was a much better option than living with my everyday chaos. I gave advice on how to establish better sharing in their long-term Hampstead relationship, skilfully eliciting the additional information. Excellent advice, but very difficult to take.

I went back a week later and was congratulated on my nourishing contribution. My suggestions for improved marital relationships seemed to be working. He asked for even more help and I recall dimly a mention of a paper he'd written recently, published by the University of Jerusalem. I didn't return for the third appointment. We never met again. So I was a big success in marital guidance if not as a lunatic, but on one level I felt cheated. This had been my big moment on the stage to talk about turbulent demons and somehow I'd been robbed. It had been a sort of judo. Without any awareness, I had been thrown to the floor, bruised but still crying. I was supposed to have been mentally hugged and analysed and...

He might be making great progress with his marriage but I still struggled on with mine. I went on to undertake a placement at the University College Hospital from the Royal Free and got some real nutrition from a well-respected practice supervisor and her medical colleagues: I made slow progress as the energy returned. Both nanna and my mother-in-law were dead within months. After nanna's funeral I never saw dad again, alive or dead. The LSE course bumbled along. It was both boring and mistaken in its mostly psychodynamic understanding of mental health issues; so I thought at the time, and even more so now. It seemed that I had great personal problems, but also something to say about the professional course. It was claustrophobic, middle-class and increasingly irrelevant to the pressing demands of the community mental health services. It was possible to have an unresolved oedipal complex and be right – or rather, have some truth. But within that structure, and in most systems, that was not possible. I felt like the mad outsider, my favourite King Lear – railing against the cruelty of the world – social work student 'more sinned against than sinning'.

For the last thirty years, I've wrestled with recurring depression, like the North Sea flowing backwards and forwards: high and low tides. It comes in immense surges; a strange mixture of grief and rage, an immense disappointment about life. Often I've lived close to suicide and even closer. More recently, I've seen it primarily as a spiritual experience; the challenging of one set of meanings by some brutal aspect of ordinary truth, so that my fragile beliefs fell down like a pack of playing cards. I've tried to express that in books like 'Zen in the Art of Helping' and 'Tao of Survival'. As a professor of social work in the last year or two, I've picked up large elements of cowardice, greed for comfort and intellectual torpor in the settings in which I've worked. Others, very understandably, experienced it as my anger, despair and bitterness and that was also true, but always rather more than that.

One social work colleague described me as 'depressed' when I was despairing. I felt the social work profession was dying: the courses were a funeral. My situation was rarely seen as anything to do with the nature of social work schools or social services. I felt strongly that, on a spiritual level, we had completely lost our way – become smug and comfortable rather than righteously angry about what was happening to those in poverty. I referred to our social work school as a nursing home. I felt so isolated and angry that it was hardly possible for people to hear what I had to say. They genuinely and very understandably didn't want to listen to this ball of bile; this particular ball felt blamed and outside.

As I was going through a long period of despair, over many months, at times close to suicide and a considerable nuisance to others, a close colleague stopped me and demanded: 'Why don't you go to the doctors and get some pills?' On one level a genuine expression of compassionate concern, but also on yet another a way of managing and dealing with me, getting me medicalised so the systemic damage could be limited within my individual pathology through the magic bullets. I didn't go to the doctors, but I couldn't carry on. Eventually when I resigned, or rather took early retirement, I made an almost immediate recovery. I felt immensely cleansed and liberated.

I saw, and still do see my various periods of despair and depression not as a psychiatric diagnosis, but as an expression of spiritual crisis. This view was not shared, nor even listened to, by most of the many mental health professionals I dealt with over the years. On the contrary, the explanation of spiritual crisis was seen by many as a form of denial. This meant we couldn't be partners in healing. The process of treatment was increasingly seen by me as benevolent oppression.

Jo Payne

I started at Durham University in October 1990. I was very stressed, tense, unhappy and lovesick, whatever that means. I had just returned from a difficult time in Germany and had mixed feelings about returning. I was anxious about Durham, about sharing a room with another person and meeting new people. The first term went really well. I found the work very positive and enjoyable. I made an impact as a bright student. The plan was to get a First in Philosophy and Politics and do a Ph.D at Cambridge. I worked hard, cried a lot from being in love – like a rubber band pulling tighter and tighter until it snapped. And snap it did!

I became very ill. I made odd comments in philosophy classes, saying that I believed in God and he made the world – not quite the thing for a discussion on Aristotle! My tutor noticed and got in touch with my personal tutor, who arranged for me to see the university doctor. In the meantime I saw yet another doctor who prescribed some tranquillisers. My personal tutor got in touch with my parents. I went home for a week without telling anyone. I spouted religious comments, got very tense and burst into tears of terror. I saw the university doctor on my return; he arranged for me to see a consultant psychiatrist. He asked me about any suicide risk; I recall every detail of the hospital room still. He was very scary: he suggested medication or going into hospital. Nothing in college was working and so I agreed to go into hospital.

I went to hospital and was started on pimozide 14mg as a daily dose. (This is a drug which was commonly used to treat schizophrenia.) The dose was reduced to 6mg after several months. My parents came to stay in Durham. Mum stayed for four weeks and contributed to my recovery. She would take me out every day, forcing me to communicate. I recall one trip to Hadrian's Wall when my legs became so stiff, I couldn't walk; a side-effect from the medication. I had to be carried to the bottom. Sheer terror. God had afflicted me. I still managed my exams in the summer. I somehow functioned for work, slept a lot, worked automatically and struggled on.

Two years after graduation, I was accepted for a social work course at Anglia Polytechnic University. In the period before the course, I had a bad bout of illness. Could I work in the caring professions? I had no idea of the boundaries between personal and professional life. I had little idea of what happened in social work. I wanted to empower and enable clients. I started with a lot of enthusiasm. I enjoyed the first term of college-based learning, but the lectures were a bit boring and empty and turned me off. Was that the schizophrenia or the medication? I had few skills and a fund of personal knowledge that nobody knew how to tap into. Later, on placement, I found that my practice teacher, a social worker in a community mental health team, had little understanding or empathy. She was busy and had no time to support a nervous budding social worker.

I was anxious and spent evenings feeling out of place. I had an office with no desk. I felt nervous making telephone calls when the office noise levels were high. I felt like a disempowered alien. I had no supervision sessions with my practice teacher and did very little. I was told in a three-way meeting that I would pass my placement. Then my academic tutor told me in the general social work office (not even in private) that I had failed. There was a general lack of consideration. How, in a busy environment, do you train a social work student who doesn't fit in because of mental illness, who has few skills, and needs time and energy to develop? I was judged to have failed to function as 'an effective member of the team'.

I attended a meeting with the university's placement advisor, my personal tutor and my practice teacher. I defended myself. My practice teacher said that she couldn't trust me to do the work because I was unable – or should it have been disabled? I felt disabled by my mental health problems. The same professionals who advocated empowerment for their clients, could not accept those problems in their colleagues. I argued the injustice of this. I was horrified about the lack of warning of failure, and the lack of liaison between practice and university.

It was suggested that I try counselling. It was effective on one level, but not in dealing with the deeper anxieties. The counsellors had little understanding of mental illness. I was given another opportunity to pass the placement and spent six weeks with David Brandon, who ran an agency called Shield, and worked at the university. He taught me to cope more effectively with my anxiety; he met me at my level. I worked in a day centre for people with head injuries and attended the groups. I learned from a teacher who understood my needs. David had begun by saying: 'Are you a

psychiatric patient or a social work student? If the latter you are welcome –
if the former you need to seek help elsewhere because here we are primarily concerned with our clients'. I worked on care plans, and passed, and
went on to do my second year placement with David.

I was nurtured and guided by David and by Lana Morris who worked
with him; they put up with me and were sensitive to my needs. I would feel
stressed and overwhelmed in the evenings, but I carried on and learned. I
did holistic care planning at a Cambridge day centre. This is a care plan
which looks at a person in an all-embracing way and identifies the needs
and visions he or she has for their life. I was supported throughout. I
passed the placement components and later went on to qualify as a social
worker.

I was offered nothing by the university except counselling. My fellow
social work students supported me and saw more value in me than the university ever did. I recall being told 'helpfully' that I was the sort of person
who would never do anyone harm. Other students recognised the role a
disabled person could play in social work, but the system did not. It
brooked no disability. There was no concept of the value of the wounded
healer, only of an efficient bureaucrat who could fill in papers, and
empathise from a distance. The question I ask still is whether there will
ever be a place for someone like me in social work? It is fashionable to be a
disabled user involved in consultation, but what happens when the social
worker becomes ill? I know I will and I fear it. Will I recover enough to
continue, or will I lose everything I've struggled for?

David and Jo

The actual experience of mental illness was very frightening and destruc-
tive of confidence, but the reactions of others and the formal treatment
magnified our fears. We learned to think of ourselves as psychiatric
patients and much later as mental health survivors. We had to deal both
with our own desperate situations and also with the often negative and
fearful reactions of many others. Stigma came from those around us – not
in some conscious way, but in the pollen of uncertainty, sometimes the
humouring and patronising. Nobody brought up in western society can

avoid the negativity surrounding mental breakdown. We were both brought up with inherent fears and believed that in some sense it was our fault. When we broke down, we felt in some sense to blame. We also felt that some judged us adversely and we were no longer listened to. We had become spoiled goods. Few people, who are not themselves survivors, can fully understand the wholly shattering nature of that experience.

Our friends and immediate family were hugely important in helping us to regain our health, although the battle for each of us is not yet over. They communicated hope, against the odds, continued to see us as unique when most others, especially professionally, seemed negative. We were often perceived as a nuisance and a burden in the eyes of professionals. At university, we were faced with services that didn't know what to do, except offer referral to counselling that was hardly sufficient. They were 'mentalist' – they 'blamed' mental health survivors for their condition. Even the systems that supported people with a disability didn't consciously see mental illness as much to do with them. There was a catch-all referral to counsellors. There is a need for a wider response, not psychiatric necessarily, that accepts the disability and also looks directly at the problems ordinary people (in our case social workers and academic tutors) experience in struggling with their inherent mentalism[1]. Such issues are readily faced with regard to racism but mentalism – seeing mental health survivors as inferior – is more contentious and more strongly denied.

We both felt that our distress was, at least in part, the consequence of the systems surrounding us. Jo felt that the nature of social work was non-accepting, that her practice teacher didn't give her enough time, that her academic tutor didn't understand. David felt that the courses he worked on were stale and uninspiring, that decisions were made about his work that didn't involve him and that turned out to be inherently unhelpful. We both felt too that from the moment we were buttonholed as 'mentally ill', very little attention was paid to the surrounding systems and settings. It is possible to be unwell and still have insight into injurious systems; but that sort of sophisticated response was rarely experienced.

We both struggled with whether our chosen profession could handle wounded healers. The textbooks are mainly antagonistic to that notion, and the range of practice competencies integral to social work training tends to pathologise vulnerabilities and personal damage. We felt that Shamanic traditions of healing from the wounds (reasonably common in medicine and nursing) were rare and increasingly unacceptable in the excessively pragmatic world of social work. For those of us who suffered fears and anxieties (the vast majority), there was no room. We had been damaged, not only by the experience of mental illness (whatever that may mean) but also by the very restricted ways in which our universities had responded.

Those fellow students around us were mostly generous and kind (if bewildered) people, who wanted to help. However, their understanding and attitudes were frequently confused or negative, and their actions thoroughly misguided. Without conscious intention, they often contributed to the difficulties we faced. We see this as part of a wider problem of socialisation rather than as a fault of particular individuals. Universities need to be much better prepared, with more relevant and participative systems. At present they tend to define the problems as existing inside the mind of a single distressed person, ignoring those created by oppressive systems.

Overall our experience of the education system was that it was benevolently oppressive: at all levels, a student was supposed to fit in. There has been a major attempt by universities to tackle issues of gender and race (whether successful or not), but scarcely any so far to tackle issues of mentalism: the ways in which these institutions contribute to the distress of those labelled 'mentally ill'.

We value ordinary human contact, but with 'illness' that becomes even harder to sustain. Without love and care from our immediate families and friends, we might never have recovered. For each of us, as 'wounded' social workers, the long experience of mental illness has been devastating but also enriching. Our understanding of being a client, patient, or distressed student is much profounder than before. It is not our fault the education system finds that hard to accept, but it is, along with many others, our problem. We have lived with the injurious consequences of it, therefore, universities need to become much more emotionally literate.

Endnote

1   The term mentalism is defined by Chamberlin (1988) in two ways: the first describes how psychiatric patients are held responsible for their condition; and the second how psychiatric patients are deemed inferior to professionals and non-psychiatric patients. Arising from these two aspects of mentalism, Chamberlin felt that only people with direct experience of psychiatric services as users should work with psychatric patients.

References

Chamberlin, J. (1988) *On Our Own: Patient Controlled Alternatives to the Mental Health System.* London: Mind Publications.

Chapter 3

Students' Perspectives

James Wade

Introduction

Mental health is an issue for all of us: we may all feel mental distress of one sort or another and some of us will experience mental ill-health. This chapter explores issues around mental health and ill-health relevant to the student community. It is informed by students' personal perspectives and concludes with the importance of the voluntary sector's role in tackling stigma and complementing campus-based services.

We all have mental health. If we take this statement on board it will play a crucial role in understanding the broader themes of this chapter and their implications for students. How do we understand mental health? The New Oxford Dictionary of English (1998, p.1157) includes references for: 'mental', 'mental age', 'mental block', 'mental cruelty', 'mental defective', 'mental deficiency', 'mental handicap', 'mentalism', 'mentality', 'mentally handicapped', 'mental set', and 'mentation'. It does *not* have a reference for 'mental health'. If there is no clear definition for 'mental health' in a con-temporary dictionary, how can we clarify what it is and what it represents? Without an easily accessible and clear definition, mental health remains intangible. The lack of 'visibility' of mental health is one of the most sig-nificant barriers to raising awareness and understanding among students and young people. At the beginning of the autumn semester or term, students can feel disorientated away from familiar surroundings, and under stress from new routines, coursework and the need to make friends. For many it is a time of fun and excitement, for others it can be daunting and fraught with anxieties. The students' perspectives discussed later in this chapter highlight ideas that students' unions and universities could consider. Asking for help can be difficult at the best of times; many of us do not wish to admit when we are in need.

Stigma

Sadly, the stigma associated with mental ill-health is frequently encountered. Mental ill-health is often a taboo and difficult to discuss. If this is how the general public may feel, consider the experience of someone who suffers mental ill-health. Knowing that people are generally unsympathetic causes untold distress to those experiencing such problems.

A student experiencing distressing and possibly frightening symptoms may find asking for help difficult. Occasionally a student or young person will not realise that something is wrong. It is precisely this that makes it imperative they have a greater awareness and understanding of mental health and ill-health. Friends sharing accommodation, halls of residence or renting privately, can be alerted to warning signs of a person's deterioration. But friends can find it difficult to ask for, or know where to find, the most appropriate help. Understanding may be sketchy, people may be reluctant to talk about feeling 'low' or 'down', and may be unsure about where to turn for information or assistance. In such situations, external sources of information will influence people's ability to understand issues and make informed decisions.

Media influences

The media continues to perpetuate misunderstandings surrounding mental health and ill-health. Of course, not all media coverage is damaging, but misrepresentation and misunderstanding of mental health and especially ill-health, occur frequently. Shock headlines serve only to perpetuate shock headlines. They grab attention but often offer little in the way of fact or balance. The use of shocking words in large and bold typefaces taps into the collective fear of 'the mentally ill'. It reinforces the public's feelings of hostility towards something it is being encouraged to reject.

Similarly, advertising uses shock tactics. Grabbing your attention, just for a few seconds, is usually enough to convey an idea or image that will influence your thoughts and perhaps encourage you to buy a product. But the means of doing this are sometimes dubious and could be considered offensive. The use of words like 'mad', 'nutter', or 'loony' reinforces misunderstanding and negative stereotypes. Classic examples include variations on a theme of: 'you'd be mad to miss this sale' or 'spring madness'. The more serious examples play on themes such as hearing voices. As I write this, a television advertisement is using the idea of 'voices' to sell a product to a young audience. Advertisers may justify such representations by claiming that the work is ironic. Humour and irony have their place, but not when used at the expense of people experiencing serious illness. If you are at all unsure of the ideas being suggested here, try applying them to other groups within society. One that comes to mind is ethnicity. How many people are willing to endorse offensive language and derogatory representations in this respect?

Media representations are often lazy in their approach to mental health and ill-health. It takes seconds to make fun of something, but a long time to turn around public perceptions based on misrepresentations. Being able to differentiate fact from fiction is crucial for students and young people but this process is hindered if the points of reference continually deliver negative or mixed messages.

Mental health messages

There are numerous health campaigns competing for our attention every day. All of them affect people's lives directly and indirectly. Similarly, in the student community, health issues such as alcohol and drug misuse, as well as meningitis, are important enough to be recognised as priorities for awareness raising and support – as they should be. Interestingly, as I write this in spring 2001, a government-backed campaign to destigmatise mental illness among young people has been announced with the backing of the National Schizophrenia Fellowship (NSF) and the National Union of Students (NUS) in the UK.

This campaign is timely, as mental health and well-being are marginalised issues, although they are as important as physical health and well-being. The two interact and support one another and yet in my experience of working with students through awareness raising sessions, many students are unaware that they have mental health. It is disconcerting that students are unaware of such an important part of their well-being.

The accounts that follow indicate that students with mental health problems encounter a range of levels of awareness and informed support within higher education. These personal perspectives highlight the variety of people encountered by students in their search for support. They were offered to the author by students who wanted their experiences to be used constructively.

Student perspectives 1

Student representatives

I ran a workshop with approximately 30 undergraduate students during summer 2000 at the NUS annual convention. I asked them, 'How many of you have got mental health?' Three hands pointed towards the ceiling with certainty, 27 students were probably feeling a little uncomfortable. I smiled at them and asked the question again; another two hands were raised. I now had five students from a total of 30 acknowledging their own personal mental health. Some of the students were looking puzzled. Perhaps they thought I meant ill-health or illness, or perhaps they just didn't know the answer. All of the students in the room were there to attend a session about being at ease with mental health and illness. They had understood enough to attend of their own free will, but many did not recognise one of the basic prerequisites of the workshop. Realising there were 25 unsure students, I hastily reorganised the workshop content with a view to encouraging them to realise that they all had mental health. Many of the students attending that particular workshop were elected welfare officers for their respective students' unions. They were gatekeepers to potentially thousands of other students who might approach them for information, support, or advice. I hope this example serves to reinforce the need for student representatives to engage with the issues.

Student perspectives 2

Tim

Tim experienced problems with depression in his late teens. The precipitating event was witnessing the suicide of a woman on a busy road during an autumn afternoon. Although he was at the scene within moments, Tim was unable to do anything constructive apart from telephone for an ambulance, which fortunately arrived quickly. Both the driver of the car and Tim himself were shocked by the suddenness and severity of the woman's actions. The police arrived and asked questions, after which the driver and Tim were able to leave the scene with the promise of a follow-up visit from the police. Tim went home and spoke of the experience to his parents later that day. Soon after the incident, he felt unable to cope and became isolated and withdrawn. Tim was persuaded to visit his local GP who prescribed anti-depressants and exercise. In time Tim made a good recovery and was able to resume everyday activities; the police did not contact him to follow-up the incident.

Tim decided to return to education in his early twenties after experiencing a period of unemployment and working at a variety of jobs. He successfully worked his way through GCSEs and A levels at an FE college before starting a degree course at university. Tim experienced one episode of acute anxiety prior to his A level exams, which required medication. As a mature student, Tim enjoyed studying at university and the first year went by without incident. All work was completed and submitted without problem. However, in the autumn semester of year two, he realised he was beginning to feel depressed. His previous experiences and coping strategies alerted him to his feelings of lethargy and isolation. Tim had good insight and he needed to find support that would allow him to continue his studies uninterrupted.

Tim thought about making an appointment at the GP's surgery near to his student accommodation, but it took him approximately one month to build up the courage to do this. He had registered with the surgery on entering university, but had had no reason to visit since. Tim saw an unfamiliar doctor who listened briefly and asked him to return once a week for several weeks to be weighed and consulted, but Tim was worried about waiting for so long. Drawing upon his past experiences and his own insight into his condition, Tim suggested he should start taking anti-depressants. The doctor, however, rejected this idea and repeated his request for Tim to visit once a week for regular weighings and consultation.

Tim left the surgery and went back to his accommodation without making a follow-up appointment. After thinking the situation through, he made an appointment with his GP at home and booked a train ticket. Three days later he kept the appointment, where the doctor prescribed anti-depressants, suggested exercise, and made a follow-up appointment which Tim agreed to keep. The local doctor knew Tim's long-term medical history and took note of his symptoms and suggestions. Tim appreciated that a prescription was not *the* answer but only *part* of the answer to improve his mental health.

At the same time, Tim approached a course tutor to discuss the impact of his depression on his coursework; unfortunately, the tutor felt unable to help in any way. Tim left feeling embarrassed and lacking the confidence to make another approach. After a few days he was confident enough to approach another course tutor, and this time was encouraged to arrange a meeting with a university counsellor while in the presence of the tutor. Tim felt able to talk about his academic difficulties, and the tutor handled the situation sensitively. A coursework extension was agreed, if needed, to meet deadline requirements.

The initial counselling session at the university was made available within a day – the first of six sessions that helped Tim to clarify difficulties and begin to resolve anxieties. He went home to his family for the Christmas vacation and completed his coursework within the extension deadline. He felt better able to cope with his studies throughout the spring semester and completed the second year without further difficulties. A year later, Tim graduated with an upper second class honours degree. Tim summarises his feelings about making the appointments with the doctors:

> I felt powerless to begin with. It took me about a month to approach the first GP and I had never visited the surgery. The GP did listen to me, but I couldn't convince him to prescribe me some medication. I understand my illness and manage it well, but the thought of possibly waiting two months for medication, and during the winter months, compelled me to

seek alternative help from my home GP. I'm glad I did. Without it, I may not have kept up with coursework or finished the course.

Tim experienced a mixed response from his university. His first attempt to broach the subject left him embarrassed and unsure of making another approach to someone else. He felt able to approach another tutor and had a better response. The second tutor listened to his difficulties and encouraged him to make an appointment with the counselling service. This tutor explained that she was unable to help with emotional concerns, but could support Tim during their impact on his studying and deadlines. The second tutor spent time helping Tim when he first approached her, and within minutes his circumstances were altering for the better. She did not need a lot of detailed information in order to offer relevant support. Excellent communication between academic and counselling staff and support from the second tutor helped Tim to find further assistance, maintain his dignity and keep up with his coursework. The university counselling service was efficient and helped him to put his anxieties in perspective and continue studying. Tim did not approach the student union as they were not particularly active at his satellite campus. There were no obvious contact points for welfare staff on this campus until his third year, when an NUS representative became available one day per week.

Student perspective 3

Gemma

Gemma started university with high hopes, but quickly found it difficult to motivate herself or fit in with others, and began to feel isolated. Living in halls of residence should have increased her social contacts, but she found it relatively easy to shut herself away without anyone noticing that anything was wrong, and she gradually began to withdraw from lectures.

Gemma started experimenting with illicit drugs and began to experience feelings of paranoia. During lectures she talked about her worries openly and found herself being ridiculed by a member of staff. Gemma started hearing voices and approached her tutor, who quickly arranged an appointment for her to see the university psychiatrist. The psychiatrist prescribed anti-depressants but unfortunately Gemma did not confide all her symptoms. She stopped going to lectures and made an appointment to see the university counselling service. An appointment was made available three weeks later where she poured out her worries to a counsellor who listened and suggested baking cakes as a way of relieving stress. Gemma did not feel this addressed her frightening symptoms and difficulties.

Some two weeks after starting to take the anti-depressants, Gemma combined them with paracetamol with the intention of overdosing in her room. At this point she felt she wanted to die. Over the following four days, her flatmates periodically knocked on her door to ask if she was okay. Gemma replied, yes, she was fine. After four days she asked a flatmate to call a doctor. Gemma woke up in hospital and found her tutor sitting by her bedside, which she found comforting.

Gemma left hospital with only a few weeks remaining before her first-year exams, but she was unable to take medication due to the fragile state of her liver. The university offered special facilities for her exams; Gemma attended some, missed others and walked out of one due to feeling unwell. Despite this, she did reasonably well, and needed to resit only a few exams to move into the second year of her course. Unfortunately, as the resits began Gemma experienced further psychiatric symptoms. Soon afterwards she was admitted to a local psychiatric ward where she stayed for two months. During this period Gemma successfully studied for and was able to pass her resits. A short while later she re-entered university without having to repeat the academic year.

Gemma contacted her student union and enquired about support while studying. The union suggested a women's group (which Gemma found 'cliquey') and a project being run by the NSF to raise awareness and understanding of mental health and ill-health in the student community. The union did not know much about the NSF, but Gemma found information through contacting them directly herself and learned coping strategies from her psychiatrist and from other students experiencing similar difficulties. During her third year Gemma became a welfare officer and Nightline (a campus-based telephone crisis and information service) volunteer to assist other students. Due to adverse side effects from her medication, Gemma's final project achieved a poor mark but, nonetheless, she successfully completed her course and graduated.

The key factor in enabling Gemma to continue her studies was her success in persuading the university to allow her to resit her exams. She summarises her situation below:

> During that time (on the local psychiatric ward) both my parents and my clinical psychologist wrote letters to the university almost begging them to let me resit my exams. The second-hand information I have had since suggested that this was very difficult.

The following are Gemma's observations for improving overall understanding and care of students' mental health and ill-health for student unions, colleges and universities. They are reproduced with her permission:

1. 'Crisis runs' (student union staff knocking on doors to check welfare) could be extended to cover every student on campus, and training should be given to those taking on this responsibility.

2. A more obvious support system could have been in place; my flat mates and I should have had somebody to contact to ask for help.

3. Part of the induction programme or handouts could have included numbers to call for support, or information for people experiencing difficulty at this vulnerable time.

4. A befriender scheme could have been in operation, whereby anybody who was feeling lonely could call their befriender and be able to talk.

5. University staff or procedures could have been a little more open-minded about my return to study.

6. It should be possible to get a more balanced mixture of exams and essays for assessment from which to grade progress at the end of the degree.

7. A disabilities officer *within* the student union: someone with either a physical or mental health problem themselves who can

advise or co-ordinate support services, perhaps with a permanent member of staff acting as their opposite number.

8.   More advertising could be provided for Nightline services.

9.   Free, confidential access to a telephone for all students; although there was an internal telephone in each student house that could be used to contact Nightline, it was difficult to hold a conversation without the rest of the house hearing.

Gemma is currently well and employed. She contributes voluntarily to NSF's work in raising awareness of severe mental illness with students and young people.

Student perspective 4

Mike

Mike acknowledges that being bullied during his school years has affected his self-esteem. He felt depressed during secondary school and harboured suicidal thoughts from the age of around 13 onwards. Despite these difficulties, Mike participated in music and debating, winning prizes for his efforts, and his examination grades were very good. Prior to university, Mike was prescribed anti-depressants and attended counselling; however, the counsellor did not feel his difficulties were indicative of severe mental illness. One month into his course, Mike experienced serious depression; he started injuring himself with razor blades taken from course practicals, and bounced from feelings of irritability to elation. He spent his entire student loan in one day.

Mike approached the student health services and asked for a psychiatric referral, taking a copy of material from a psychiatric handbook with him to support his case. An appointment was made available within a week at the outpatients' clinic at the student health service. At this point Mike started on anti-depressants once again, but very quickly manic symptoms became evident. Manic depression was mentioned in passing during consultation and alternative medication prescribed. A change in student health service staff meant that Mike began to take lithium, which helped many of his symptoms and overall functioning. He learned of his diagnosis through seeing a medical certificate.

Mike has found it relatively easy to talk about his illness. He wanted to make a difference for other students in similar situations and worked to establish a Nightline service. His university does not formally recognise him as disabled, therefore he makes arrangements with individual academic departments to recognise the limitations his ill-health occasionally brings. This has been successful and Mike feels well supported. Mike's perspective differs from the others described in this chapter in one significant way; he has used and speaks very highly of internet-based resources:

> It was really the regular support of the mailing lists 'Walkers in Darkness' and 'Roses and Thorns' that helped me through, kept me going, and suggested that I seek a psychiatric referral.

The following are Mike's suggestions for improving overall understanding and care of students' mental health and ill-health, for student unions, colleges and universities. These good practice and coping strategies are reproduced with his permission:

- 24-hour access to the internet for researching and seeking support from mailing lists (NOT chat rooms)

- rapid referral to psychiatric services, through the student health service

- an outpatients' clinic on campus and continuity of care

- psychiatric staff who understand student lifestyles and recognise the value of 'suggesting' admission, or 'offering admission if you feel you need it'

- acceptance of applications to use disbursement from university access funds to cover financial losses incurred during mania

- course co-ordinators who are genuinely pleased to help

- exceptional relationship with adviser of studies who, as well as being a doctor, was more supportive than he needed to be

- flexibility on credit requirements during manic depressive episode

- LEA paying repeat year cost of tuition fees in full, on advice of psychiatrist

- making contact with the local branch of the Manic Depression Fellowship

- becoming more the supporter than the supported on mailing lists.

Difficulties and obstacles:

- the halls of residence environment: no support or information available during times of mental distress

- some lecturers were less willing than others to make special allowances.

Mike is currently well and actively working in the student community to improve understanding of disability issues.

Conclusion

These students' perspectives provide snapshots of a range of experiences, coping strategies and assistance sought. It is not the aim of this chapter to represent experiences of the whole of the broad student community. However, those outlined above help to make what can often seem intangible tangible.

Two of the three students have successfully graduated and the other is on track to graduate. Between them they have diagnoses of depression, schizophrenia, and manic depression. During their student careers, one declined to talk openly with peers, one talked about difficulties, often at inappropriate times arising from her illness, and the other was confident enough to use his experiences to actively campaign on behalf of fellow students. One has made effective use of internet resources at times of concern for himself and others. All three refuse to be defined by their respective illnesses.

Student unions can make a real difference in their respective communities by acknowledging that everyone has mental health and that we can all do something to help ourselves and others. While mental health and ill-health continue to be misunderstood, students with mental ill-health difficulties will refrain from identifying their needs prior to admission and while studying for fear of the stigma incurred. Concentrating on mental health and well-being are excellent stepping-stones to understanding and exploring the more difficult issues of mental ill-health. I would like student unions to explore what it is that makes a mentally healthy environment. This can be constructive, shifting the focus from 'other' people who have 'problems' to viewing mental health as an issue for all of us. Understanding symptoms and being able to ask for assistance, whether it is for oneself or a friend, are small but crucial steps that may help someone to help themselves and successfully complete their studies.

Each student union has different demands on its resources; while identifying funding to improve overall awareness can be difficult, much can be achieved by utilising community-based resources. The possibilities are broad and include: sources of further information, awareness raising, assisting current and future students, training, volunteering and community partnerships. Raising awareness on World Mental Health Day, 10 October, is an obvious starting point.

Voluntary agencies can complement campus-based services. Voluntary agencies are not there to do the job of services on campus, but can work with them to improve students' mental health and well-being. The NSF runs projects ranging from information and advice to advocacy, sheltered housing and employment. There is a wealth of knowledge and expertise waiting to be tapped. Individual projects are unable to respond with unlimited resources, but building bridges with student communities and projects may help to raise awareness, provide opportunities to reduce stigma and inform development of service provision.

The NSF has been active in the UK student community for several years and its initial work was recognised by the government as good practice in the National Mental Health Service Framework (Department of Health, 1999). Since then the NSF has been developing a website with young service users called @ease (www.at-ease.nsf.org.uk) specifically for *all* young people. The website aims to raise awareness of mental health and ill-health, dispel stigma, and offer signposts to further assistance. It is an information resource and does not, at the time of writing, provide a crisis service. We are keen to encourage student unions, Nightlines, and university welfare services to link with @ease. Many student unions already provide health-related information via their respective websites, and we believe @ease will be a welcome addition.

Acknowledgment

The author would like to thank those students who contributed their experiences to this chapter.

Note

Those interested in commenting on or contributing to developing @ease can write c/o NSF @ease, 30 Tabernacle Street, London, EC2A 4DD, telephone +44 020 7330 9100 or fax +44 020 7330 9102.

References

Department of Health (1999) *National Service Framework for Mental Health: Modern Standards and Service Models.* London: Department of Health.

Chapter 4

When Our Children Kill Themselves
Parental Perspectives Following Suicide

Margaret Harvey

All of the contributors to this chapter have lost a son or daughter to suicide. Each of our stories is unique, as are our attempts to understand what led up to our child's death. Some of us feel that we can piece together a sequence of events, at least with hindsight, while for others it remains a shocking mystery. Probably we all accept that we can never know the full, true story. As parents, we recognise that the departure of a son or daughter to college or university marks a significant shift in the dynamics of our family. Our children are adults; they lead independent lives, and the family home becomes a place to visit, rather than to live. Some of us find it easier than others to adapt to this new 'equal adult' relationship than others; all of us still see ourselves as parents and our concern and wish to support our children continues, albeit in a different form. When our children take their own lives, we scour the past, unpicking their childhood in an attempt to understand, and we ask ourselves the question: 'how did it happen, when did it all begin?'

Our children's stories
Many of our children were high achievers who set themselves high standards and met with conspicuous success:

> She was an extremely bright little girl with a voracious appetite for knowledge, life and people. Her career at school covered a wide spectrum of interests, both academic and in all other fields.

Some of us look back with hindsight and see shadows:

> Most of the time Jim was happy and cheerful, always ready to get the most out of life, but he did have times of depression. At these times, he would become unmotivated and find it hard to complete his work on time. He would spend a lot of time sleeping. However, he could recover from these times very quickly and soon got back on track.

Even incidents remembered as markers are only defined as such with hindsight:

> Our four-year-old, Ben, painted a totally black piece of paper and said it was 'his bedroom with the light off'; it was only recalled as a key to latent depression, rather than artistic awareness, when he had killed himself.

All of us who do look back and see shadows ask ourselves this question:

> How does one judge if a teenager is being 'normal', keeping things to himself and not wanting to share everything with his parents and siblings? Isn't that what adolescence is about – becoming independent, knowing more about everything, sometimes feeling superior? He was popular, thriving, busy – a little self-contained and demanding. Had everything turned out well, I would not have remembered this.

All of our children died while at college or university or just afterwards. For some families, the late teenage years were a rollercoaster ride, knowing that our child was depressed, trying to help them find effective help, hoping that counselling or new medication would be the solution, but knowing that we could only go so far. Some of us watched helplessly, as treatments and medications were tried in turn, or in combinations, in an attempt to find something which was effective while still giving an acceptable quality of life. We discovered that our able and articulate children were not prepared to live a stupefied existence merely to stay alive, and they were often intolerant patients. We learnt that this was not something we could 'fix', like a plaster on a knee. Some of us had already had to support our child after a suicide attempt: 'At the age of fifteen Robert took an overdose of paracetamol. He would not see a GP or a counsellor after his first suicide attempt.'

Even at this age, when we are faced with refusal and it is our first real contact with depression, we are at a loss to know what to do for the best. We look back and remember these times. When our children are older, it is no easier to help:

> I was aware that Guy was very miserable. We talked about this. He said something had happened a short while before but that he could not talk about it. I asked him if he needed help and suggested he could have some counselling. This was met with a quizzical smile and a refusal. He was uncertain if he wanted to go back to college. I left the decision to him after discussing various possibilities. He seemed to have thought things through rationally.

Some of us, in the face of a polite refusal to let us help directly, agonised over what else we could do:

> Two days before he died, I had such an uneasy feeling about him that I went to the phone to contact the polytechnic counselling service. I did not trust my instinct enough and felt that Ashley would be annoyed if I interfered in his life. Suicide never once entered my head. I just felt he was struggling and needed some expert help. I never made that call.

Other families found they could offer help that was accepted. Some of our children felt isolated and unhappy, for a wide variety of reasons: 'From a hall of residence, he had moved into a rented house with friends from his first year. None of them took his subject or had to work hard for exams during that year.' Difficulties in communication can become real obstacles:

> He did not have a phone in his Hall so had to go out to use a public phone box. He told me later that he really missed us after we left and felt homesick and unsettled for a while, although this was not evident to his friends or to the college.

It seems that for some of our children, it is regular contact with home that enables them to continue:

> At home that Christmas she became very anxious about her 'writer's block', and all through the spring term would ring in tears about not being able to put the work on paper. Each call was agony, but by the end of spring she was calmer (perhaps on prozac again), and was awarded a

scholarship for her first year's attainment as well as being voted vice-president of the Junior Common Room [college students' union] in charge of accommodation and welfare.

But even when quite openly asking for support, and clearly in deep distress, it is not always possible to get the help needed:

> The first time we knew she was really ill … she told us that she felt a 'compulsion' to wade into the reservoir near her flat. She broke down and we were completely devastated. She had wet clothing with her and we knew it was true … I took her to the family GP next morning but stayed outside as she wanted privacy. I regret that I didn't go in as I later heard from him that she had presented a radiant smile and said her exams were a worry and he prescribed mild tranquillisers.

This highlights one key issue that comes through in so many of our stories: frequently our children employ a massive cover-up that may include friends, tutors and family – even health care professionals. Often we do not realise that this is going on, that even their closest friends perhaps do not know that they are depressed. Sometimes we only discover later, maybe by chance, that our child has been taking anti-depressants for years, that they have made one or more suicide attempts of which we knew nothing. Even when we do know the seriousness of the problem, we find it almost impossible to approach the issue:

> At this stage there had been no contact between us, the family, and the university… I didn't know what to do and felt the need to discuss things with a health care professional, but didn't know how I could do this without compromising Kate's need for confidentiality. I rang a local mental hospital to discuss the pros and cons of psychiatric help.

Some of us do feel that the university was constructive in supporting time out, keeping course enrollment open and giving our child time to recover from a severe episode of mental illness or breakdown. What seems to be missing from all our accounts is any real sense of partnership – of support services, tutors and parents being able to work together with a student in crisis. We will return to explore this later in the chapter.

When our child dies

The world changes for ever when we hear that our child is dead. For each of us, the circumstances are unique yet equally devastating; for some it is a totally unexpected shock, while others have lived in the shadow of suicide attempts, perhaps for years. Some families have had to endure a period when their child was missing, fearing the worst, but waiting weeks before a body was found. Even those of us who knew of earlier suicide attempts were never prepared for the reality when it came. Our experiences of the police are varied in the extreme, but are not relevant here. Our first direct contact with college or university often only begins at this point, when it is too late to work together, when our child is dead. For some of us the contact was straightforward: 'Friends, neighbours, colleagues, tutors, the police – all were kind and supportive, as were his peers and friends. We had no struggle to get answers to questions.'

And some of us met great openness and a willingness to talk:

> We wanted to meet his art tutors to see if they knew any reason why he had taken his life. They were stunned at the news and told us he had been doing very well at his course, had completed work on time and had a lot of friends.

Sometimes contact was maintained in an imaginative and thoughtful way:

> Ashley's tutor wrote to say that his attendance and marks had been good, there had been no obvious problems. The student counselling service promised to review support services available to students on halls of residence. They prompted a friend to write to me, outlining Ashley's last movements.

For others, the communications and dialogue were less satisfactory:

> After the announcement of my daughter's death, the university seemed to want to fade out of the picture. The doctor and therapist treating her in the last two months of her life were not forthcoming and I was the one who had to make the effort to investigate... We received an official letter of condolence from the vice-chancellor 'on behalf of all the staff who knew Kate', but nothing more personal was ever written to us... When I look back, I find the 'wall of silence' extremely hurtful to the bereaved family. Equally, when I asked to meet a favourite tutor to talk about my daughter I was discouraged. None of her course work could be found

anywhere when I asked. The university did not help the bereavement process. I now feel they were frightened of doing so by legal constraints.

This is not the only example where the family feel that anxiety about possible criticism of the care given to their child prevented the college or university giving them full information. Sometimes we are told that an enquiry will take place but, although we have asked specifically to be informed of the actions taken, we are told nothing. Sometimes, the university or college has been much more direct than the health care services:

> A full independent inquiry was set up, the results and recommendations of which were sent to us. They now have in place a high-profile welfare policy and use the money from a fund set up in her name, to send students on welfare training courses.

Thus, in some instances, parents are able to make suggestions which result in specific help being made available, such as articles in student newspapers on stress and exam preparation. In one instance, volunteer examination 'advisors' were set up to help students under stress and help them to find the right support network. It seems clear from these few examples that dialogue with parents can be both supportive and fruitful.

With hindsight

All of us wish that our child's story had not ended in death by suicide, and all of us, as we unpick the past, can see times when things should have been handled differently. Some of these are personal to our family: the times we did not manage to say what was in our hearts, pick up the phone when we were worried, check whether someone was alright. Most of us, though not all, feel that our child's death represents a failure of parenting at some level:

> We knew, we would always know, that the burden of guilt was ours, totally and completely. I, her mother, had not protected my child; I had not saved her from the black demons of despair and her despair was now mine for ever.

This feeling is not one grounded in logic, to be proved or disproved; it is simply a graphic statement of how we feel when our child takes his or her own life. But hindsight is more than guilt; it can teach us lessons that may be of practical importance to others.

All of us wish that we had known more about depression and other mental illnesses, and feel that such knowledge would have helped:

> I regret that the possibility of suicide did not enter my thoughts, so I never asked him about suicidal feelings. I feel that to have helped my son I needed to be more aware.

There are two issues here: the need for better understanding and the need for openness, so that these matters can be discussed, both within and outside the family.

> Why is it that depression is particularly a 'no-go area'? – ME and epilepsy are now understood and accepted by most people. Depression carries a sort of guilt with it, and a fear... Perhaps its name should change as it is too easily confused with having a low day 'so buy yourself a cream bun and have a relaxing bath'. Perhaps it should have a name like cancer of the mind, except that implies no cure.

This desire for greater awareness encompasses our children and their friends, not just ourselves as parents. For the young it clearly needs to begin at school, so that young people go on to higher education knowing that suicidal thoughts and dark depression are not unique to them, nor are they shameful. We know that this knowledge cannot of itself prevent tragedies occurring, anymore than knowing about depression stops an individual suffering from it. However, we do want our children to be able to help each other, to know what to look out for and to have some idea about how to help.

Similarly, we wish we could have been better equipped to help:

> As parents we must find ways of keeping the lines of communication open with our adolescent children. If we do not, we may fail to recognise, or to respond appropriately, when things have reached crisis point. When our children go away to university we must find acceptable ways of supporting them and keeping in touch. Young men, in particular, may feel they should stand on their own feet and deal with problems of accommodation, finances, work and blending socially all on their own. Traditional role models do not encourage young men to reach out when problems arise.

Closely allied to this wish that we had been more successful in supporting our children, is the wish that we had better understood at the time the role concealment can play in mental illness. We all wanted to trust our children, to believe that they were in control of the decisions they were taking, to treat them as the equal adults that they were. But few of us realised to what extent the illness itself makes it impossible to seek the help needed. Even when we knew something of the severity of our children's problems, most of us did not feel able to contact tutors, health professionals, friends or student services against their wishes. We felt, at the time, that to do so would be to betray our children's trust, to step outside the perceived boundaries of our role as parents. Some of wish with hindsight that we had acted differently.

Diagnosis of our child's illness is seen by some of us to have been inadequate: too little and too late. With hindsight, and sometimes after considerable research, we believe vital clues were missed. Sometimes this was because those we confided in were not sufficiently knowledgeable to pick up the clues and refer them to an appropriate source of help. For example: a persistent sense of being followed, together with other symptoms, can be an indicator of schizophrenia. Perhaps with more information, tutors, counsellors – even friends – might have been able to help.

Many of us also wish that the treatment our children received had been more effective, less fragmented, and more directly targeted at their needs. The bottom line is, of course, that we wish it had been able to keep them alive through the crises they experienced, that they had had time to recover. There often seems to have been a lack of co-ordination between the various sources of support available. When we try to unravel the course of events, it seems that the communication between services at home and at university or college was often inadequate, sometimes even non-existent. As we try to understand what happened, there seems sometimes to have been a lack of communication between various agencies within the university. This may well have been compounded by the concealment strategies mentioned above; when students do not say that they have already been receiving treatment for their problems from another source, then connections may not be made. But that does not negate the fact that many of us think that better exchange of information might have resulted in more effective care. This is especially true when judgements have to be made about the risks of self-harm and, ultimately, suicide. There is also an urgent need for some form of swift response when a crisis looms; an appointment in six months' time is of little help.

At the core of these problems is the issue of confidentiality. Many of us now feel that, had we known more, the outcome might have been different:

> Far too much is made of confidentiality. It is like not putting a broken leg in plaster in case someone finds out it is broken! I wanted to go to the doctor with Simon but needed his permission, which he withdrew at the last moment. This was a life-threatening illness; confidentiality is pointless when things are really serious.

It seems that, if secrecy, isolation, and an inability to talk about the severity of a problem are part of the illness itself, then there is a Catch 22 situation. Health care professionals feel that their relationship with the patient must be based on trust, and that this involves not breaching a confidence without their explicit consent. But there is a real sense in which the illness itself impairs the ability to give consent. The complexities of this issue need wider discussion, but most of us feel that the current balance does not always give the best outcome. Because our children were adults, that does not mean there was no positive role for us, had we known more. Some of us, ironically, learnt about self-harm – why some profoundly suicidal people view death as a friend rather than an enemy, and why cutting can seem to release insupportable mental tension – only after our child had died. It would have been more useful to have understood these things earlier. And many of us wish there had been support services available to us, when we were in a caring role, to advise on ways of living alongside and supporting a deeply depressed person.

When our children were hospitalised, sometimes after a failed suicide attempt, many of us wish that more recognition could have been given of their particular needs. To say this is not elitist, it merely recognises that there are differences:

> We rang to find out why she had been released in a state of self-harm. We were told that she had appeared to them to be a borderline case and they dealt with many cases every day, applying the same criteria for everyone. But surely highly intelligent young people need to be judged by different

criteria; they are used to words and ideas and are more adept at covering up their feelings?

Similarly, those of our children who were placed in a secure psychiatric ward found it an impossible place to be: 'They are all mad here. I cannot talk to anybody'. The extremes of behaviour can be profoundly disturbing, especially to a young person in a fragile mental state who has never witnessed anything similar before. The care staff often appear to be in a custodial rather than a supportive role, and the ward is seen as a place to avoid returning to at all costs. This in turn creates more anxiety, and severe problems may be concealed from doctors when they attend for appointments and consultations. Anything, including death, is better than going back into hospital. We recognise that there is massive under-funding in this area, but it is another where, with hindsight, we feel our children were not given the help they needed, nor an appropriate place of safety in which to recover.

When our child died while in the care of the psychiatric services (perhaps having been in hospital and not wishing to return there), some of us were asked whether we wished with hindsight that they had been detained under the Mental Health Act. Our responses are varied and uniquely personal, though we all wish that our child had been able to stay alive and recover. For those of us who witnessed a long battle with a seemingly incurable and ultimately terminal depressive illness, our thoughts are complex. We respect our child's right to choose, and in that sense, see theirs as a 'complete' life, however tragically cut short and however deeply we wish that the outcome had been otherwise. Some of us have more than one perspective:

> As a long-serving Samaritan, I believed that people have the right to take their own life. I still do, but – and this is a big but – I also believe that we should do everything possible to support the person in crisis. Some crises do pass and people can come through the other side. Samaritans cannot break their code of confidentiality, but they encourage people, by every means in their power, to explore those dark demons that make living seem so futile. No judgements are made and no stigma attached. One of the main debates I would like to see opened out is a willingness to talk about feelings of suicide. Many of us have them, but we have had to learn, painfully, to walk beside them without shame and guilt. The young do

not always have the life experience to bring to bear on these things and they need to be nurtured, by every means possible, until they can manage.

The need for regular and frequent contact to be maintained at many different levels is also something we recognise more fully with hindsight. First year students, away from their familiar base for the first time, need to be supported; perhaps mobile phones should be seen as a necessary link and not a luxury. Gemma's account in the previous chapter (p.53) testifies to the difficulty of relying on public phone boxes. Students need to be able to receive calls from family and friends in private so that they can talk freely. Students do feel isolated, especially when their place of residence is far from the campus and travel is difficult and expensive, when there are no obvious support services locally, and when they have yet to make new friends. These things are doubly true for those with depression. To put up a poster with a phone number is not enough, although it is better than nothing. There is a real need to be proactive, both with student support services and with health care. If an appointment is missed, it should not be assumed that the problem has resolved itself; rather, it should be seen as a cause for concern.

One issue lies at the heart of all these thoughts and is summed up by this parent:

> The whole thing really comes down to lack of communication between all concerned – school, university, doctors, counsellors, friends and family ...and Simon, of course. In fact, it is the total impossibility of communication and the fact that it is virtually forbidden that is the problem. Simon's wishes had to be respected – but he was ill. That is why he saw suicide as the solution.

The way forward

Nothing is static and new initiatives are taking place all the time. However, there is still much to be done. From our experiences as parents of children who took their own lives, we offer these suggestions:

1. Young people must be educated about mental illness so that they recognise the symptoms in themselves or in someone they

know. Young people must know how to respond if someone they know is suffering, and there must be support services in place that are immediately and easily accessible. The discussion of these issues needs to begin at school. Time should be built into the national curriculum, and a proper delivery of study programmes should be supported by adequate funding and effective training for those teachers responsible. As well as tutor group sessions, personal, social and health education programmes and drama should be used as vehicles to explore these subjects. Discussion needs to cover both what it feels like to be depressed or suicidal oneself, and also how to support and get help for a friend who is troubled. Research has refuted the myth that we should not speak about suicide because then we 'put the thought into their heads'; there is ample evidence that it is there already (Pritchard 1995).

2. When putting programmes and services into place in universities and colleges, it is vital to consult with the students themselves about appropriate courses of action. We need to understand their needs and fears, to listen to them when they tell us about the things they believe would work, and not to waste resources on schemes that will be of no use. By raising these issues, we are also taking a significant step in changing the climate of opinion and opening out discussion.

3. There needs to be considerable support at the very beginning of a new student's life, even before they start their course. This should build on school education programmes, perhaps with shared conference sessions of sixth formers and current local students. Induction weeks should include information about support services available and how to access them. Written information needs to be backed up by personal contact. No one can guarantee that this will result in everyone getting all the help they need, but it does enlarge the safety net.

4. There should be thorough, compulsory and properly funded training for all tutors who have a pastoral responsibility for students; it is not enough to leave it to people's good

intentions. If there are clear requirements, for example that all first-year students should be contacted personally by their pastoral tutor in their first month at college, then there is at least a case to be made for funding this.

5.   In some areas there are concerns about the new student's contact with local health care provision. Perhaps all students should be required to register with either the student health service or with a local GP, with formal notification of this so that each is aware of the other's existence.

6.   If students are required to register with the student health service, then perhaps some strategy could be agreed to address issues of confidentiality and contact should a crisis occur. Some counselling centres ask clients to sign a 'personal safety' clause, giving permission for next of kin or other named person to be contacted if, in the doctor's opinion, they pose a threat to their own or another's safety. This would not guarantee such contact, but it would at least offer the possibility of discussion with family during a crisis.

7.   Further to the central issue of confidentiality: there should be clearly defined protocols for the sharing of information between the various support services within the college or university. There are complex questions to be resolved about privacy and the rights of an individual. These need to be discussed widely, not least with the students themselves. If attitudes within society changed, if mental illness was no longer stigmatised, but became just another illness like diabetes, then it would become easier to move forward on these issues.

8.   There is also a case for support systems at times of high stress, particularly during examinations. Trial schemes have provided specific help through exam 'advisors'. Students who leave examinations early are told of the help available to them, and there has been a good response to such a direct approach.

9.   If we are to reach more students with problems, then there needs to be a wide range of services available, not all linked

directly to health care, using a variety of approaches. The work of the Samaritans has pioneered the model of a confidential phone service combined with a drop-in contact point. Schemes such as '42nd Street' in Manchester offer services to meet recognised local needs that can be useful to students.

Night-time phone support lines and internet chat rooms offer initial contact to an individual who feels unable to seek out face-to-face professional treatment.

10. Underlying all these above is the huge issue of education – both to raise the level of basic awareness, and to change the current climate of opinion about mental illness, including depression. This will be a long process, but schools and higher education institutions seem logical places to initiate new programmes and target funding.

Awareness is growing all the time, but more needs to be done if future generations of students are to get the support services they need to survive in an increasingly pressured world.

Acknowledgements

Contact was made with families through Papyrus, an organisation founded by parents who have lost a child through suicide, and also through the Compassionate Friends, a national organisation of bereaved parents. We would like to thank all those who told their stories to make this chapter possible. Some have wished to remain anonymous, but those who have shared their stories include: Jacquie Kingston, mother of Ashley; Janet Roques, mother of Simon; Angela Napuk, mother of Sarah; Fred and Helen Segar, the parents of Robert; Stephanie, mother of Kate; Pauline and Charles, parents of Jim; and Arthur Thomlinson, father of Leon.

Useful contacts

The Compassionate Friends

> 53 North Street
> Bristol
> BS31EN
> Helpline: 0117 9539639
> Office: 0117 9665202
> website: www.tcf.org.uk
> e-mail: info@tcf.org.uk

PAPYRUS: Parents Association for the Prevention of Young Suicide

> Rosedale GH
> Union Road
> Rawtenstall
> Rossendale
> Lancashire
> BB4 6NE
> Tel and fax: 01706 214449

References

Pritchard, C. (1995) *Suicide – The Ultimate Rejection? A Psycho-Social Study.* Birmingham: Open University Press.

PART TWO

Exploring the Problems

Chapter 5

Identifying Students' Concerns
Taking a Whole Institutional Approach

Annie Grant

Introduction

In the UK, the transformation of a relatively well-funded elite higher education system into a comparatively poorly funded mass system has resulted in significantly worse staff–student ratios, requiring a rethinking of both teaching methods and the way that pastoral and other personal support are delivered. The consequent reduction in the amount of personal contact between academic staff and students has been offset, to some extent, by an expansion in the range of specialist central student services provided in many institutions, although the ratios of support staff to students have not necessarily improved. Academics are gradually relinquishing their role in respect of personal support, and referring students with personal concerns and problems to the central service providers.

At the University of Leicester, the expansion of central provision for students included the creation, in 1995, of the Educational Development and Support Centre (EDSC). This unit brings together a range of development and support services for students (careers, welfare and counselling services, AccessAbility centre, sick bay and Student Learning Centre) and a Teaching and Learning Unit that offers services for staff to encourage the development of their teaching. This particular grouping of provision makes explicit the link between effective teaching and appropriate support for learning. MacFarlane (1995) defined education as the 'design, manage-

ment and creation of environments which support the learning process'
(p.54). At Leicester, the provision of that learning environment is viewed
as the joint responsibility of the academic departments and the central
academic and pastoral support providers, with its effectiveness for the
student learners predicated on the strength of the partnerships and
inter-relationships that exist between these different groups. It is this
model and approach that underpins the work undertaken at Leicester in
respect of students experiencing mental health difficulties.

The Leicester Student Psychological Health Project

When the 1996–9 'Special Initiative to Encourage High Quality Provision
for Students with Learning Difficulties and Disabilities' was announced by
the Higher Education Funding Council for England (HEFCE 1996), staff
at Leicester had already identified provision for students experiencing
mental health difficulties as a priority area for development. A successful
bid was made by the EDSC to HEFCE for a project that aimed to improve
support for these students. The specific objectives were to raise the awareness, knowledge and skills of the whole university community and,
through the production of training and study support guidelines and
materials, to enhance provision.

A number of earlier HEFCE-funded projects at Leicester had been
located within specialist student service units, but the framework of the
infrastructure for this new project was much broader, and involved the
whole institution. The rationale for this approach was twofold. First, it
would help to overcome the difficulties of identifying those students
whose views needed to be heard and who might most benefit from the
work. Mental ill health is not clearly defined nor even, in very many
instances, clearly visible to others and there is still a very strong stigma
attached to mental illness that frequently inhibits disclosure. Psychological
distress can have an effect on every aspect of functioning, from academic to
personal, social and economic. Locating the project within the disability
unit or counselling service would have helped us to understand and
respond to the needs of only those students who had chosen to seek help
and perhaps, although not necessarily, those with some of the severest dif-

ficulties. It would not have helped us to determine and respond to the full extent of student difficulties or to understand the issues and concerns that were having the greatest impact on students' well-being.

Second, it would allow us to work on a much broader front, consistent with our views about the importance of the relationship between the centre and the academic departments in the creation of an effective learning environment. If the project was to be successful in achieving its aims, it was crucial that it was embedded within the systems and structures of the institution, and that it involved a wide range of staff.

Although the focus of the three-year project had to be on implementation and not primarily on research, establishing a robust evidence base was fundamental. Many of those involved in higher education believe that there are now more students experiencing mental health problems than in the past (for example, Rana *et al.* 1999). Declining staff–student ratios and some improvement in social attitudes to mental illness will inevitably have contributed to this perception. However, whether or not this equates to an increased incidence in the student population is not possible to say in the absence of robust longitudinal studies. A longitudinal study was not possible, but establishing a baseline was, and from the outset it was felt that a survey would be the only way to identify the nature and extent of mental health problems in the student population, and to understand the issues that were causing students the most concern. A quantitative approach was chosen in order to obtain the broadest view possible. However, the potential value of qualitative information obtained through interviews was also recognised and a number of focus groups were run after the initial analysis of the survey data to clarify issues raised.

A review of the literature revealed that previous work on student well-being had concentrated mainly on particular issues such as alcohol and drug use or eating disorders, and there was very little prior work that had attempted to look broadly at the wide range of issues that might impact on students' mental well-being. An exception is a survey that was undertaken at Columbia University in the US in 1986 and 1988 (Bertocci *et al.* 1992), and their questionnaire was adapted for one section of our own survey instrument so that we could have some basis for comparison.

The questionnaire designed by the survey team was divided into a number of sections. The first section sought wide-ranging demographic information: Table 5.1 summarises the responses most relevant to the following discussion.

Table 5.1. Demographic characteristics of the University of Leicester student survey sample

Demographic characteristic	N*	%
Sex		
Male	722	46
Female	845	54
Age		
18 – 21 years	1334	84
22 – 25 years	176	11
Over 25 years	81	5
Ethnicity		
White	1267	80
Non-white	324	20
Fee status		
Home	1345	87.5
International	192	12.5
Year of study		
first year	297	18
second year	1156	71
third year	99	6
fourth/fifth year	33	2
other	35	2

* *Students who did not provide the relevant information are excluded.*

The next major section was based on the Columbia University survey (Bertocci *et al.* 1992), slightly modified to make it appropriate and relevant for students in Britain. The questions were designed to identify the extent to which a wide range of issues impacted on the respondent's own self-perceived stress levels. Sixty-one questions were included relating to a wide range of concerns including academic study, careers, general health, sexual health, interpersonal relationships, self confidence and family problems.

Further sections included questions on alcohol and drug use, eating and weight control and the extent to which students' drug and drinking habits, personal problems, physical health and psychological problems impacted on their academic and personal responsibilities. The final section asked about students' help-seeking behaviour. Included with the in-house instrument was a copy of the Brief Symptom Inventory (BSI). This is a self-report instrument that has been extensively used in both clinical and research practices to provide an initial evaluation of a comprehensive range of mental health problems (Derogatis and Melisaratos 1983; Boulet and Boss 1991; Derogatis 1993; Hayes 1997). The BSI comprises an inventory of 53 items designed to reflect psychological symptoms. Respondents are asked to rate on a 5-point scale the extent to which they were distressed by each of the items (Derogatis 1993).

The primary target of the survey was second-year undergraduate students (see Table 5.1), both on grounds of practicality (students in later years of their courses are often less accessible as they are largely taught in smaller groups on option courses) and to ensure that the responses reflected a significant experience of studying in the higher education environment. In order to ensure a good response rate, whenever possible the questionnaire was administered and completed within scheduled lecture time. The co-operation of academic staff was essential and generously offered. This survey method ensured a very high response rate of 77 per cent of our target population; 1620 students completed the questionnaire, which was administered in February and March 1998.

Student concerns

Analysis of the survey results has provided insights into a wide range of student concerns and behaviours, only some of which can be discussed here. This section concentrates on academic and career concerns, psychological well-being and alcohol consumption, but a general overview of the issues that were of particular concern to students is given in Table 5.2.

Table 5.2. Issues impacting on student stress levels

Concerns reported by students	*%* of students identifying significant impact on stress levels*
Study concerns	
concentration	58
study skills	53
ability to manage and complete coursework	60
ability to set priorities, make decisions and manage time	59
overcoming fears about taking exams	51
ability to clarify and meet academic and/or career goals	63
Careers issues	
dealing with concerns about preparing for a career	61
overcoming specific fears about finding a job/career	55
Adjustment to student life	
getting used to university life	40
coping with inadequate/ unsatisfactory housing	41
dealing with severely inadequate finances	58
General and psychosocial health	
general worry about health	26
managing vague anxieties, phobias or panic attacks	23
coping with sadness, depression or mood changes	40
Personal development	
being assertive	49
improving my self-esteem and confidence	48
understanding and coping with loneliness	32
Relationships	
developing trust in friendships	50
maintaining a love relationship	41

* Percentage of respondents who indicated that the issue had a crucial or very important impact on their stress levels.

The overall levels of stress and anxiety reported were generally high. For example, 40 per cent of the respondents, most of whom were already in their second year of study, reported that getting used to university life was having a crucial or very important impact on their stress levels. The very high level of stress in respect of inadequate finances should also be noted; student financial concerns are discussed in detail in Chapter 6.

Academic and career concerns

There were eight questions in the section on stress factors that related specifically to academic or career concerns (see Table 5.2). Reported stress levels were high for each of these issues, with over 50 per cent rating them as having a crucial or very important impact. It is not surprising that students feel stressed by academic pressures, but the levels of reported stress were higher than were predicted by the project team. It was more surprising that career preparation issues were rated so highly by the predominantly second-year student group (see Table 5.1). The levels of concern about career preparation and finding a job were not significantly different between different year cohorts, but students expressing the greatest levels of concern about career preparation were more likely to have used the university's careers service than those who were less concerned, suggesting that for some students their concerns had led to productive behaviour. Students' use of support services is discussed in more detail below.

Of particular significance are some other differences that emerged when further detailed analyses were undertaken of the responses of different groups of students. There were significant differences (chi-square tests, $p < 0.01$) between males and females on four of the eight issues: managing coursework, dealing with concerns about taking exams, preparing for a career and finding a job. A higher proportion of female students found these issues crucially or very concerning. Age was a significant factor for four of the issues, with a higher proportion of the oldest age group, the over 25 year olds, finding managing coursework and dealing with concerns about exams particularly stressful, and a higher proportion of the 22 to 25 year olds rating finding a job and preparing for a career particularly stressful. A higher proportion of students from ethnic minority back-grounds (38% of whom were international students) rated all eight academic and career issues crucially or very concerning (chi-square tests, p<0.001).

Some degree of stress and anxiety may be considered normal in the student population, particularly about academic issues. However, an experimental study by Fransson (1977) in the 1970s showed that students were more likely to use surface learning and reproductive methods of recall when they felt threatened. Our survey was anonymous, and we were not able to correlate the results with student academic performance, but levels of stress that may have a serious impact on academic functioning must be a matter of concern for the HE sector, particularly if some groups of students are more likely to be adversely affected than others. The Leicester results do not appear to indicate a specifically local problem: on the contrary, very similar results were obtained by Bertocci and colleagues (1992). This is discussed in more detail below.

Mental health problems

The survey was not designed to diagnose specific mental health problems, although the BSI was used to gain some indication of overall levels of psy-chological functioning and of the types of difficulties that students were experiencing. The BSI results were scored on the six factors that Hayes (1997) derived from an analysis of the results of a survey of 2078 American college and university counselling centre clients. Means for each of Hayes' sub-scales are given in Table 5.3 for the total Leicester student sample, and separately for those who had used the counselling service in order to provide a more appropriate comparison with Hayes' (1997) results, which are also included in the Table. The average ages of the two student groups from America and Leicester were, respectively, 23.2 years (SD = 6.2) and 20.6 years (SD = 3.7).

The highest scores were on the depression, hostility, social comfort and obsessive-compulsive subscales, although the means for all subscales were below 1, indicating that on average students were only 'a little bit' distressed by the items included in each of the dimensions. However, the average for depression was close to 2 (moderately distressed) for the group of students who had consulted the counselling service.

Table 5.3. Brief Symptom Inventory subscale means and standard deviations for University of Leicester students and US college and university counselling service clients

	University of Leicester students (total sample) (N =1549)		University of Leicester students using the counselling service (N = 108)		USA college and university counselling service clients (Hayes 1997) (N = 2078)	
BSI Subscale*	M	SD	M	SD	M	SD
Depression	0.94	0.89	1.71	1.03	1.53	1.08
Somatisation	0.47	0.59	0.73	0.70	0.42	0.59
Hostility	0.73	0.78	1.07	0.98	0.78	0.84
Social comfort	0.85	0.82	1.38	0.93	1.01	0.92
Obsessive-compulsive	0.97	0.81	1.48	0.92	1.09	0.89
Phobic-anxiety	0.28	0.55	0.75	0.92	0.35	0.59

* Hayes 1997.

There is still no clear view as to the point on each of the subscales that indicate psychopathology (Hayes 1997, p.365), making it difficult to determine the incidence of very serious mental health problems among the student population. Table 5.4 indicates the proportion of students whose scores on each of the subscales were 2 or above. Approximately one in six students is likely to be experiencing at least moderately distressing symptoms of depression (including feeling blue, feeling lonely, feeling no interest in things and feeling hopeless about the future). Similar, and partly overlapping proportions are likely to be at least moderately distressed by symptoms of the dimensions defined as obsessive-compulsive (including trouble remembering things, difficulty making decisions, trouble concentrating and having to check and double-check what you do) and social comfort (including feeling disliked, feeling watched or talked about, feeling inferior and feeling easily hurt). Such feelings may well impact on students' academic performance and their ability to achieve their potential.

	BSI score ≥2
Table 5.4. Proportion of University of Leicester students with scores of 2 (moderately distressed) or more on the Brief Symptom Inventory subscales	
BSI Subscale *	%
Depression	14
Somatisation	3.5
Hostility	9
Social comfort	12
Obsessive-compulsive	13
Phobic-anxiety	3

* *Hayes 1997.*

Analysis of the BSI results indicated differences between male and female respondents. Mean ranks were significantly higher (Mann-Whitney, $p<0.01$) for women on the depression, somatisation, social comfort and phobic anxiety subscales. Mean ranks were significantly higher (Mann-Whitney, $p<0.001$) for students from ethnic minorities on all six dimensions (depression, somatisation, hostility, social comfort, obsessive-compulsive and phobic anxiety), confirming other survey findings about stress levels for these students.

Alcohol consumption

Two of the survey questions were about alcohol consumption. The first asked how much alcohol was consumed each week and the second asked how often the respondent drank over 10 units of alcohol on a single occasion. A unit of alcohol was defined as being equivalent to a single measure of spirits, a glass of wine or half a pint of beer, and is roughly equivalent to 80g of ethanol.

According to the UK *Sensible Drinking* guidelines, the levels of alcohol consumption unlikely to cause health damage are defined as below 3 to 4 units per day for men, and 2 to 3 units per day for women, that is, respectively, 21–28 and 14–21 units per week. Levels of alcohol consumption above these limits are considered to be abusive (ICAP 1996). The survey results indicate that over 25 per cent of male and 14 per cent of female students are drinking well above the maximum recommended levels, and a further 17 and 31 per cent, respectively, may also be drinking at levels that are harmful. Thus although, in general, women students reported drinking significantly less alcohol than men, a higher proportion of women may be drinking at harmful levels.

Perhaps of even more concern is the proportion of students who report frequent heavy drinking episodes. 'Binge' drinking is variously defined, but is 'characterised by the consumption of alcohol to intoxication within a short period of time' (ICAP 1997). For the Leicester survey, students were asked how often they consumed 10 units or more of alcohol on one occasion. The results suggest that a significant proportion of students' alcohol consumption is in heavy drinking bouts. Fifty-eight per cent of students claimed to drink heavily at least once a month, and over 50 per cent of male students and 25 per cent of female students were drinking the equivalent of five pints or more on a single occasion at least once a week. Again, the effects of these levels of drinking are likely to be even more serious for the women drinkers than for the men. There is not surprisingly a significant correlation between high levels of overall consumption and binge drinking. However, some of the modest drinkers reported weekly or monthly binge drinking – the 'Saturday night' effect.

There were no significant differences between the mean ranks of BSI scores for five of Hayes' (1997) six dimensions for those who reported drinking at least 30 measures of alcohol per week, and for the more moderate drinkers and abstainers. The same was true for four of the dimensions for those who reported drinking 10 units or more on a single occasion at least once a week. The exceptions were for the phobic anxiety dimension for which significantly lower mean ranks (Mann-Whitney, $p<0.005$) were found for the heavy drinkers and the frequent binge drinkers. There were also lower mean ranks (Mann-Whitney, $p<0.01$) on the obsessive compulsive dimension for the frequent binge drinkers.

The drinking behaviours of British and, in particular, American students have been much discussed (for example, Meilman *et al.* 1989; Carey 1995; see also Roberts and Zelenyanszki, this volume) and are a matter of considerable concern for the higher education sector. Binge drinking in particular is strongly discouraged by health promotion experts who cite the increased risk of accidents and injuries, including traumatic injury and violent death (Roizen 1989) in addition to increased risks of a number of serious medical problems. Such drinking appears to be considered 'normal' amongst a significant proportion of the student population. However, a cross tabulation of amounts of alcohol consumed, against responses to a survey question on levels of concern about alcohol usage, showed a significantly higher level of concern by those who reported drinking more than 10 pints a week, suggesting that some students are very concerned about their alcohol consumption and may be receptive to help and advice.

There is no evidence from the Leicester survey that heavy drinking is a symptom of mental health problems, but it may sometimes be difficult for non-specialist staff to distinguish between symptoms of depression or other psychological health problems and those of heavy drinking.

Help-seeking behaviour

The section of the questionnaire on help-seeking behaviour was designed to enhance our understanding of students' use of both central and departmental provision as sources of help and advice. The responses to this section (Table 5.5) confirmed the strength of the 'whole institutional' approach by demonstrating unequivocally that students in difficulty sought advice from a very wide range of sources, both 'official' and 'unofficial': from personal tutors and student services personnel, to porters and cleaners. The primary source of advice for the majority of students was their friends and family. Within the institution it is the staff in the students' academic department to whom students most commonly turn, particularly to the personal tutor (see also the first chapter in this volume). The significance of these results was reinforced by further analysis. For those specifically seeking help for psychological problems, advice from personal tutors was only marginally less commonly sought than advice from the professional counselling service. Students are no different to the rest of us: when they need help they are most likely to turn first to those they already know.

Table 5.5. Students' help-seeking behaviour	
Source of advice	% students seeking advice
Friends and family	65
Personal tutor	54
Other academic staff	35
Departmental secretary	21
Student health centre	40
Careers service	23
Welfare service	11
Student learning centre	8
Counselling service	7
AccessAbility centre	3
Student union	3
Chaplaincy	2
Porters, cleaners and security staff	3
Other/community services	4

Further analysis revealed differences in the help-seeking behaviour of particular student groups. Those using the counselling service had higher means on each of the six BSI subscales defined by Hayes (1997) (Table 5.3). However, although students with the severest difficulties, as measured by the BSI, were more likely than other students to seek such professional help, approximately three-quarters of the former had not used the counselling service.

There were also differences in the help-seeking behaviour of students from ethnic minority backgrounds, who were significantly (chi-square tests, $p < 0.05$) less likely than other students to consult academic staff (other than their personal tutors), departmental secretaries and the university health service, but more likely to consult the welfare service where there is a specialist adviser for international students. The differences between male and female students were less pronounced, although female students were more likely to use both the counselling service and the health centre (chi-square tests, $p < 0.01$).

Our survey also suggested that the older the student, the more likely he or she was to consult their personal tutor, departmental secretaries and the welfare service. This may not indicate that they have more psychological problems (none of those over 25 years of age had scores within the top tenth percentile of the BSI scores), but that they have more confidence and are better able than younger students to seek help when they require it. This view is also supported by comparisons of the scores of the over 25 years group on the social comfort dimension of the BSI: their mean score was significantly lower (Mann-Whitney test, $p < 0.01$) than that for younger students.

Staff attitudes

At the same time as the student survey was being undertaken, a survey of staff was conducted. All categories of staff were sent a brief questionnaire by university internal mail; 642 completed forms were returned. Approximately half the respondents were academic staff and the rest included clerical, library, computer, student services and administrative staff, and porters and cleaners. Although the overall response rate was only just over 20 per cent, for academic staff it was almost 50 per cent. The questions on the staff survey instrument focused on their experiences of students with mental health problems, their behaviours (gauged through their responses to two brief scenarios), referral to other sources of support, and their training and information needs. Ninety-five per cent of the respondents who undertook a personal tutor role – and at Leicester this is the majority of academic staff – thought that supporting students with personal problems was an important or necessary part of their work. However, in response to a question about attendance at a training session only 45 per cent of academic staff said 'yes' they would attend such a session, and a further 6 per cent said 'perhaps'.

The problems of persuading academic staff to attend any kind of training course have been well rehearsed in staff development fora, and we should not necessarily particularise the reluctance expressed to attend the training offered as part of the project. The competing pressures of research, teaching and administrative duties create considerable tensions for academics: indeed, a number of the staff respondents indicated that they would value support in respect of their own problems and concerns.

Developing provision

The primary purposes of the surveys were to provide robust data to inform the development of provision, and our efforts focused initially on two main areas: training programmes for staff and resource materials for staff and students.

The project team developed a new staff development programme including workshops that focused on raising awareness of mental health issues, challenging prejudice, promoting positive attitudes, building confidence in responding appropriately to students, and knowing how and to whom to refer (see Dogra 2000; EDSC 2000). The use of case scenarios, developed specifically for training sessions for individual staff groups, has proved to be particularly effective. Participants work in groups to discuss their responses to the particular scenarios presented. Through discussion they are able to begin to differentiate between students who may have mental health problems and those who may be distressed, to develop understanding of their limitations in terms of both their skills and their remit and to understand how, when, and to whom to refer students for further help. Staff from the university counselling service played a major part in developing and delivering the workshop, and their knowledge and understanding of the issues and of the academic context have been invaluable.

Despite the fairly negative message about training from the staff survey there was a better response than was predicted to the staff development programme. There has been particular interest from departments whose Quality Assurance Agency (QAA) subject reviews are impending. Despite the many criticisms of the QAA process, it has been very effective in focusing attention on learning and teaching issues, and in stimulating interest in training for staff in their academic and pastoral roles. One outcome of the QAA review is a strengthening of the relationships between academic departments and student services at Leicester.

Workshops have also been run for careers staff, library staff and secretarial and clerical staff and these groups have tended to be particularly willing to attend, and be enthusiastic about training events. These staff groups had not previously been offered such training, as the assumption is often that it is not their role to support students in other than an administrative sense. However, as the help-seeking section of the student survey demonstrated (Table 5.5), students seek advice from staff across the institution. Training events have also been run for porters and security staff, who are often involved in crisis situations involving students. Feedback from participants indicated that they were particularly pleased to be offered guidance.

The work of the project derived great benefit from being part of a wider network of HEFCE-funded projects working in similar areas. Collaboration with the University of Nottingham was particularly fruitful (Grant and Woolfson 2001). Project teams from the two institutions met on a regular basis to exchange ideas and findings. Leicester was able to draw inspiration and ideas for a staff guide, 'Helping students in difficulties: a guide for personal tutors and other staff' (Grant 1999) from Nottingham's 'Identifying and responding to students in difficulty: a guide for personal tutors' (Woolfson 1999). The Nottingham guide was adapted and developed to incorporate knowledge and understanding gained from the Leicester student and staff surveys, and information of particular local relevance.

The Leicester guide, which includes sections on student difficulties, the pastoral role of university staff, identifying and responding to problems, confidentiality and internal and local support services, was distributed across the institution to all categories of staff following a launch event and an article in the university's staff bulletin. Responses to the guide, both at Leicester and at many other institutions, have suggested that the information included has met a very real need from staff who are increasingly concerned by some students' behaviour but unsure about their own roles and the best action to take. A number of presentations has also been made to individual departments, often at staff meetings, in which the results of the student survey are outlined, and key issues from the guide summarised. These sessions have stimulated a great deal of useful discussion and have provided a means of reaching staff who might not be willing to attend more formal training sessions. Having hard survey data to present has also proved effective in engaging the attention of an academic audience.

The university has also reviewed its examination procedures, and made some changes to ensure that these are fair to all, but also sensitive to those experiencing particular difficulties prior to or during exams. Students have for several years been able to sit their exams in small rooms or in the sick bay. Project staff collaborated with the academic office in developing guidelines for invigilators to help them respond to students who have panic attacks or become 'frozen' during exams.

Resources developed specifically for students include leaflets on exam stress and coping with interviews and presentations, and a series of leaflets on specific difficulties including depression, bereavement and self harm. Other developments included a first-year mentoring scheme, which is trying to tackle concerns about adjustment to university life, and an eating disorders self-help group. Further developments in response to project findings are underway or at the planning stage.

Conclusion

An understanding of the concerns of students and of their help-seeking behaviour is crucial to the development of institutional provision that is responsive and sensitive to the needs of a diverse student body and offers targeted and effective services and resources. There is every reason to suspect that the results of the Leicester University survey, although conducted in a single institution, have relevance for the rest of the higher education sector. The Columbia University findings were almost identical to the Leicester results for many of the questions, including, for example, those on concentration, time management and meeting career goals, even though this survey was conducted a decade earlier (Bertocci *et al.* 1992). Comparisons between the results of the two surveys were also very similar in other areas. For example, the relative proportions of students reporting concerns about depression and suicidal thoughts as crucially or very important were almost identical in the two surveys.

The Columbia survey also showed higher levels of concern amongst students from ethnic minorities, and more reluctance amongst this group to seek help. Table 5.3 indicates general similarities between Hayes (1997) and the Leicester survey, particularly in the relative importance of each of the dimensions identified. These similarities encourage us to believe that the causes of stress and the pattern of psychological disturbance cannot necessarily be related to the systems and structures of any individual institution, but may be related to more fundamental and intrinsic factors.

This does not, however, relieve us of any responsibility for ensuring that the learning environment in each institution is as responsive as possible to the needs of the full range of students. Widening participation brings with it a particular set of challenges, but also responsibilities. The challenge is in the way that we deal with these concerns and enhance the learning environment to try to ensure that all students are able to achieve their potential.

Crucial as student services are, the solution does not lie merely in improving provision centrally. The Leicester project has shown that students are most likely to seek help for a wide range of concerns from those with whom they have the most frequent contact on a regular basis: friends and family and, crucially, their personal tutors. For a smaller proportion of students, other academic staff and departmental secretaries also play an important role. This indicates the importance of giving attention to the environment in which students spend most of their time: their academic department.

This is by no means to suggest that academic staff should get deeply involved in the personal concerns of students. On the contrary, the training programmes that we have developed as part of this project have focused in particular on referral and on boundary issues. There is, however, a responsibility for all staff to be aware of the signs and symptoms of psychological disturbance, to know how to respond appropriately, and how and to whom to refer students for specialist support. Providing that staff are clear about their boundaries, the limits of their own expertise, and of the time they have available, then they can play a very appropriate role in helping students to manage their concerns and anxieties. Students who are experiencing difficulties may have particular problems with undertaking and completing their academic work, and may require guidance on managing their time and defining their priorities.

The levels of stress in respect of academic concerns also suggest that in developing curricula, HEIs should be looking seriously at the nature and structure of academic courses, the practical skills training offered to students, the modes and frequency of assessment, and their arrangements for particularly stressful events such as examinations.

Analysis of the differences in responses to the survey by particular student groups has helped the EDSC staff to begin to redefine some of its priorities. Mature students have often been singled out for special attention, both in terms of funding and general pastoral support. But the survey has suggested that these may be a relatively more robust group in several respects, and better able to seek help than many of both the younger students and those from ethnic minorities.

Other studies have also shown the difficulties that students from ethnic minorities may face. A small-scale study undertaken by Osler (1999) in the mid-1990s highlighted the sense of isolation that such students may feel. She drew attention to a number of issues, including a tendency by teaching and academic staff to underestimate such students' capacities – something that may contribute to the very high levels of anxiety about academic issues revealed by our study. Student services may be able to take action to improve their sensitivity, but unless such efforts are matched by moves across HEIs to encourage better representation from ethnic minorities amongst staff at all levels, and the development of more inclusive curricula, these groups of students may continue to be disadvantaged by the British higher education system.

Addressing the needs of students with the most severe mental health problems may be more difficult, not least because such students can be very difficult to identify. Although the proportion of students with the highest BSI scores were more likely to have used the counselling service than those with lower scores, only 27 per cent of the former group had used the counselling service, and a significant proportion of these students had not sought any professional help for psychological or personal problems. Again, a whole institutional approach is vital if these students are to be identified, responded to appropriately, and offered the right support when it is needed. The survey results have also highlighted the need to develop ways to reduce student alcohol consumption, perhaps as part of wider health promotion initiatives.

A role for student services that has perhaps been under-developed in higher education is in providing consultancy and training for other staff. The counselling service at Leicester has played a crucial role in delivery of the workshops developed as part of the psychological health project, and requests for advice from academic staff are now more frequent than before the project began. It is important that training becomes embedded within staff development programmes, including those on learning and teaching offered to new lecturers. Training and information should also be made available to all staff groups, not just academics. It is also vital that relevant information and advice are provided for the whole student body. The friends of students with psychological difficulties are often the first to notice the signs of distress, and may themselves need advice as to how best to respond. Some of the students who completed the survey noted that their help seeking had been on behalf of friends and not for themselves, a point discussed by Lago in this volume (Chapter 8). The difficulties of living with other students who are seriously ill should not be underestimated, particularly if self-harm is involved, as the personal accounts included in Chapter 3 illustrate. Many of the Leicester student guidance leaflets now include sections on how to respond if friends appear to be experiencing difficulties.

The whole institutional context of this project was fundamental in its formulation and has underpinned the work undertaken. The EDSC structure, which explicitly links teaching with learning, has also been crucial in establishing effective relationships with academic staff. Its location within the university's administration section also means that there are no structural barriers to impede productive working relationships with those who are responsible for admissions, examinations and quality assurance. University systems and structures are frequently more effective vertically (up and down hierarchical structures), than they are horizontally, across different academic, academic service or administrative units. If student services are to maximise their contributions to the well-being of the student and, indeed, the staff body, then they should not be isolated from the mainstream teaching and research activities of their institutions.

The cross-institutional networks that were created as a result of HEFCE initiatives have also proved to be valuable, particularly in respect of the work undertaken to improve provision for students experiencing mental health difficulties. If higher education is to be effective in ensuring that its diverse student body is able to gain maximum benefit from academic study, then more collaborative and inclusive working practices are essential.

Acknowledgements

The work of the University of Leicester Student Psychological Health Project was undertaken by a cross-institutional team. Members of the team were: Annie Grant, Project Director (Educational Development and Support Centre (EDSC)); Paula Mawson, Project Officer (EDSC); Carol Whitehouse, Project Administrator (EDSC); Nisha Dogra, Senior Lecturer and Honorary Consultant (Division of Child and Adolescent Psychiatry, Department of Psychiatry); David Stretch, Lecturer in Mathematical Psychiatry (Division of Child and Adolescent Psychiatry, Department of Psychiatry); Matthew Davis, Project Statistician (EDSC); and Catriona Walker,

Head of the Counselling Service (EDSC). The project's achievements are due to the hard work and commitment of all members of the team.

References

Bertocci, D., Hirsch, E., Sommer, W. and Williams, A. (1992) 'Student Mental Health Needs: Survey Results and Implications for Service.' *Journal of American College Health 41*, 3–12.

Boulet, J. and Boss, M. (1991) 'Reliability and Validity of the Brief Symptom Inventory.' *Psychological Assessment 3*, 3, 433–437.

Carey, K. (1995) 'Heavy drinking contexts and indices of problem drinking among college students.' *Journal of Studies on Alcohol 56*, 287–292.

Derogatis, L. (1993) *BSI Brief Symptom Inventory. Administration, Scoring and Procedures Manual* (3rd edition). Minneapolis: National Computer Systems.

Derogatis, L. and Melisaratos, N. (1983) 'The Brief Symptom Inventory: An Introductory Report.' *Psychological Medicine 13*, 596–605.

Dogra, N. (2000) 'Mental health awareness training: a pilot programme for university staff.' *International Journal of Mental Health Promotion 2*, 4, 29–34.

EDSC (Educational Development and Support Centre) (2000) Student Psychological Health Project: Mental Health Awareness. www.le.ac.uk/edsc/sphp/sphp-33.html

Fransson, A. (1977) 'On qualitative differences in learning IV – effects of intrinsic motivation and extrinsic test anxiety on progress and outcome.' *British Journal of Educational Psychology, 47*, 244–257.

Grant, A. (1999) *Helping students in difficulties: a guide for personal tutors and other staff.* Leicester: University of Leicester.

Grant, A. and Woolfson, M. (2001) 'Responding to students in difficulty: a cross-institutional collaboration.' *AUUC Newsletter and Journal 1* (February 2001), 9–11.

Hayes, J.A. (1997) 'What does the Brief Symptom Inventory measure in college and university counselling centre clients?' *Journal of Counselling Psychology, 44*, 1, 360–367.

HEFCE (Higher Education Funding Council for England) (1996) *Special Initiative to Encourage High Quality Provision for Students with Learning Difficulties and Disabilities.* London: HEFCE.

ICAP (International Centre for Alcohol Policies) (1996) *Safe Alcohol Consumption: A Comparison of 'Nutrition and your Health: Dietary Guidelines for Americans' and 'Sensible Drinking.'* ICAP Reports 1. *www.icap.org/publications/report1.html*

ICAP (International Centre for Alcohol Policies) (1997) *The Limits of Binge Drinking.* ICAP Reports 2. www.icap.org/publications/report2.html

MacFarlane. A. (1995) 'Future patterns of teaching and learning.' In T. Schuller (ed) *The Changing University.* Buckingham: SRHE and the Open University Press, 52–65.

Meilman, P., Yanofsky, N., Gaylor, M. and Turco, J. (1989) 'Visits to the college health service for alcohol-related injuries.' *Journal of College Health, 37*, 205–209.

Osler, A. (1999) 'The educational experiences and career aspirations of black and ethnic minority undergraduates.' *Race, Ethnicity and Education, 2*, 39–58.

Rana, R., Smith, E. and Walkling, J. (1999) *Degrees of Disturbance: the New Agenda.* Rugby: British Association for Counselling.

Roizen, J. (1989) 'Alcohol and Trauma.' In N. Giesbrecht, R. Gonzalez, M. Grant, E. Osterberg, R. Room, I. Rootman and L. Towle (eds) *Drinking and Casualties: Accidents, Poisonings and Violence in an International Perspective.* London: Tavistock/Routledge, 21–66.

Woolfson, M. (1999) *Identifying and responding to students in difficulty: a guide for personal tutors.* Nottingham: University of Nottingham.

Chapter 6

Degrees of Debt

Ron Roberts and Christiane Zelenyanszki

Introduction

The landscape of higher education within the UK has changed beyond recognition. Few people can be unaware of this – however, some of the serious consequences of these changes have yet to be fully appreciated, by the public at large, by academics and indeed by policy makers. The restructuring of higher education has been justified on the grounds that, in order to remain economically competitive, the country needs to possess a 'modern' system capable of delivering mass higher education. One of the obvious signs of this drive to competitiveness has been the rapid expansion in numbers of students enrolling in further and higher education in the UK; the bulk of this expansion occurring in the early 1990s when numbers in full-time education increased by 55 per cent. This expansion was most pronounced amongst women, whose numbers increased by 72 per cent. Amongst part-time undergraduates, enrolments for women increased by 88 per cent, in comparison to an increase of only 9 per cent for men. This strongly suggests that the forces responsible for restructuring the wider labour market toward more part-time casual employment – chiefly of women in low-paid work (Hutton 1995) – have also been active in the arena of higher education.

As numbers of students have rocketed, successive governments have failed to match this with real spending (Central Statistical Office 1997). Academic salaries have declined in relation to comparable professions, and the state's financial provision for students has come under progressive attack. This began with the maintenance grant being frozen; it continued with yearly reductions of 10 per cent, and culminated in the introduction of tuition fees and abolition of the mandatory grant, contrary to the explicit recommendations of the Dearing Report (1997).

Prevalence of financial difficulties in student populations

To date, little research has been conducted on the effects of these changes on student well-being. This is surprising given that several studies, both in the UK (Windle 1993; National Union of Students 1994; Berry 1995; Rickinson and Rutherford 1995) and internationally, have documented financial problems in students. Prior to the introduction of tuition fees, a survey by the National Union of Students (NUS 1994) found over half (53%) of the students sampled were in debt. Still in the UK, Berry (1995) found that over 90 per cent of women attending a northern English university were unhappy with their financial resources. Many of this sample also considered the prospect of abandoning their course of study because of their own financial difficulties. Lower figures have been reported by Rickinson and Rutherford (1995), who described just under a fifth (18.5%) of those surveyed as reporting severe financial problems. The discrepancy between this figure and others is probably explained by the fact that their sample comprised first-year students, who had not had sufficient time to accumulate higher debts.

The picture from inside the UK mirrors that found in other countries. Wherever information has been gathered, students appear to be under financial strain. This has principally come from two countries: Ireland and the United States. In a survey of Irish undergraduate students by Tyrrell (1992), managing money was seen as the most important stressor amongst first-year students, with just under a half (44 %) describing this as severely stressful. Further issues such as academic problems, time pressures and interpersonal relationships were also reported as stressful, though to a lesser degree.

Despite the cultural differences (until now) between the UK and the US systems of funding students in higher education, two American studies also describe financial problems in high percentages of students. Forty per cent of Dunkel-Schetter and Lobel's (1990) students described their financial responsibilities as frequently overwhelming, and, in another study, six out of every ten students reported experiencing financial problems within the previous six months (Frazier and Schauben 1994).

Given the diverse composition and locations of these studies, differences in the proportions of those experiencing financial difficulties should not be unexpected. All are consistent, however, in showing financial problems in a relatively high proportion of students. Work by Sands and Richardson (1984) should, in addition, remind us that as well as being a source of stress during study, low income stands in the way of those wishing to return to study. In one of the very few studies to examine any health correlates of financial problems in students, they also reported elevated levels of depression and anxiety among those with such difficulties.

Health and low income in students

Despite the above picture of extensive financial problems, we discovered almost no work had been undertaken to ascertain the consequences for students' mental and physical well-being. One possible reason for this omission may be the widely held stereotypes of student life, such as: young people always enjoying themselves, doing little work, going to parties and engaging in a range of hedonist activities. In short: students have fun, they do not get ill, and they tend to be drawn from the more well-off sections of society.

A considerable body of work, however, has existed for many years which repeatedly attests to strong relationships between financial stress and ill-health. These show relationships which are directly causal, as may arise from poor nutrition and bad housing, or which are indirectly causal, stemming from the social meanings and implications of having relatively little money (Wilkinson 1996). Difficulty in paying bills, for example, was found to be a major factor in explaining social class inequalities in depression and psychological well-being among British civil servants (Marmot *et al.* 1997).

As students in the UK have turned to the student loan system, many have moved into sizeable debt, and need to work long hours to maintain a viable standard of living. One study by Lindsay and Paton-Saltzburg (1993) found almost 60 per cent worked regularly during term time, with a third of these working over twenty hours each week. In 1997 the NUS estimated the mean debt for final year students at almost £5000 (Swanton 1997). The possibility that the resulting financial stresses could deter people from higher education and increase the risk of dropping out has also not gone unnoticed (Edmundson and Carpenter 1995).

This then was the picture we found on beginning our own work. We began with a smallish study of approximately 100 students from one of the new universities in London, the University of Westminster. Results from this (Roberts, Golding and Towell 1998) appeared to confirm our suspicions of health risks to students, and led to a larger scale study encompassing students from both Westminster and Imperial College – one of the established 'old' universities in London. Our overall aims were to examine the relationships present between students' economic and occupational circumstances, their health behaviours (smoking, drug and alcohol consumption), lifestyle, mental and physical well-being, the possibilities of dropping out, and some indicators of academic performance: attendance and meeting coursework deadlines. Preliminary and final results from this study were published in two further papers (Roberts, Golding, Towell and Weinreb 1999; Roberts *et al.* 2000). Below we summarise the principal findings to emerge from these and highlight some further as yet unpublished analysis from one of the authors.

The evidence

Economic and social circumstances

In all we received completed questionnaires from 482 students: 162 from Imperial College and 320 from Westminster. Although our study made no claims to be a random sample of the UK student population, where comparisons were possible, results were broadly similar to representative national student surveys in terms of: average ages (23.4 years for men and 24.2 years for women), the percentages in debt (43.4 %), and the amount of money owed. The overall average of money owed was £3403, though the average amount increased progressively through years one

(£2403.93), year two (£2638.57) and year three (£5593.02) of under-graduate study, and with the proportion working in addition to studying (47.1 %). The sample were predominantly undergraduates (87.4 %) and mainly comprised those in full-time education (85.9 %). We found no dif-ferences in level of debt between different ethnic groups or by social class (measured either by parents' occupation or self-described by respondents), but gender was important. Men were on average almost £717 deeper in debt. This remained (£711.31) even after adjustment for level of drug, alcohol and cigarette use.

Although just under half were in debt, a large majority (72 %) experi-enced some difficulty paying bills, with 12.2 per cent reporting great or very great difficulty. We noted with some concern that among those of our sample who had children, an even greater proportion (79 %) reported dif-ficulty in paying bills, with 46.2 per cent stating they were in debt. Economic hardship for students who are parents therefore is likely to entail hardship for their children too. With a direct link between poor childhood socioeconomic conditions and future morbidity shown by many research-ers (Barker 1990; Lundberg 1991; Wright, Waterson and Aynsley-Green 1994; Roberts 1997), our data suggests that adverse consequences of student hardship on the health of future generations may ensue, with increased costs to the health service. With around 2.5 million people cur-rently in further and higher education in the UK (for 19–20 year olds, around one-third of the available population: Wisniewski 1997), the potential burden of ill-health cannot be ignored. Plans to increase further participation rates whilst not addressing the health consequences of student hardship must be viewed as irresponsible.

For those working in addition to studying, the average working week amounted to just under 19 hours. Over 20 per cent were working at least 30 hours per week, and we found some who were working up to 50 hours. Little wonder then that many admitted to missing lectures because of working (71 % of those working) and handing in coursework late (11.5 % of those working). Though as yet there is no hard evidence that working to make ends meet affects degree performance, it is difficult on the face of this kind of evidence to imagine that it does not.

A little under 10 per cent (n=42) of the sample indicated that they had seriously considered dropping out of study for financial reasons. These students were also more than five times more likely to miss lectures because of the demands of outside work, more than three times more likely to be late handing in coursework, and twice as likely to be working in addition to studying. Among those working, those considering dropping out worked on average four hours more each week than those who did not, and were around £2000 more in debt.

General health

A number of measures were used to determine the health and well-being of our sample, designed to cover physical, psychological and social well-being. We used seven subscales of the UK version of the SF-36, a widely used generic health measure that includes scales to measure physical functioning, social functioning, role limitations caused by physical problems, role limitations resulting from emotional problems, vitality, bodily pain and perceptions of general health (Ware et al. 1993). Higher scores on these are indicative of better health. To measure mental health we employed the 12–item version of the General Health Question-naire (GHQ) (Goldberg and Williams 1988).

In comparison to population data for people of comparable age and sex – we made comparisons with the Health and Lifestyle Survey (Cox 1987) for the GHQ and for the SF-36 a large-scale survey by Jenkinson, Coulter and Wright (1993) – we found bodily pain, role limitations due to both physical and emotional problems, vitality, social functioning, perceptions of general health and mental health (as indexed by the GHQ) all to be sig-nificantly worse than established norms. Scores of physical functioning were similar. Thus, it is within the psychological and psychosocial dimen-sions of health (Roberts, Hemingway and Marmot 1997) where substan-tially poorer functioning is evident. For example, 43.5 per cent of respon-dents produced social functioning scores more than one standard devia-tion below the population mean. This compares with 16 per cent in a normal population.

As mentioned already, a range of health-related behaviours were also assessed. These included alcohol use (units of alcohol consumed during the preceding week, and the CAGE alcohol problems screening test (Mayfield, McLeod and Hall 1974)), smoking (numbers of cigarettes smoked) and recreational drug use (a summary score was calculated based on the number of different drugs used). Average weekly alcohol consumption for men was 16.7 units, and for women 9.3 units. Approximately one in three men (30.2 %) and one in five women (21.1 %) were drinking above the 'sensible' limits recommended by the Medical Royal Colleges (Royal College of Physicians 1995), and analysis of CAGE scores showed almost one in five (19.8 %) met the criterion for problem drinking (Zelenyanszki 1999). In all 32.3 per cent of women were current smokers and 23.4 per cent of men. Just over one in five (20.4 %) were currently using illicit drugs.

Correlates of debt

We performed a series of multivariate analyses to examine in greater detail the correlates of poor economic circumstances. Several variables were found to correctly predict problem drinking status, including amount of debt and mental health problems. In addition, white rather than non-white students, male rather than female students, and home rather than international students were more likely to meet criteria for problem drinking. These variables enabled the correct classification of 80 per cent of the sample. Amount of debt predicted both smoking status (smokers were on average £800 more in debt) and current drug use.

As anecdotal evidence (Barrett 1997) has suggested, some female students may be drawn towards prostitution as a way of making ends meet. We asked whether respondents knew of any students (male or female) who had engaged in drug dealing, prostitution or crime to help support themselves financially. A number reported knowing someone involved in prostitution (3.1 %), crime (10.2 %), and drug dealing (22 %). Those in debt were almost three times more likely to answer in the affirmative for each of these.

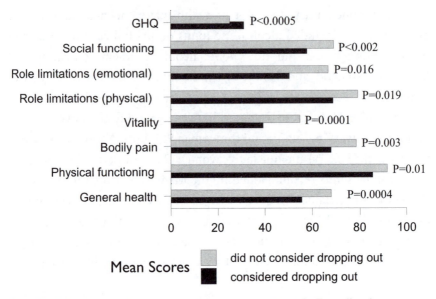

For GHQ higher scale scores indicate poorer health. For all other scores higher scales indicate better health.

Figure 6.1. Health status by whether students had considered abandoning study for financial reasons (means adjusted for age and sex).

Poorer mental health was related to longer working hours outside university and difficulty in paying bills. Students who had considered abandoning study for financial reasons had poorer mental health, greater role limitations caused by emotional problems, lower levels of social functioning and lower vitality. Their physical health as indicated by physical functioning, bodily pain, role limitations caused by physical problems and their perceptions of general health was also poorer. Interestingly, they were also heavier cigarette smokers and engaged more in recreational drug use (see Figure 6.1). Because of the possibility that elevated cigarette and drug use within this group was responsible for the health problems observed and had contributed to dropping out, we performed further analyses to control for the possible contribution made by these poorer health behaviours. This analysis continued to show significant differences between respondents who had considered dropping out for financial reasons and those who had not, with little or no change in the magnitude of these effects originally observed.

Amount of debt was unrelated to whether students had consulted a GP during the preceding two week period, but the larger the debt the greater the dissatisfaction with their most recent visit. This finding is consistent with adverse effects on psychological well-being that have been observed, and could be an indication that financial stresses increase students' propensity to complain. If so, this may also manifest itself through increasing complaints about their academic management.

Pathways to ill-health

To piece together the picture which was emerging we turned to structural equation modelling (Dunn, Everitt and Pickles 1993; Bentler 1998), a tool that has been developed in recent years and that has considerable power (both statistical and descriptive) to examine the combined actions of separate linear models. On the basis of the earlier results a model describing two distinct pathways from financial stress to impaired mental health was developed. This was found to provide an extremely good fit to the data and is illustrated below.

The structural equation model presented here describes two pathways through which financial stress can impact on students' mental health: for simplicity we have refrained from presenting a range of statistical parameters which ordinarily accompany presentation of a model (for a fuller pre-

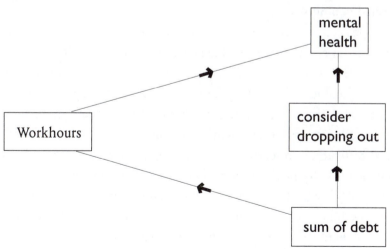

Figure 6.2. Pathways linking financial circumstances to mental health

sentation see: Roberts *et al.* 2000). First of all, as debts rise, the likelihood increases of considering abandoning study, which consequently impacts negatively on mental health. Second, as debt increases, longer hours are worked, which subsequently impact negatively on mental health.

Conclusions

Our analyses showed indicators of physical ill-health and psychological well-being in the current sample are poorer than the population norms established for people of the same age and sex. Furthermore, there appears to be good evidence to link this adverse health to the experience of financial difficulties, mediated through the stresses of longer working hours and worry about abandoning study. This builds on previous work which has found financial problems in students related to poor academic performance, poor psychological functioning and depression (Hodgson and Simoni 1995).

Naturally there are some caveats that must be placed on these findings. The cross-sectional nature of the study means the results must be interpreted with caution. It is feasible that the cultural context of higher education in the UK contributes to the observed patterns. In other national contexts where the self-financing of students has been long established, the impact of financial stress may be mediated differently or attenuated by established coping strategies.

It is possible for relationships between poor health and financial problems to arise in two ways. Financial stresses could directly affect health or alternatively people with poorer health may be more prone to financial difficulties – most likely through the denial of opportunities for work. Although the possibility of health being causally related to financial difficulties cannot entirely be eliminated in this study, the observation that financial difficulties are correlated with longer working hours makes it unlikely. Principally because there is no obvious explanation as to why those with poorer health, whether of a mental or physical nature, would work longer hours. An established body of work already indicates that in modern competitive economies such as our own, it is people with poorer health who are likely to be denied the opportunity to work (Fox 1990; Bartley and Owen 1996).

Certainly much more work in this area is required, not least because the impact of tuition fees has not been systematically investigated, and our own study began prior to their introduction in 1998. Further work, where changes in both health and financial circumstances could be tracked, is desirable to elucidate the causal mechanisms behind the relationships we observed. At present, however, these data suggest that the magnitude of any adverse effects resulting from economic circumstances are greatest within the psychosocial domain. Given this, it must be considered disappointing that the considerable concern these results have provoked appears not to have been taken seriously everywhere. Despite a great deal of positive feedback about the merits of this work – from students, parents, colleagues, counsellors in higher education and the wider scientific community – there were some quarters from which it was not greeted with enthusiasm.

Within the new university where some of the work was conducted, the authors consider that steps were taken to make further research in this area difficult. Additionally and not surprisingly, the UK government did not welcome the findings. When questioned in the House of Lords during the early part of 1999 about the disturbing implications of these data, higher education minister Tessa Blackstone responded:

> I do not believe that the study adequately attributes stress and poor health to financial problems; it does not really make the links. However that does not mean that the Government should not be very careful to look at the impact of the new arrangements. My department has asked for research based on a very large sample – 2,000 full-time and 1,000 part-time students – to be undertaken this summer. We shall be reporting on that study next spring… We shall certainly want to look at any health problems experienced by students. (Hansard)

At the time of writing (December 2000) the government has neither undertaken nor reported on any study commissioned into links between students' financial circumstances and their health, despite a growing national interest in student mental health (Rana, Smith and Walkling 1999; CVCP 2000). In the opinion of the authors this is a disgrace. The ubiquitous nature of the links between financial status and ill-health that have been established in epidemiological research worldwide suggests that similar relationships will be found in student populations, given their financial predicaments. Students are not isolated from the rest of society and poor student health carries implications for the provision of health and support services within higher education and the wider community. Widespread psychological ill-health among students is more than likely to affect the quality of life of a substantial section of the population. The issues of crime and prostitution in student life, which have until now remained largely anecdotal, urgently require investigation. That these may appear to some students to be necessary choices must be considered a tragedy. The potential cascading effects of debt in early adulthood into later life seem also to have been ignored in the rush to get students to 'pay their way'. The recent expansion of higher education may carry significant risks for the psychological and physical health of large sections of the population, including many children. The extent of these risks appears not to have been calculated in what must be considered to be a large-scale, ill-thought out social experiment.

Acknowledgments

We would like to thank Antje Mueller and Mary Cronin for helpful discussion, as well as all those who provided data for the study.

References

Barker, D.J. (1990) 'The fetal and infant origins of adult disease.' British Medical Journal 301,1111.

Barrett, D. (1997) 'Students on the Game.' The Times Higher Education Supplement, 18 July.

Bartley, M. and Owen, C. (1996) 'Relation between socioeconomic status, employment and health during the economic change, 1973-1993.' British Medical Journal, 313, 445–449.

Bentler, P.M. (1998) EQS: Structural Equations Manual. BMDP Statistical Software.

Berry, M. (1995) 'The experience of being a woman student.' British Journal of Guidance and Counselling 23, 211–218.

Central Statistical Office (1997) Social Trends 27. London: HMSO.

Cox, B.D. (1987) Health and Lifestyle. ESRC Data Archive. Colchester: University of Essex.

CVCP (Committee of Vice-Chancellors and Principals) (2000) Guidelines on student mental health policies and procedures for higher education. London: CVCP.

Dearing, R. (1997) *Higher Education in the Learning Society – Report of the National Committee of Enquiry into Higher Education.* London: The Stationery Office.

Dunkel-Schetter, C. and Lobel, M. (1990) 'Stress among students.' *New Directions for Student Services 49*, 17–34.

Dunn, G., Everitt, B. and Pickles, A. (1993) *Modelling Covariances and Latent Variables using EQS.* London: Chapman and Hall.

Edmundson, T. and Carpenter, C. (1995) *Students' financial circumstances 1994. A Report.* London: University of Westminster.

Fox, J.W. (1990) 'Social class, mental illness, and social mobility: The social selection drift hypothesis for serious mental illness.' *Journal of Health and Social Behaviour 31*, 344–353.

Frazier, P.A. and Schauben, L.J. (1994) 'Stressful life events and psychological adjustment among female college students.' *Measurement and Evaluation in Counselling and Development 27*, 280–292.

Goldberg, D.P. and Williams, P. (1988) *A User's Guide to the General Health Questionnaire.* Windsor: NFER-Nelson.

Hansard (1999) Student Debt. House of Lords, 4th March, Column 1791–1793.

Hodgson, C.S. and Simoni, J.M. (1995) 'Graduate student academic and psychological functioning.' *Journal of College Student Development 36*, 244–253.

Hutton, W. (1995) *The State we're in.* London: Vintage.

Jenkinson, C., Coulter, A. and Wright, L. (1993) 'Short form 36 (SF36) health survey questionnaire: normative data for adults of working age.' *British Medical Journal 306*, 1437–1440.

Lindsay, R.O. and Paton-Saltzburg, R. (1993) *The Effects of Paid Employment on the Academic Performance of Full-time Students in Higher Education.* Oxford: Oxford Brookes University.

Lundberg, O. (1991) 'The impact of childhood living conditions on illness and mortality in adulthood.' *Social Science and Medicine 36*, 1047–1052.

Marmot, M., Ryff, C.D., Bumpass, L.L., Shipley, M. and Marks, N.F. (1997) 'Social inequalities in health: next questions and converging evidence.' *Social Science and Medicine 44*, 901–910.

Mayfield, McLeod and Hall (1974) 'The CAGE questionnaire: Validation of a new alcoholism screening instrument.' *American Journal of Psychiatry 131*, 1121–3.

National Union of Students (1994) *Values for Money: NUS Survey of Student Finance and Attitudes to Money Management.* London: NUS.

Rana, R., Smith, E. and Walkling, J. (1999) *Degrees of Disturbance: The New Agenda.* Rugby: British Association of Counselling.

Rickinson, B. And Rutherford, D. (1995) 'Increasing undergraduate student retention rates.' *British Journal of Guidance and Counselling 23*, 161–172.

Roberts, H. (1997) 'Children, inequalities and health.' *British Medical Journal, 314* 1122–1125.

Roberts, R., Hemingway, H. and Marmot, M. (1997) 'Psychometric and clinical validity of the SF-36 in the Whitehall II study.' *British Journal of Health Psychology 2*, 285–300.

Roberts, R., Towell, A. and Golding, J. (1998) 'Student finance and mental health.' *The Psychologist 11*, 10, 489–491.

Roberts, R., Golding, J., Towell, T. and Weinreb, I. (1999) 'The Effects of Students' Economic Circumstances on British Students' Mental and Physical Health.' *Journal of American College Health 48,* 103–109.

Roberts, R., Golding, J., Towell, T., Reid, S., Woodford, S., Vetere, A. and Weinreb, I. (2000) 'Mental and physical health in students: The role of economic circumstances.' *British Journal of Health Psychology 5,* 3, 289–297.

Sands, R.G. and Richardson, V. (1984) 'Educational and mental health factors associated with the return of mid-life women to school.' *Educational Gerontology 10,* 155–170.

Swanton, O. (1997) 'Burden of Debt.' *Guardian Education, iii,* 3 June.

Tyrrell, J. (1992) 'Sources of stress among psychology undergraduates.' *The Irish Journal of Psychology 13,* 184–192.

Ware, J.E., Snow, K.K., Kosinski, M. and Gandek, B. (1993) *SF-36 Health Survey: Manual and Interpretation Guide.* Boston, MA: The Health Institute, New England Medical Center.

Wilkinson, R.G. (1996) *Unhealthy Societies.* London: Routledge.

Windle, R. (1993) 'Student Income and Expenditure Survey 1992/1993.' *London Research Services Limited.*

Wisniewski, D. (ed) (1997) *Annual Abstract of Statistics.* London: HMSO.

Wright, C.M., Waterson, A. and Aynsley-Green, A. (1994) 'Effect of deprivation on weight-gain in infancy.' *Acta Paediatrica 83,* 357–359.

Zelenyanszki, C. (1999) *Problem Drinking in Students.* London: University of Westminster.

Chapter 7

Identifying Students' Mental Health Problems in Primary Care Settings

Lionel Jacobson

Introduction

The period of life as a student in higher education can encompass many ages, but usually starts from the age of 16 years and upwards. There is no formalised and defined upper limit, although most students in higher education will have completed A level or equivalent examinations by 19 years, and their undergraduate degree courses by the age of 23 years. Clearly, older people can still be students, either as post-graduates or entering higher education as mature students up to any age. Furthermore, there are child 'prodigies' who do attend university at increasingly younger ages. This chapter will focus mainly on the primary mental health needs of students in the typical age range of 16 to 23 years, although it is worth emphasising that, in many ways, some of the issues will have relevance for other age groups.

Higher education is seen as a more stressful experience for present-day students in many ways, with apparent increasing competition for places, increasing competition with and between peers while on any course, and more perceived pressures to obtain good grades. Allied to this is the perennial problem with poor finances for students (as described by Roberts and Zelenyanszki in this volume), problems of living either at home or away from home (each has difficulties for young people), and pressures to find and maintain relationships. It is not surprising that for many students the pressures are too great; they find themselves under stress and experiencing mental and emotional turmoil. This aspect of the less-than-idyllic student lifestyle has been noted recently, with even the national press commenting on recent student suicides and investigating student life further (Wright and Charter 2000).

Studies of stress in young people have shown that some 15 per cent of adolescents aged 16–19 years are found to be disturbed at any one time (Jacobson and Wilkinson 1994; Walker and Townsend 1998); however most studies have focused on teenagers as a generic group, without studying student groups in particular. There have been further studies indicating increasing rates of depression with more suicides and parasuicides (deliberate self-harm) among people aged under 25 years (Appleby et al. 1996; Walker and Townsend 1998). Therefore, all health professionals need to be able to recognise, manage and follow up mental health problems in young people, and to be able to distinguish the normal self-limiting emotional reactions of young people from problems that are likely to have significant impact on their immediate or long-term future. This chapter will mostly focus on the role of the General Practitioner (GP) and the Primary Health Care Team because this is often the first medical port of call for young people with any health problems (Jacobson and Wilkinson 1994; Macfarlane and MacPherson 1995; RCGP/NASHU 1996; Walker and Townsend 1999).

The majority of health care in the UK is provided by a primary care service available to all irrespective of age, gender, social status, or disease process. The role of primary care is to manage most problems presented, but to use specialist services when appropriate. Most primary care involves GPs who care for a defined practice population of roughly 1800 patients each, which includes approximately 150 young people aged between 16 and 23 years. Most GPs work in partnership in practices to provide care for a larger population (approximately 9000 patients with 900 young persons on average) and have other health professionals, such as nurses and health visitors, who act in concert as a Primary Health Care Team (WHCSA 1996).

Some practices are based on university campuses, although this is rare. Some practices within a town or city will see many students due to their proximity to halls of residence or other student accommodation. Most GPs will have experience of treating university or higher education students at some time, because many students will return to their family home during vacation time and may be seen by their family doctor, either because they are still registered there or because they are seen as temporary residents. Many young people are relatively unaware that they can be seen under these circumstances by a doctor with whom they may be more familiar (McPherson *et al.* 1996).

This chapter examines how primary care can help in providing a service for young people; it is aimed at a non-specialist, and non-medical, audience and will largely focus on common presentations of distress, rather than rarities requiring specialist medical involvement. The author has used his experience of working with young people as a GP and the knowledge base accrued from relevant work on the health of older adolescents. There is a large body of work on the educational experiences of students in future health professional careers and their training in working with patients' emotional distress, but this is specialised material pertinent only to health professional training and will not be discussed further. Some aspects of health care covered in the available research on students and mental health problems are discussed here, although it will quickly become apparent that there is little available on the mental health of students in general, and UK students in particular. The chapter also aims to highlight unanswered questions, to stimulate awareness, provide direction for future research, and to encourage provision of appropriate training, resources and services.

The scale of mental health problems

In 1995, Meltzer and colleagues reported OPCS data which showed that 7 per cent of men and 19 per cent of women aged 16 to 19 years living at home in 1993 had a neurotic disorder; approximately 9 per cent had alcohol dependency and 7 per cent had a drug dependency (Meltzer *et al.* 1995). These data are broadly in line with trends over recent decades. A second feature of these data is that they appeared at a time when many students were not living at home, although recent demographic shifts would suggest that more students are living in their family home in recent years.

A continuing trend is that rates of most mental health disorders increase with age and are significantly higher amongst women (Harrington 1994; Meltzer *et al.* 1995). Clearly, there is much psychiatric morbidity in any population of young people at any one time, but clinically it is important to distinguish symptoms from disorder. Symptoms of psychological distress are more prevalent than disorder for all age groups, and it is important to recognise that emotions are still relatively labile among young people. Despite the difficulties inherent in determining the true prevalence of psychological morbidity amongst young people, rates do appear to be increasing.

Research is needed to determine whether any increase in mental health problems among young people is due to increasing recognition or increasing prevalence within the population of young people in general. Roberts and colleagues' study of British university students, described in the preceding chapter, found that there were higher levels of mental health problems compared to a non-student population matched for age and sex. Further, this poorer mental health was associated with financial problems and the need for outside work to pay bills, representing the first formal evidence that financial deprivation has a major deleterious role in students' mental health (Roberts *et al.* 1999).

Further interesting findings have emerged from outside the UK. A study from the United States indicates that 43 per cent of 737 students at the University of Texas had some form of suicidal ideation during the previous year (Rudd 1989). Six per cent of the 737 had acted on these thoughts with episodes of deliberate self-harm, and a further 2.4 per cent had made serious suicide attempts. Similar data has emerged from a later study of 1678 students in Queensland, Australia (Schweitzer *et al.* 1995). Again from the United States (New Hampshire) data indicates that depression and mental health problems are important reasons for withdrawals from university (Meilman *et al.* 1992).

However, there are still gaps in knowledge of the scale of mental health problems for students in higher education. For instance, further research is needed to determine formal prevalence rates of mental ill health within any student population in the UK. More research is urgently needed on the effects of financial hardship upon students in general. Also, the influence of other factors such as potential extra problems for younger students, mature students, and students who have young children, needs to be more formally assessed.

Pattern recognition of mental health problems

As noted above, mental health problems are common among the population as a whole. Most GPs see mental distress frequently, and will recognise common patterns of depression, anxiety or other aspects of psycho-emotional distress. However, many GPs and other health professionals also accept that pattern recognition may also require assessment of other 'domains' of morbidity, namely individual and contextual issues; this point will be addressed later.

Symptoms of mental health problems may include a feeling of having difficulty sleeping. Clearly, students experience poor sleep, sometimes as a result of their study, and sometimes as a result of their extra-curricular activity, but a reported symptom and a request for something to assist in sleep may indicate anxiety, and would suggest the need for a fuller assessment. A feeling of being under increasing stress, low mood, increased anxiety, crying easily, and reduced interest in usual activities could point to a diagnosis of depression. These may indicate that the student needs to be seen and assessed by a health professional, most commonly a GP. A GP can assess psychological functioning as part of a mental state examination and can look for clinical features such as objective lowering of mood, poverty or excess of speech, avoidance of eye contact, dishevelled appearance or clinical features of agitation. These may all support the hypothesis that the student may be experiencing a depressive illness.

More worrying features of mental illness would include delusional beliefs or thoughts. These may include paranoid ideation (that the person is being persecuted), ideas of reference (that news or other information carries special and individualised meaning for the person), effects on thought processes including a perceived transfer of thoughts or control of the individual's thoughts. Further, some people with severe illness experience delusions of being a different, usually better, person such as a guru, a religious figure, or a popular music icon. Some may experience unusual experiences, most commonly in the form of hallucinations: hearing voices either talking to them or commenting about them. Each of these indicates psychotic breakdown in the form of a presentation of a severe mental illness such as schizophrenia or hypomania. The first presentation of each of these illnesses frequently occurs in the age range of 15 to 25 years, and therefore the first breakdown may occur while in higher education (Katona and Robertson 2000). Each may also indicate the use of recreational drugs such as ecstasy or amphetamine. In any instance, management by a psychiatrist is usually indicated and thus referral to secondary health care services is the norm. If the individual is seriously disturbed and a risk to him/herself or to others and also declining treatment, detention in hospital under the 1983 Mental Health Act may be warranted, but this is uncommon.

There are also specific conditions such as obsessive-compulsive disorder (characterised by a compulsion to perform the same task repeatedly), anorexia nervosa (involving poor body image), panic disorder (where the person experiences an overwhelming feeling of panic, often featuring physical symptoms during an attack). A further specific condition among higher education students is attention deficit and hyperactivity disorder (ADHD), which is characterised by restlessness and poor concentration. These may require specialist referral as well as supportive primary care management and follow-up.

Not all those with psychological distress will report psychological symptoms, and many people may present with non-specific physical symptoms, which may defy biomedical explanation. This situation may pertain to those with established diseases too, so frequent attendance does not of itself indicate psychological distress. Nonetheless, it is well recognised by GPs that people who consult frequently may have more psychological distress (McWhinney 1996), and that frequent attendance at the surgery may indicate a non-reported psychological condition.

The scope of the problem

The specific aspect of mental ill health that has captured most public attention in the UK has been the rise in suicide rates amongst young men. In 1995, the rate of suicide and undetermined verdicts amongst 15–19 year old men was 8.63 in every 100,000, double the rate of 1971. The equivalent rate amongst women is 2.98. The lifetime prevalence of self-harm in the community as a whole is 7–14 per cent by the age of 19 years, but 20–45 per cent have experienced suicidal thoughts at some time. These are worrying trends and may indicate that there are high levels of severe psychopathology at the more extreme end of the spectrum (Shaffer and Piacentini 1994).

At the less severe end of the spectrum in terms of life-risk, Whitaker et al reported that common diagnoses amongst older teenagers were mood disorder (4.9 %); major depression (4.0%), generalised anxiety (3.7%), obsessive compulsive disorder (1.9%), bulimia (2.6%), panic disorder (0.6%), and anorexia nervosa (0.2%) (Whitaker et al. 1990). In 1998, Kramer and Garralda reported that 12 per cent of general practice attenders aged 13–19 years had major depression, 11 per cent had dysthymia or other depression, 3 per cent had overanxious disorder, and 6 per cent had disruptive (externalising) disorder (Kramer and Garralda 1998). Many disorders occur in combination, and there is no reason to suppose that students will have less mental distress than the general population figures noted above.

Many disorders affecting adults start during adolescence, as has been noted above with regard to schizophrenia and hypomania. Fully 50 per cent of patients with obsessive compulsive disorder reported that their symptoms began by the age of 15 (Rapoport 1986), and similar data has been reported for panic disorder (von Korff et al. 1985), and for antisocial disorders (Earls 1994). Poor mental health requiring hospital treatment during adolescence has been linked with suicide attempts, and with adult mental health problems (Brent et al. 1990; Kandel and Davies 1986; Kazdin 1989; Harrington et al. 1994; Rao et al. 1993). In addition, children and adolescents with a diagnosis of depression have been shown to be significantly more at risk of depression and hospitalisation in later life (Harrington et al. 1990).

Within the primary care arena, adult rates of mental disorder have been found to be more than double amongst those who had a psychiatric problem as teenagers. These data emerge from a study involving follow up of a cohort of continuously registered young people from early adolescence to adulthood (Smeeton *et al.* 1992). Whilst these studies provide good evidence of an association between adolescent and adult mental ill health, further research is required to determine whether early diagnosis and management will reduce later risks in adulthood; this would have implications for those moving on to higher education.

Inter-relationship of mental health problems with other health behaviours

Whilst adolescence in general, and student years in particular, are known to be periods of exploration and experimentation, students with mental health problems have been shown to indulge in higher levels of 'risk-taking behaviour'. For example, cigarette smoking is associated with higher rates of depression and anxiety. It is suggested that this is possibly consistent with smoking as self-medication for the condition (Patton *et al.* 1996). This would tie in with adult behaviour patterns where, for example, many young mothers turn to tobacco as something to do while feeling trapped, lonely and isolated (Graham 1992). This also applies to students experiencing financial hardship according to the University of Westminster study reported in Chapter 6 (Roberts *et al.* 1999).

Substance misuse itself has shown increases in prevalence in most developed countries since 1990 (Bauman and Phongsavan 1999). This trend applies to students according to a study from Valladolid, Spain, carried out in 1984, 1990 and 1994; the study further demonstrates that illicit drug use does have effects on the mental health of university students (Martinez *et al.* 1999). Other work has confirmed that depression, suicidal ideation, conduct disorder, attention deficit disorder, post-traumatic disorder, anxiety and a schizophrenia-like illness are all more common in drug-using adolescents and young adults (Hovens *et al.* 1994; Zeitlin 1999). Illicit drugs themselves are associated with injury, violence, unwanted pregnancy, sexually transmitted diseases and adverse mental health (Sells and Blum 1996). Clearly there is the issue of whether the mental health problem came before the substance misuse or vice versa, and of whether this is an association or some part of a causal link (Swadi 1999), but it is apparent that the conditions co-exist. It is noteworthy that the incidence of both has been rising in recent decades.

There is convincing evidence that depression and substance misuse are risk factors for suicide. A 1988 study carried out 'psychological autopsies' of completed suicides in young people, and found the combination of mood disorder and substance misuse to be far more common in suicide victims (81 %) compared to age and sex matched controls who had not undertaken any self-harm (29 %) (Shafii *et al.* 1988). A short report has noted that self-harm in the form of taking an overdose has an association with termination of pregnancy in some young women; there is no apparent causative link in either direction, but risk factors for both do show similar characteristics (Houston and Jacobson 1996).

In view of these associations, it is important for primary health care professionals who encounter any young people with mental health problems to consider other health risks and behaviours. Conversely, an assessment of mental health could usefully be undertaken in any young person presenting with other associated risk-taking behaviours. This applies to all young people, and students clearly come into this category. It appears to be a useful rule-of-thumb that students with deleterious effects of risk-taking behaviour should have a brief mental health assessment by a health professional. There exist research questions for health professionals of how to quantify the level of risk, how to better promote drug-free student culture, how to communicate effective health promotion messages for distressed students, and how to apply the above to a primary care situation.

Risk factors for mental health problems

A number of factors have been shown to be associated with an increased risk of mental health problems during adolescence, which will affect students' lives at the time, or as young adults. These include being cared for by the local authority; parental disharmony and divorce; physical and sexual abuse; bullying and family history of mental disorder (Hill 1989). Further risk factors include relationship problems (which may well be exacerbated by student life), lower socio-economic class, and poor educational attainment; this latter risk factor is unlikely in higher education.

Adolescents who are 'looked after' will have had significantly higher levels of psychiatric disorder compared to those living with their families (McCann et al. 1996). In this Oxfordshire study, 67 per cent of 13–17 year old adolescents living in the care system had psychiatric disorder, compared to 15 per cent in a control group; depression and anxiety were both very common. As noted above, these problems are likely to persist into adulthood and GPs should be aware of this particular risk factor wherever possible.

GPs are still often considered to be family doctors, although it is uncertain whether they always have sufficient contextual and background information about individuals to be able to proactively identify young people at risk of mental disorder. This applies to all young people, who tend to be viewed from the relatively narrow confines of seeing the patient as an individual, without necessarily seeing them in the context of their family or social circumstances. However, this is particularly so for students who have moved to the area solely for the purpose of entering higher education. Their sense of isolation, vulnerability, and potential absence of any contextualising family information make the holistic perspective sought by many GPs even more difficult to achieve. A useful research area would be to evaluate whether improved primary care information provision about family and contextual risk factors could improve early detection and management of mental ill health.

Students seeking help from general practice

There is increasing evidence that young people who are frequent attenders at the GP surgery are more likely to have a mental health problem (Kramer et al. 1997; Kramer and Garralda 1998). However, only a small proportion talk explicitly about symptoms of psychological disorder. It is likely that many young people with significant mental health problems either never encounter primary health care professionals, or are not recognised as having mental health problems. However, the impact of such morbidity on future emotional, psychological and social development may be significant.

When students visit the GP with overt signs of mental distress it may be in the context of a crisis, when domestic or educational circumstances have deteriorated sufficiently to a point of requiring outside help. Paradoxically, it may be in such extreme situations that GPs feel least able to provide effective intervention. One such form of crisis presentation is the student who has taken an overdose or self-harmed, in which case care needs to be directed at the physical well-being of the student in the first instance.

Since, like many older adults, young people perceive GPs to be more concerned with physical rather than emotional illness, they may legitimise their distress by presenting with physical symptoms such as headaches, fatigue or sore throats (Kramer *et al.* 1997). Such symptoms are widely prevalent amongst the younger population, making it difficult to identify those with a deeper need (Royal College of General Practitioners 1995). Other problems, such as sleep disturbance, may be directly symptomatic of a psychological disorder.

Hill noted the following symptoms could indicate a depressive pattern for older teenagers and younger adults: affected sleep pattern, separation anxiety, antisocial behaviour, a falling off in academic performance, apathy and boredom, hallucinations, running away from home and hypochondriacal symptoms (Hill 1989). Some of these symptoms may involve the student recognising potential illness, but some are usually noted by other people, including parents or tutors, but most often by their peers. There have been no formal studies examining the presentations of young people in general, or students in particular, with mental health problems in primary care, or the extent to which such presentation may be influenced by personal, peer-led or parental beliefs. There is scope for further research in this area.

Recognising potential turmoil in the consultation

It is apparent that a large proportion of young people with mental health problems remain unrecognised and untreated, and this applies to all adolescents and young adults (Williams 1993). A community study reported that only 1 out of 28 teenage girls suffering from major depressive disorder, as detected by direct interview, had been previously identified (Goodyer and Cooper 1993). Therefore, an aim of primary care might be to improve the mental health of late adolescents and young adults by earlier recognition of problems (Jacobson and Wilkinson 1994; Walker and Townsend 1998; Walker and Townsend 1999).

A diagnosis of depression for any individual is still associated with stigma (Priest *et al.* 1996) (see also David Brandon and Jo Payne's accounts in Chapter 2). Assigning such a diagnosis to a student may be hampered by a reluctance to stigmatise the particular student. There may be an inherent hope that this is a phase that they may grow out of, or that the condition may resolve spontaneously. This denial of the diagnosis and fear of stigmatisation may come from the doctor, the tutor or student counsellor who asks the student to attend the GP, or students themselves. The stigma can be attached to both the diagnosis of depression and the involvement of secondary psychiatric services, or to the need for anti-depressant medication.

A recent trend within primary care is to provide screening clinics within general practice, which may include some clinics for older adolescents and younger adults of undergraduate student age. These are offered as a means of attempting to see all young people within a practice at least once, and to screen for unrecognised morbidity. The majority of these clinics would not attract payment for the practice and may not be attractive because of the inherent costs involved. Nonetheless, several reports have indicated favourable uptake and useful identification of ill health, including mental ill health, which may be amenable to management and health improvement (Campbell and Edgar 1993; Donovan and McCarthy 1988; Walker and Townsend 1998; Westman and Garralda 1996). The main concern of clinics within primary care is that they tend to attract the 'worried well'. In other words, the people who attend are usually those who have few health needs, not those for whom the clinics were originally intended. Those with more 'health need' tend to avoid the clinics; thus the service may not fulfil its main function of detecting important morbidity.

This concept has been enshrined within primary care as one of the features of an 'inverse care law' (Hart 1971). Briefly, this work suggests that many health resources do not go to areas of great health need, but are rather diverted to those with less covert need, but more overt anxieties. It is not the role of this chapter to discuss clinics for young people in any great detail, but it does point to an interesting area for future investigation within a student population as to whether potential benefits outweigh any costs of having such clinics.

Is the student ill or is there a psychosocial problem?

Having recognised a potential mental health problem doctors need to categorise it. A Canadian academic family practitioner, Ian McWhinney, has provided medicine in general, and primary care in particular, with the notion of a triple stage diagnosis involving physical, individual and contextual diagnosis. Whenever a patient presents to a doctor, the clinician must consider the problem in biomedical, individual (psychological) and contextual (social) terms (McWhinney 1996). This appears even more necessary within the assessment of a potentially troubled student.

Some problems can be clearly explained or classified. For instance, psychosocial issues may be indicated by (we hope temporary) problems with friends, relationships or other clearly delineated issues. An indication of more serious mental health problems may include symptoms of depression or features that follow on for some time after these 'temporary' problems should have been resolved. There will always be grey areas and clinicians should be aware of overlap. This is even more so in the areas of potential newer diagnoses such as ADHD, conduct disorder, eating disorder or even seasonal affective disorder, which is now known to affect adolescents and young adults (Rosenthal *et al.* 1986). The GP must use some element of judgement as to whether there may be psychosocial pressures, which do not amount to illness, or whether the possibility of such illness exists. For instance, some (although not the author) may argue that there is some benefit for a student to be diagnosed as having ADHD rather than poor conduct, in that it may afford more 'understanding' of the troubled individual.

What is not known within the primary care situation is whether psychosocial problems inevitably progress to biomedical diagnosis, or the prognosis (eventual outcome) of either. This needs more research, although clearly there may be difficulties associated with this. There are clear methodological difficulties on agreeing a truly objective consideration of whether a presentation is of illness alone, psychosocial problem alone, or a combination of both. Furthermore, what is not known is in what way the implications and stigma of attributing a psychiatric diagnosis are, or are not, helpful.

The primary care response

The management of any condition in general practice starts even before a diagnosis is reached. Consultation skills such as empathy and active listening are recognised as having a therapeutic effect, irrespective of the nature of the problem (McWhinney 1996). Where adverse circumstances and sustained negative attitudes have contributed to the development of a psychological disturbance, the value of attention, interest, and a positive approach should not be understated. The danger of an increasingly reductionist and medicalised approach to the provision of care in general, and primary care in particular, is that such simple time-honoured interventions can be neglected. Although the same applies to adult consultations, the challenge is greater in relation to teenagers and young adults who may have developed negative views of the older adult population, and require greater input before any trusting relationship can develop (Jacobson and Wilkinson 1994). Paradoxically, although young people may require more time in the consultation for this purpose, they actually receive less (Jacobson et al. 1994).

Psychological problems requiring active treatment in adults are usually managed with drugs, psychological treatments, or a combination of both. In relation to depressive disorders there is evidence that adults strongly favour psychological approaches because of the belief that antidepressants are addictive (Priest et al. 1996). The belief that doctors are likely to prescribe such treatment may inhibit help-seeking behaviour and also reduces the likelihood that the individual will take such medication, even when it is recommended. Specific psychological therapies, such as cognitive approaches, have been shown to be equally effective as anti-depressants for depression in adults, although more commonly used non-directive counselling has not been fully evaluated (Churchill *et al.* 1999). Problem-solving approaches have also been suggested, and some recent evidence suggests they are helpful (Mynors-Wallis *et al.* 2000).

Young people with psychological disorders requiring active treatment may also be treated with drugs or psychological approaches. In relation to depression it has been suggested that tricyclic anti-depressants are less effective than in adults (Hazell *et al.* 1995). As a result, young people are probably less likely to be prescribed such treatment, although there may also be an inherent reluctance on the part of GPs to use such an approach, reflecting possible concerns about risk-taking behaviour in young people. Newer Selective Serotonin Reuptake Inhibitors (SSRIs), such as Prozac, appear to be better tolerated and, possibly as a result, more effective (Carrey *et al.* 1996), although there have been no trials in the primary care setting to confirm this.

As stated above, there may be a role for preventive management. The potential benefits of social skills training, family therapy and cognitive therapy as management options are outlined by Crome (1999). Others have reported interventions that could be used in primary care to act as management options for families with potential dysfunction, in the form of divorce, or in families with affective disorder (Beardslee *et al.* 1993; Grynch and Fincham 1992). Either may have relevance for students with family problems affecting them while in higher education. These preventive management options will need to be evaluated further.

In practice, the importance of a particular treatment modality depends not only on its efficacy and effectiveness, but also on its availability. Student psychological services vary widely in their availability and ability to respond quickly to the needs of troubled individuals. Further, even when counsellors and psychologists are present in general practice, they are usually only experienced in dealing with older adults, and may not have the relevant expertise to deal with students, especially if the practice population includes only small numbers.

Clearly, some students may have serious pathology; one management option is to consider a referral to secondary care or other services, commonly professionals in psychiatric services. All GPs are aware of the difficulty of accessing mental health services for adults. However, it becomes especially difficult for disturbed 16 and 17 year olds who do not neatly fall into the requisite age for adult services, but may be too old for child and adolescent mental health services. It is imperative that more referral resources are made available for all young people, and several recent reports have drawn attention to the need for more services (Audit Commission 1999; Yamey 1999).

The benefits of treatment depend on uptake which, in turn, relates to preferences and understanding. There has been little research into teenagers' or young adults' understanding of psychological disorders and treatment. Further, there is little knowledge of whether students may feel that to reveal any mental distress to a GP could result in medical information being given to the university or educational authorities. These are important areas in terms of recognising their concerns and potential barriers to presentation and treatment uptake. However, this is not to imply that the role of the educational institution is necessarily a negative one. Frequently, the institution can be involved in therapeutic intervention by way of befriending the troubled student, by assisting in taking a medication regime, or by having a tutor inform others and make allowances for their apparently poor academic performance at the time. Family members may also have a supportive role to play, and it is important to ask the student permission to involve family members also if this appears to be helpful.

However, this brings the notion of patient confidentiality into sharp relief. The nature of the ethical considerations which underpin confidentiality is a broad subject. It needs to be stressed that in the majority of instances any information revealed to a GP or other primary care provider is confidential and may not be revealed to a third party without the express consent of the individual patient. In this context third parties include the university or educational authorities and/or parents. Occasionally, confidentiality may be broken (examples would include a patient who continues to drive despite having epileptic fits, in which case the DVLA may be informed, or reporting a consultation where a patient informs a doctor that they are the perpetrator of a major crime), but these are rarities. Most GPs are aware that from time to time they need to seek expert guidance from their medical defence organisations on issues of divulging information to a third party.

There are many unanswered questions in the form of relevant follow-up of people with mental distress. For instance, there is no evidence available on how often GPs should follow up people in general, and students in particular, with mental health problems, or the relevance of appointments made but not kept. Some management options have been outlined, but clearly there needs to be ongoing research in primary care on how best to manage students with mental health difficulties, and how to provide care which is supportive but not overly intrusive.

Training needs

Most UK GPs receive poor training about the period of youth in general, and some have poor awareness of the health needs of young people beyond the more publicised areas of drug use and teenage pregnancy (Richardson *et al.* 2000). The request for more training pertains across other areas of the world too, with Australian and American doctors providing primary care noting a need for more training (Blum and Bearinger 1990; Fleming *et al.* 1994; Veit *et al.* 1995; Veit *et al.* 1996). GPs can be encouraged to think of younger people's health needs more appropriately. Within the UK, Bernard and colleagues have demonstrated better recognition of depression and more confidence among a group of GPs exposed to a brief training programme (Bernard *et al.* 1999). Recent Australian work has demonstrated the benefits of a training programme for educating Australian GPs on the health of adolescents with improved knowledge and self-reported skills, although it is of note that patients involved in the programme did not report any improvements (Sanci *et al.* 2000).

The most important health risk is of suicide, and the greatest risk factor for young adult and adolescent suicide is a previous attempt, with over 40 per cent of completed suicides preceded by a previous attempt (Slap *et al.*

1992). Many adult suicide victims see their GP before their death and it has been suggested that primary care doctors with more enhanced skills may have a role to play in preventing more suicides (Matthews *et al.* 1994), although this link can never really be proved (Walker and Townsend 1998). However, many young people report problems establishing rapport with their GPs. Young people do not see GP services as sensitive to their needs, and this could apply equally to any student population (Bewley *et al.* 1984; Donovan *et al.* 1997; Epstein *et al.* 1989; Jones *et al.* 1997; Kari *et al.* 1997; MacPherson *et al.* 1996; Richardson *et al.* 2000). These reports do not distinguish between young people with or without mental health problems, but do indicate a need for GP services to be more approachable and sensitive to all young people.

The main findings of recent research directed towards finding better services for young people have pointed to a need for an approachable, easily accessible, confidential, supportive, non-judgmental service, which values young people as people in their own right (Donovan *et al.* 1997; Jacobson *et al.* 2000; Jacobson and Kinnersley 2000; Richardson *et al.* 2000). This should continue to be the subject of research relating to young people within primary care.

Conclusions

There are several gaps in our present approach to student mental health. The first gap is one of awareness, and suggests that the notion of student turmoil indicating potential mental health problems should be made more of a priority for primary care. To date, this has received only scant attention within the medical profession in general, and primary care in particular. This may in turn lead to a second gap, namely that there is a need for more training for primary care professionals to attempt to better meet the health needs of their younger adult patients. The research and development work from outside the UK described above, and some early developmental work from within the UK, suggests this may be feasible, easily carried out, and not overly time-consuming.

A third main gap is one of research. This chapter may contain a great number of referenced papers, reports and articles, but the careful reader will note that most research has not been conducted with any focus on students in relation to primary medical care. Clearly there are huge gaps in our knowledge base and these would benefit enormously from more research and more evaluation. This evaluation may not be easy, and the author has noted such difficulties in relation to teenage health, which has broadly similar features and much overlap with student health (Jacobson *et al.* 1998). The fact that evaluation for both may be difficult should not detract from the fact that this work is of profound importance.

Fourth, there is a clear need for more resources and services to be made available, both within primary care and within other strands of care provision, to allow for better services for students in general and troubled students in particular. The vagaries of the NHS are well known, but there are many impressions of a devalued service for young people. They are one group in need of better service provision.

References

Appleby, L., Amos, T., Doye, U., Tomenson, B. and Woodman, M. (1996) 'General Practitioners and young suicides. A preventive role for primary care.' *British Journal of Psychiatry 168*, 330–333.

Audit Commission (1999) *Children in Mind.* London: The Audit Commission.

Bauman, A. and Phongsavan, P. (1999) 'Epidemiology of substance use in adolescence: prevalence, trends and policy implications.' *Drug and Alcohol Dependence 55*, 187–207.

Beardslee, W., Salt, P., Porterfield, K., Rothberg, P., van de Velde, P., Swatling, S., Hoke, L., Moilanen, D. and Wheelock, I. (1993) 'Comparison of preventive interventions for families with parental affective disorder.' *Journal of the American Academy of Child and Adolescent Psychiatry 32*, 254–263.

Bernard, P., Garralda, E., Hughes, T. and Tylee A. (1999) 'Evaluation of a teaching package in adolescent psychiatry for general practitioners.' *Education for General Practice 10*, 21–28.

Bewley, B., Higgs, R. and Jones, A. (1984) 'Adolescent patients in an inner London general practice: their attitudes to illness and health care.' *Journal of the Royal College of General Practice 34*, 543–546.

Blum, R. and Bearinger, L. (1990) 'Knowledge and Attitudes of Health Professionals Toward Adolescent Health Care.' *Journal of Adolescent Health 11*, 289–294.

Brent, D., Kolko, D., Allan, M. and Brown, R. (1990) 'Suicidality in affectively disordered adolescent inpatients.' *Journal of the American Academy of Child and Adolescent Psychiatry 29*, 586–593.

Campbell, A. and Edgar, S. (1993) 'Teenage screening in a general practice setting.' *Health Visitor 66*, 365–366.

Carrey, J., Wiggins, D. and Milin, R. (1996) 'Pharmacological treatment of psychiatric disorders in children and adolescents.' *Drugs 51,* 750–759.

Churchill, R., Dewey, M., Gretton, V., Duggan, C., Chilvers, C. and Lee, A. (1999) 'Should general practitioners refer patients with major depression to counsellors? A review of current published evidence.' *British Journal of General Practice 49,* 738–743.

Crome, I. (1999) 'Treatment interventions – looking towards the millennium.' *Drug and Alcohol Dependence 55,* 247–263.

Donovan, C. and McCarthy, S. (1988) 'Is there a place for adolescent screening in general practice?' *Health Trends 20,* 64–66.

Donovan, C., Mellanby, A., Jacobson, L., Taylor, B. and Tripp, J. (1997) Members of the Adolescent Working Party, Royal College of General Practitioners (RCGP). 'Teenagers' views on the GP consultation and their provision of contraception.' *British Journal of General Practice 47,* 715–718.

Earls, F. (1994) 'Oppositional-Defiant and Conduct Disorders' In M. Rutter, E. Taylor, L. Hersov (eds) *Child and Adolescent Psychiatry: Modern Approaches,* (3rd edition). Oxford: Blackwell Scientific, 308–329.

Epstein, R., Rice, P. and Wallace, P. (1989) 'Teenagers' health concerns: implications for primary health care professionals.' *Journal of the Royal College of General Practice 39,* 247–249.

Fleming, G., O' Connor, K. and Sanders, J. (1994) 'Paediatricians' Views of Access to Health Services for Adolescents.' *Journal of Adolescent Health 15,* 473–478.

Graham, H. (1992) *Smoking among working class mothers. Final report.* Coventry: Department of Applied Social Studies, University of Warwick.

Goodyer, I. and Cooper, P. (1993) 'A community study of depression in adolescent girls II: The clinical features of identified disorder.' British Journal of Psychiatry 163, 374–380.

Grynch, J. and Fincham, F. (1992) 'Interventions for children of divorce: Towards greater integration of research and action.' *Psychological Bulletin 111,* 434–454.

Harrington, R., Fudge, H., Rutter, M., Pickles, A. and Hill, J. (1990) 'Adult outcomes of childhood and adolescent depression: I. Psychiatric status.' *Archives of General Psychiatry 47,* 465–473.

Harrington, R. (1994) 'Affective Disorders.' In M. Rutter, E. Taylor, and L. Hersov (eds) *Child and Adolescent Psychiatry: Modern Approaches.* (3rd edition). Oxford: Blackwell Scientific, 330–350.

Harrington, R., Bredenkamp, D., Groothues, C., Rutter, M., Fudge, H. and Pickles, A. (1994) 'Adult outcomes of childhood and adolescent depression: links with suicidal behaviours.' *Journal of Child Psychology and Psychiatry 35,* 1309–1319.

Hart, J.T. (1971) 'The inverse care law.' *Lancet 1,* 405–408.

Hazell, P., O'Connell, D., Heatcote, D., Robertson, J. and Henry, D. (1995) 'Efficacy of tricyclic drugs in treating child and adolescent depression: a meta-analysis.' *British Medical Journal 310,* 897–901.

Hill, P. (1989) *Adolescent Psychiatry.* London: Churchill Livingstone.

Houston, H. and Jacobson, L. (1996) 'Overdose and termination of pregnancy: an important association?' *British Journal of General Practice 46,* 737–738.

Hovens, B., Cantwell, D. and Kiriakos, R. (1994) 'Psychiatric comorbidity in hospitalised adolescent substance misusers.' *Journal of the American Academy of Child and Adolescent Psychiatry 33*, 476–483.

Jacobson, L. and Wilkinson, C. (1994) 'A review of teenage health: time for a new direction.' *British Journal of General Practice 44*, 420–424.

Jacobson, L., Wilkinson, C. and Owen, P. (1994) 'Is the potential of teenage consultations being missed? : a study of consultation times in primary care.' *Family Practice 11*, 296–299.

Jacobson, L., Matthews, S., Robling, M. and Donovan, C. (1998) Members of the Research Sub-Committee, Adolescent Working Party, RCGP. 'Challenges in evaluating primary health care for teenagers.' *Journal of Evaluation in Clinical Practice 4*, 183–189.

Jacobson, L., Mellanby, A., Donovan, C., Taylor, B., and Tripp, J. (2000) Members of the Adolescent Working Party, RCGP. 'Teenagers' views on general practice consultations and other medical advice.' *Family Practice 17*, 156–158.

Jacobson, L. and Kinnersley, P. (2000) 'Teenagers in primary care – continuing the new direction.' *British Journal of General Practice 50*, 947–948.

Jones, R., Finlay, F., Simpson, N. and Kreitman, T. (1997) 'How can adolescents' health needs and concerns best be met?' *British Journal of General Practice 47*, 631–634.

Kandel, D. and Davies, M. (1986) 'Adult sequelae of adolescent depressive symptomatology in adolescents.' *Archives of General Psychiatry 43*, 255–265.

Kari, J., Donovan, C., Li, J. and Taylor, B. (1997) 'Adolescents' attitudes to general practice in North London.' *British Journal of General Practice 47*, 349.

Katona, C. and Robertson, M. (2000) *Psychiatry at a glance.* (2nd edition). Oxford: Blackwell Scientific.

Kazdin, A. (1989) 'Developmental psychopathology: current research, issues and directions.' *American Psychologist 44*, 180–187.

Kramer, T., Iliffe, S., Murray, E. and Waterman, S. (1997) 'Which adolescents attend the GP?' *British Journal of General Practice 47*, 327.

Kramer, T. and Garralda, M. (1998) 'Psychiatric disorders in adolescents in primary care.' *British Journal of Psychiatry 173*, 508–513.

Macfarlane, A. and MacPherson, A. (1995) 'Primary health care and adolescence.' *British Medical Journal 311*, 825–826.

Martinez, J., Del Rio, M., Lopez, N. and Alvarez, F. (1999) 'Illegal drug-using trends among students in a Spanish university in the last decade (1984-1994).' *Substance Use and Misuse 34*, 1281–1297.

Matthews, K., Milne, S. and Achcroft, G. (1994) 'Role of doctors in the prevention of suicide: the final consultation.' *British Journal of General Practice 44*, 345–348.

McCann, J., James, A., Wilson, S. and Dunn, G. (1996) 'Prevalence of psychiatric disorders in young people in the care system.' *British Medical Journal 313*, 1529–1530.

MacPherson, A., Macfarlane, A. and Allen, J. (1996) 'What do young people want from their GP?' *British Journal of General Practice 46*, 627.

McWhinney, I. (1996) *A Textbook of Family Medicine.* Oxford: Oxford University Press.

Meilman, P., Manley, C., Gaylor, M. and Turco, J. (1992) 'Medical withdrawals from college for mental health reasons and their relation to academic performance.' *Journal of American College Health 40*, 217–223.

Meltzer, H., Gill, B., Pettigrew, M. and Hinds, K. (1995) *OPCS Surveys of Psychiatric Morbidity: The Prevalence of Psychiatric Morbidity in Great Britain.* London: The Stationery Office.

Mynors-Wallis, L,. Gath, D., Day, A. and Baker, F. (2000) 'Randomised controlled trial of problem solving treatment, antidepressant medication, and combined treatment for major depression in primary care.' *British Medical Journal 320*, 26–30.

Patton, G., Hibbert, M., Rosier, M., Carlin, J., Caust, J. and Bowes, G. (1996) 'Is smoking associated with anxiety and depression in teenagers?' *American Journal of Public Health 86*, 225–230.

Priest, R., Vize, C., Roberts, A., Roberts, M. and Tylee, A. (1996) 'Lay people's attitudes to treatment of depression: results of opinion poll for Defeat Depression Campaign just before its launch.' *British Medical Journal 313*, 858–859.

Rao, U., Weissman, M. and Hammond, W. (1993) 'Childhood depression and risk of suicide: a preliminary report of a longitudinal study.' *Journal of the American Academy of Child and Adolescent Psychiatry 32*, 21–27.

Rapoport, J. (1986) 'Childhood obsessive compulsive disorder.' *Journal of Child Psychology and Psychiatry 27*, 289–300.

Richardson, G., Parry-Langdon, N., Jacobson, L. and Donovan, C. (2000) *Bridging the gap: How do teenagers and health care providers view each other?* London: NHS Executive, January.

Roberts, R., Golding, J., Towell, T. and Weinreb I. (1999) 'The effects of economic circumstances on British students' mental and physical health.' *Journal of American College Health 48*, 103–109.

Rosenthal, N., Carpenter, C., James, S., Barry, B., Rogers, S. and Wehr, T. (1986) 'Seasonal affective disorder in children and adolescents.' *American Journal of Psychiatry 143*, 356–358.

RCGP, Office of Population Censuses and Surveys, Department of Health (1995) *Morbidity Statistics from General Practice: 4th National Study, 1991–1992.* London: HMSO.

RCGP, National Adolescent & Student Health Unit (NASHU) (1996) *The Health of Adolescents in Primary Care.* London: Royal College of General Practitioners.

Rudd, M. (1989) 'The prevalence of suicidal ideation among college students.' *Suicide and Life Threatening Behavior 19*, 173–183.

Sanci, L., Coffey, C., Veit, F., Carr-Gregg, M., Patton, G., Day, N. and Bowes, G. (2000) 'Evaluation of an educational intervention for general practitioners in adolescent health care: randomised controlled trial.' *British Medical Journal 320*, 224–229.

Schweitzer, R., Klayich, M. and McLean, J. (1995) 'Suicidal ideation and behaviours among university students in Australia.' *Australian and New Zealand Journal of Psychiatry 29*, 473–479.

Sells, C. and Blum, R. (1996) 'Current trends in adolescent health.' In R. DiClemente, W. Hansen and L. Ponton (eds) *Handbook of Adolescent Health Risk Behavior.* New York: Plenum, 5–29.

Shaffer, D. and Piacentini, J. (1994) 'Suicide and attempted suicide' In M. Rutter, E. Taylor and L. Hersov (eds) *Child and Adolescent Psychiatry: Modern Approaches* (3rd edition). Oxford: Blackwell Scientific, 407–424.

Shafii, M., Steltz Lenarsky, J., McCue-Derrick, A., Beckner, C. and Whittinghill, J. (1988) 'Comorbidity of mental disorders in the post-mortem diagnosis of completed suicide in children and adolescents.' *Journal of Affective Disorder 15,* 227–233.

Slap, G., Vorters, D., Khalid, N., Margulies, S. and Forke, C. (1992) 'Adolescent suicide attempters: do physicians recognise them?' *Journal of Adolescent Health 13,* 286–292.

Smeeton, N., Wilkinson, G., Skuse, D. and Fry, J. (1992) 'A longitudinal study of general practitioner consultations for psychiatric disorders in adolescence.' *Psychological Medicine 22,* 709–715.

Swadi, S. (1999) 'Individual risk factors for adolescent substance use.' *Drug and Alcohol Dependence 55,* 209–224.

Veit, F., Sanci, L., Young, D. and Bowes, G. (1995) 'Adolescent health care: perspectives of Victorian general practitioners.' *Medical Journal of Australia 163,* 16–18.

Veit, F., Sanci, L., Young, D. and Bowes, G. (1996) 'Barriers to effective health care for adolescents.' *Medical Journal of Australia 163,* 131–133.

von Korff, M., Eaton, W. and Keyl, P. (1985) 'The epidemiology of panic disorder: results from 3 community surveys.' *American Journal of Epidemiology 122,* 970–981.

Walker, Z. and Townsend, J. (1998) 'Promoting adolescent mental health in primary care: a review of the literature.' *Journal of Adolescence 21,* 621–634.

Walker, Z. and Townsend, J. (1999) 'The role of general practice in promoting teenage health: a review of the literature.' *Family Practice 16,* 164–172.

Welsh Health Common Services Authority (WHCSA) (1996) *General Practice Morbidity Database Project.* Cardiff, Welsh Health Common Services Authority. Personal communication.

Westman, A. and Garralda, M. (1996) 'Mental health promotion for young adolescents in primary care: a feasibility study.' *British Journal of General Practice 46,* 317.

Whitaker, A., Johnson, J., Shaffer, D., Rapoport, J., Kalikow, K., Walsh, B., Davies, M., Braiman, S. and Dolinsky, A. (1990) 'Uncommon troubles in young people: prevalence estimates of selected psychiatric disorders in a nonreferred adolescent population.' *Archives of General Psychiatry 47,* 487–496.

Williams, R. (1993) 'Psychiatric morbidity in children and adolescents: a suitable cause for concern.' *British Journal of General Practice 43,* 3–4.

Wright, O. and Charter, D. (2000) 'Under pressure; are we pushing our students to death?' *The Times,* 10 May, Section 2, pp. 3 and 4.

Yamey, G. (1999) 'Mental health services are failing children and adolescents.' *British Medical Journal 319,* 872.

Zeitlin, H. (1999) 'Psychiatric comorbidity with substance misuse in children and teenagers.' *Drug and Alcohol Dependence 55,* 225–234.

Chapter 8

The University
and the Wider Community

Colin Lago

Introduction

> 'The new student', opines the conventional wisdom, is a more troubled
> person; more likely to face emotional challenges, more frequently experi-
> enced with counselling, more likely to have been treated with
> psychotropic medication, with a greater probability of having more
> serious and severe psychological problems. Many student affairs profes-
> sionals share the belief that emerging generations of students therefore
> do, and will, require more elaborate, extensive and varied psychological
> services on campus. A higher proportion of today's students warrant
> diagnoses of true mental illness, and the work of counselling centres
> perforce now includes more case management, medication monitoring,
> and psychiatric consultation. (Keeling 2000)

The above quotation is the opening paragraph of an article considering the
contemporary situation facing 'student affairs' departments in American
universities in their attempts to respond appropriately and sensitively to
the issue of student 'psychological diversity.' Viewed from a British perspective, the above claims might appear as a somewhat exaggerated
description of present-day students. Nevertheless, a wide range of
evidence is increasingly available that begins to substantiate a view that the
mental health profile of students has now become a source of great
concern to institutions of further and higher education in the UK. Indeed,
this book provides powerful evidence of this developing perspective.

This chapter commences with a review of current research in relation to student mental health before proceeding to explore the links between higher education institutions (HEIs) and the local communities within which they are located. These two key strands inevitably intertwine throughout the rest of the chapter where explorations are made into facilitating the optimum referral pathways for students whose circumstances, at the point of intervention, are considered to be more serious than is possible to respond to within the confines of the educational setting. Systematic reductions of mental health services within the NHS over the last decade mean that the treatment facilities in local areas are frequently severely stretched and the care often does not materialise easily, except in the most serious of cases.

The wide range of student services that normally exists within higher education institutions is considered here, as are the voluntary and statutory agencies usually available within urban regions. Particular difficulties often exist in relation to lengths of waiting times for community services, while student counselling services may have waiting lists of several weeks at particular times of year, accessing local psychotherapy and related specialist services may entail waits of up to eighteen months. Such delays mean that students may well have to temporarily or indeed permanently withdraw from their studies.

The point of referral between organisations can often prove somewhat complex in the different perspectives brought to bear upon problems and these are discussed later, as are the needs expressed by the supporters of 'troubled' students who often become anxious themselves. There are many references in this chapter and others in this book to a set of mental health guidelines published by the UK national body representing universities and colleges. The guidelines (CVCP 2000) constitute a significant statement of concern for students with mental health problems in higher education and provide a general stimulus for those institutions in drawing up codes of good professional practice.

Included in this chapter are brief case scenarios exemplifying the points under discussion. These give an insight into some of the challenges facing higher education staff involved in assisting students in difficulty. The chapter encourages higher education institutions to draw up sets of policies to assist their support of students and to facilitate conducive and formal working relationships with the wide range of agencies in the surrounding locale whose concern is that of mental health.

The incidence of student mental ill health

There is increasing evidence that student life now requires a degree of psychological robustness. A set of findings is presented below to substantiate this argument, first providing more general data for the population at large, and then more specifically quoting from various studies conducted on the student population. Recent research has indicated that:

- Some form of mental health problem will affect one in four people in any one year (Mental Health Foundation 1999a).

- Depression Alliance conducted a survey of 1069 people aged between 15–34 which revealed that one in three considered they have suffered from depression, while nearly half admitted to knowing someone who has either contemplated or committed suicide (Currie 2000).

- There is a clear consensus amongst all those working in the field that there have been substantial increases in identified psychosocial disorders of youth since World War II in nearly all developed countries (Mental Health Foundation 1999b).

- It is calculated that, at any one time, 20 per cent of all children and adolescents experience psychological problems (Mental Health Foundation 1999b).

- Prevalence of psychiatric disorders in 16–25 year olds has increased and disorders such as depression, schizophrenia and eating disorders are likely to be in their most acute phase during this stage of life (Rutter and Smith 1995).

- Since 1995/1996 university counselling services have reported an increase in psychological disturbance among their clients (annual surveys of the Association for University and College Counselling).

- In a study conducted at the University of Wisconsin, 92 per cent of students who presented to the University counselling service showed signs of academic impairment, 16 per cent were mildly depressed, 43 per cent moderately depressed and 41 per cent had severe depression (Woolfson 1997).

- 40 per cent of student respondents were concerned with issues relating to depression and 23 per cent were worried about managing anxiety, phobias or panic attacks (Leicester University 1999) (see Chapter 5 in this volume).

- A study at a traditional university revealed that 17 per cent of students were 'clinically lonely', suffering self-doubt and isolation, a higher rate than in the population at large (Wojtas 2000).

In a major study conducted between 1995 and 1998 at the University of Cambridge, based upon an initial sample size of 25 per cent of the overall student intake, the following findings emerged:

- around 20 per cent of students reported at least one problem causing substantial worry at each of the three annual academic assessments

- around one in five women and one in ten men reported an episode of either depression or anxiety during each of the assessment periods

- psychological morbidity appeared to peak at times coinciding with university examinations

- 6 per cent reported suicidal ideation and 1 per cent of students annually reported actual suicide attempts

- 6 per cent of women reported multiple problems with diet

- around 10 per cent of students reported a level of alcohol use suggestive of alcohol-related problems (Surtees, Wainwright and Pharoah 2000).

Disturbed mental well-being and mental ill-health in students are significant inhibitors, if not barriers, to academic achievement and success. For many students, the experience of being anxious or depressed or preoccupied with problems will detract from their capacity to focus and work well. As one student recounted recently in a counselling session:

> When I sit down to work, my mind fills up with my worries and I sit there for hours staring and worrying but not engaging with the work in front of me.

The consequences of such experiences may lead students, in the short term, to under-perform academically, to fail assessments, or to consider withdrawal from university. In the long term, such experiences may adversely affect career and life patterns, a costly affair in both human and economic terms.

In recognition of these widespread concerns affecting the student community, the Committee of Vice Chancellors and Principals (CVCP) published its set of *Guidelines on Student Mental Health Policies and Procedures for Higher Education* (2000). A key statement from this report reads as follows:

> There is a growing concern that where once the provision of counsellors, medical centre staff and other staff working in a supportive capacity could be expected to address any mental health difficulties encountered within the institution, this is no longer sufficient. Whilst these services will continue to support the work of HEIs, a more coherent institutional structural approach is required, together with the involvement of specialist professionals from outside the sector, for example, psychiatrists, clinical psychologists, GPs and mental health teams. (CVCP 2000, p.9)

The above extract not only conveys the essential message of this landmark report, but also constitutes the political, philosophical and clinical underpinning of this chapter.

'Town and gown': partnerships and referrals

> The development of partnerships between HEIs and external agencies is essential. It is important to recognise that institutions will need to work within the parameters of local health service resources, which can be limited in certain areas. By building up relationships with external agencies, cross referrals can be facilitated and increased dialogue can help institutions develop their expertise. (CVCP 2000, p.22)

The University Counselling Service (of which I am Director), in its annual report for the academic year 1999–2000 recorded that 10 per cent of the students who had used the service were referred on to other sources of help and support. In some cases, these would be to colleagues working within the university, for example, personal tutors, resident tutors (in halls of residence), the university health service, the students' advice centre (in the student union) and so on. In other cases, referrals would be made to a range of other agencies within the city or region who offer more specialised assistance with a student's problems. Although the above figure would not represent a large number of students, it would increase if it was added to all the external referrals made by all the other support agencies and personnel (some of them having been mentioned above) in the university.

Such a figure would be extremely problematic to calculate with any accuracy for any HEI if it is considered that, in addition to the helping departments named above, other students might also be referred by lecturing, technical, secretarial, portering, cleaning and security staff to a wide range of voluntary and statutory organisations in the locale. From a variety of staff training activities, it has become clear to our counselling service just how extensive are the range of 'kindnesses' extended to students in need by all staff involved in the institution, not just those formally charged through their job roles with specific elements of pastoral care.

This latter group we might term the informal carers within the HEI community and there are many accounts indicating that such colleagues have been instrumental in suggesting referral to, and then providing ongoing support for, troubled students. In many cases, these relationships and acts of caring will not appear in any reports or statistical tables. Nevertheless, if they are combined with all the formal statistics of referral, a substantive pattern of connections between the university and the local community is revealed.

The interconnectedness of 'town and gown' (city and university) has long been recognised by HEIs through activities such as civic planning, consultancy and social events. There is also a major economic impact on a city or region due to the presence of an HEI. However, this author is not aware of any studies that have attempted to quantify the extent of such connections and pressures within the field of mental health. A significant report by Stewart-Brown *et al.* (2000) concluded that students attending three different institutions of higher education experienced more ill health than equivalent aged young people in the same geographical area. This research is sobering and clearly has considerable implications for NHS resources in areas that include institutions of higher education.

Given the seriousness of the statistics and findings related to student health and mental health, this interface of need and resource is one requiring consideration by health service planners. Stewart-Brown *et al.* (2000, p.492) report that: 'young people are an under-researched group and there are few surveys of the health of students at universities and other higher education institutions.' There are many cities, for example, which contain not only one, but two universities (and a range of further education colleges). The impact upon local provision of both voluntary and statutory services for mental health is likely to be considerable from this transient population that dramatically ebbs and flows with term time dates.

An additional dimension here, though it is not formally under consideration in this chapter, is the impact of academic and other staff upon these services. There have been a number of significant reports on staff stress in higher education over recent years (Harrington 1996; AUT 1994; Lodge 1996; Fisher 1994) and informal feedback from a range of medical, counselling, support and guidance agencies to this author indicates considerable levels of use of these services by university staff.

Though the overall emphasis of this chapter reflects internal HEI concerns that require specialised support from other services in the community, there is also a reciprocal response. First, external agencies strive to ensure, in a general way, that students they have helped or treated are supported when they return to the academic environment. Second, students who have been treated, sometimes in an emergency, by hospital casualty departments for serious self harm or attempted suicide, are then referred directly back to a university's counselling or health service.

Levels of resourcing nationally for the whole range of psychological services within the community have long been inadequate. Indeed, the proportion of NHS expenditure on mental illness went down from 15 per cent in 1958 to 10 per cent in 1993 (Linklater 2001). In 1991, more than £2 billion was saved through 'care in the community' (the policy at that time dedicated to moving a greater proportion of hospitalised patients with mental illness back into the community). This under-funded policy led to inadequate psychiatric provision and long waiting lists (sometimes in excess of a year for clinical psychology or psychotherapy services), factors that can often prove extremely difficult both for the student needing help and the university staff providing support in the interim (Lago and Shipton 1994). In more serious cases, such as the onset of schizophrenia or psychosis, delays in hospital admission and drug treatment can have considerable deleterious consequences for the development of the condition (Howe 1998, p.71). The recent National Service Framework now embodies a commitment to early intervention services: it is hoped that the consequences of this policy will produce more rapid and appropriate responses to those in acute psychological distress (Department of Health 1999).

Needs, connections and routes of referral

One university counselling service had been working for two years with a student with increasingly severe mental health problems. These culminated in a number of incidents involving the police and a long period in a psychiatric unit. The counselling service was not approached by medical staff treating the student and was therefore surprised to receive a long medical report stating that the student had been diagnosed with a personality disorder, was about to be discharged and that the university counsellor who had been working with her would now be responsible for her care. (Rana *et al.* 1999)

In summarising the preceding section, it may be seen that there is some substantial cause for concern in relation to student mental well-being and that the link between this and successful academic outcome is manifestly apparent. HEIs are right to be concerned about these issues and are to be encouraged in adopting appropriate support structures and referral mechanisms to ensure speedy, sensitive and relevant help is extended to all students so troubled.

Though one is somewhat cautious about making a special plea on behalf of students over and above the demands made on the various mental health support agencies by the general population, it does have to be recognised that students are in a situation of particular pressures. These include not only those due to student status (culture shock, homesickness, loneliness, anxiety, parental expectations, poverty and so on), but also the demands of an educational system that requires consistent academic and exam performance over three years. A lapse of performance over a relatively short time might require repeat years of study, demanding a further financial commitment that may already be over extended. Three key themes emerge from the above:

1. There exists a need for a seamless service within colleges and universities that may be accessed and activated appropriately in response to student distress and crisis.

2. The interconnectedness of the HEI with the wider mental health community needs to be well established in order to optimise external referrals when students' mental ill health, distress and crises cannot be contained or assisted by the institutions' own services.

3. Primary health care professionals (GP surgeries) represent the formal gateway through which all formal referrals to other NHS facilities (e.g. psychiatry) have to proceed. The GP with whom the student is registered is therefore an important, and indeed crucial figure in facilitating access to specialised services, particularly in the face of significant crisis or breakdown.

Confidentiality

One of the key issues arising from a range of agencies communicating with each other is their different codes and practices of confidentiality. Helping agencies may wish to share these before misapprehensions arise over particular cases (the numerous inquiries into mental health tragedies have frequently alluded to difficulties over confidentiality: Stanley and Manthorpe 2001). It is equally important to share such principles with the users of services. In our counselling service, cards outlining our policy on confidentiality are available to service users in the waiting room. This policy defines confidentiality as keeping discussions private, but advises that counsellors work to the British Association for Counselling and Psycho-therapy (BACP) Code of Ethics and Practice. It is noted that this means counsellors will discuss their cases with supervisors in confidence or at times with their colleagues.

Stressing that 'confidentiality is paramount', the policy warns that normal practice will be changed in rare circumstances such as harm to self or others. Even in such exceptional events, the counsellor will try to gain the person's permission to breach confidentiality. However, noting again that these events are 'very rare', the service recognises the balance between 'best interests' and autonomy, and its duty to others. Such a policy is not unique to this service; the BACP Code is widely adopted. It needs to relate to the practice of academic supervision or personal tutoring within the HEI, which expects staff to pass on information about students in many instances, as well as offering appropriate opportunities for discussion of matters affecting learning and study. HEI staff, for example, need to know that a counselling service is confidential and can pass this on to any student they refer. However, they should not expect the service to break its own code when the academic is seeking evidence of a student's well-being.

Likely referral resources

> Not that it was going to be plain sailing into the middle-class sunset. The very fact of Mullan's success at university – in his second year he won both his class prizes – started, he said, to 'destabilise' him. He hadn't been programmed, either by his background or his father, for achieve-ment. And in the middle of his finals – working a regime of 15 hour days, seven days a week – he suffered a nervous breakdown... Mullan has spoken before of how he was working at home when suddenly he lost all concentration, started crying and couldn't stop. He was in hospital for a week. He talks now...of becoming phobic, having panic attacks. 'I just put a ridiculous pressure on myself', he recalls, 'I was terrified of failure, and paralysed by the idea of success'. (Matheou 2000)

One of the major outcomes of the publication of the CVCP guidelines on mental health is likely to be a consolidation of knowledge of, and commu-nication with a range of agencies operating within the community that offer different mental health services. As noted above, these guidelines encourage HEIs to strive towards the establishment of sets of operational procedures and guidelines for use in relation to students with mental health needs. In essence, such departmental and institutional protocols will describe appropriate procedures to be implemented in different sets of circumstances. The CVCP guidelines offer each HEI therefore the opportunity to create systems of consultation and referral relevant to their own organisational structure. The resulting interpretations, unique to each institution, will provide the framework from which working links with relevant other agencies may be established.

One of the challenges of writing this chapter is to suggest or highlight various recommendations, while respecting a range of institutional differences in structures and practices. For example, some HEIs have an embedded on-site health service with medical teams who serve only that community. In others, students may register with different local GP practices in the surrounding locale or near their accommodation. The extent to which the primary care medical structure serving the student population can itself therefore be considered as internal or external to the institution, creates different challenges to any formal communications between the two. The immediate knock-on effect of this relationship between health services and the institution is likely to be the ease with which referrals to specialist NHS mental health services may be made. There exists a general belief that where health services are internal to the HEI, communication patterns between both sets of staff will already be established. Communication between people where there is a previous connection is normally easier. Case scenarios such as the following often strain both those involved and referral routes:

> Sarah is a second year student who confided in her tutor the fact that she had controlled her weight through inducing vomiting and taking laxatives since she had started her A levels. She was now, she admitted with considerable embarrassment and shame, bingeing every evening and was increasingly distressed. It seemed clear to her that her difficulties had intensified in the build-up to the exams. Her family and friends were not aware of the problem and Sarah was concerned that no one in the university, including her GP, ever find out. She was visibly underweight and the tutor was also concerned for her general health. What should the tutor do? (From a training exercise developed at Sheffield University.)

The scenario presented above provides an insight into the dilemmas faced by a tutor (or any other staff member) who is trying to secure the most appropriate and effective support for a troubled student. Reference has already been made to the range of student support facilities that may exist. As noted above, however, there is a wide range of difference between HEIs in terms of facilities, levels of resourcing, student union activities and services, and the organisational structures that bind them. Normally, the following services exist in some form:

- advice and welfare
- careers advice and guidance
- counselling service
- disability support
- financial hardship
- health service
- housing services
- personal tutoring
- resident tutoring (in student residences)
- special facilities for exams
- student union support and representation facilities
- student welfare organisations, e.g. Nightline (student-run, all night, information and support phone lines), lesbian, gay and bi-sexual societies.

To some extent, all welfare departments within HEIs act as symbols of the organisation's collective anxiety about students with mental health problems. The difficulties these departments experience come to the fore when they themselves are pushed beyond their competency and capacity to cope, either through excessive demand or by individual students in extremely serious circumstances. Such circumstances now occur more frequently than before:

Undoubtedly students are in poor mental shape and counselling services are unable to cope with the volume, …the student population is far greater and made up of a far wider spectrum of people than ever before and the pressures are higher with people having to work very hard outside university to make money. There is evidence that their general health is poorer than non-students (Dr Pauline Fox, quoted in McVeigh 2001.)

When the levels or specifics of distress in the student are such that referral to an external agency is deemed desirable, or indeed necessary, then two broad routes are possible: through the statutory sector, or through the voluntary/independent sector. Statutory agencies may include the complete range of possible NHS and local authority services (see Table 8.1).

The police are of particular interest in the discussion of mental health services. Two studies are reported in Howe (1998) that assert the importance of police involvement by carers and families in enabling mentally ill people to access formal help. Similarly, the security services within universities can often provide valuable intervention support in crisis situations and may themselves have good working relations with the local police. In addition, there may be agencies funded by local authorities that provide specific services: e.g. drugs units, youth counselling services, etc. (see Table 8.1). In major urban areas there exists a wealth of such organisations, many of which will be listed in Yellow Pages and other similar directories. Libraries and information centres provide information about local provision, while some HEIs have produced their own lists of local helping services.

One of the enormous challenges facing those HEI staff likely to refer students regularly is the formidable, if not impossible, task of communication with such agencies: to establish a working relationship, to understand their criteria for referral and to have a general sense of the length of their waiting lists. In Sheffield, our service has approximately 70 different agencies on file that theoretically, (depending on the client), could be approached by us for a referral. Even over the very long term, establishing close working contact with so many agencies is unfeasible, especially considering the often few staff of student support services. Nevertheless, such a range provides some creative possibilities for direct referrals. Good working relationships can often develop through the referral process itself, and these may have to be sufficient in the majority of cases. Professional relationships with those services most frequently used will have priority.

Table 8.1. Statutory and voluntary services

Statutory	Voluntary
• primary care (where these are external to the university) • psychiatry • clinical psychology • community psychiatric nurses • specialist psychotherapy services e.g. long-term psychotherapy, eating disorders units, cognitive behavioural departments, etc. • local social services support • art, drama or music therapy	• agencies for drug treatment • organisations for alcohol-related concerns • Relate (formerly Marriage Guidance) • church-based counselling organisations • Samaritans • Rape Crisis • self-help organisations specialising in specific themes e.g. abuse, victim support, bereavement, and so on • independent counselling and psychotherapy practices and practitioners • a wide range of other complementary approaches including aromatherapy, acupuncture, naturopathy and meditation

Questions of opinion, diagnosis and treatment

A student had a really difficult time at university, and his department, because of his impoverished circumstances (no immediate family, no local friends, heavily in debt and clearly 'troubled'), had really rallied round for quite some time, eventually turning a blind eye to him even sleeping in the department as he couldn't face going to his bed-sit! Referral to the student's doctor had, unfortunately, in the opinions of the departmental staff, been very disappointing, as they were convinced of the existence of a psychological condition that they had neither the expertise nor the skill to help with. The doctor had apparently considered there was no basis for this view. Later, the student, whilst visiting another city had been urgently referred to a psychiatrist after an incident, and had been diagnosed as suffering from schizophrenia. Upon return to the university and the re-emergence of all these difficulties, he was again referred to the doctor, who, again, did not change his original view, even when he was in receipt of the psychiatrist's report. A thorny problem remained, therefore. How was the student to be helped? How was the department to be advised and supported? (From a tutor training exercise)

Freud is commonly attributed with the phrase that diagnosis is a mutual form of reassurance between the doctor and the patient. Within the field of counselling and psychotherapy, however, there is a very strong view that any attempt to 'diagnose' is not helpful to self-exploration, as this reinforces only the expertise of the counsellor at the expense of the client's own credible view (Stewart 1997). Daines *et al.* (1997), while acknowledging this perspective amongst some therapists, also point to the importance of counsellors being able to recognise and respond to serious mental health issues.

Unfortunately, diagnoses of some psychological states can often prove extremely difficult to ascertain, achieve or agree upon – as illustrated by the training scenario above. Inevitably, different staff may vary considerably in what they consider to be serious, urgent or pathological. Their evaluation will reflect their own experiences, their role and expertise, often combined with their own and their department's capacity to contain a student with difficulties. Certain types of student distress generate considerable anxiety in others (both in staff and in other students). Relationships can deteriorate very quickly within an academic department exposed to a student who is 'acting out.' Pressures on senior staff to act, to remove the 'problem' quickly intensify.

Diagnoses are the domain of medical staff, doctors and psychiatrists. Even within the medical framework there are difficulties, as illustrated by the extracts below from Daines *et al.* (1997, p.66):

So when does a psychiatrist use the term 'mental illness'? Generally when a clear syndrome can be identified, there has been a definite change from how the person used to be and there is a deterioration in the person's ability to function effectively. This is important in differentiating illness from 'personality disorder' which is not viewed as 'illness.' Dependence on alcohol or drugs is similarly not viewed as being mental illness, but again psychiatrists are often involved in treatment in order to attempt to relieve suffering either as experienced by the person themselves or those around them.

Daines and colleagues go on to differentiate mental illness from the broader category of serious mental health problems which, for them, encompass mental illness, addictions and personality disorder:

> Diagnosis is useful only if it can be helpful in predicting the use of effective treatment... Psychiatrists have spent many years inventing categorical labels for abnormal personalities but people rarely fit one exactly. Use of these labels should be exercised with some caution as labels tend to be very sticky and the presence of a personality disorder does not preclude the additional development of mental illness.

There is, inevitably, a vast spectrum of different behaviours, relationships and psychological states amongst today's students; these may be particularly evident in the case of international students. For many there may be the shock of transition or of a different culture. The effects of such uprooting may be immediate or long-term and can affect health, mood and capacity to study. These effects are experienced differently, and it is often impossible to predict their impact or duration. It is difficult for academic and other staff to distinguish between adjustment to a different culture and to higher education, and serious mental health problems. Some students will be very anxious about referrals to a counselling service (Bradley 2000) for fear of stigma and repercussion – often well-founded.

Given the very wide range of serious mental health issues prevalent in the student population and the difficulties described above in relation to psychiatric diagnosis, academics and other staff will frequently require support in their care and management of the disturbed student (as well as other students affected) for some time after original access to medical help or psychiatric assistance. This point brings us to the next section, that of the importance of 'caring for the carers.'

Attending to the needs of the student's support community

> We share a house with Sarah and we know she's getting help but we would like to know how we might help her? (Student housemates)

> Can you advise me what to do next, this student is behaving very worryingly, and particularly after drinking, and he has assured me that he's consulted the doctor. I'd like to know if he really has, and I'd like to know how to help his neighbours, because though they have been very understanding of him up until now, they are getting somewhat tired of his antics. (A personal tutor)

> Hello, is that the student's advice centre? I am the mother of John Smith who is studying engineering at your university... I am very worried about him...he keeps phoning us at home...and he's got his exams coming soon...he seems to have no friends, says he's being bullied... and I'm worried, you know, in case he will, well, you know, he will...but I don't want him to know that I phoned you. (A worried parent)

The panoply of student services frequently receives contacts such as these from a wide range of people close to a student who is in distress. Such requests for assistance are inevitably heartfelt, often coming from people who have tried all they can to support the student and are now themselves beginning to feel the burden of this responsibility. From their perspective, the saying 'a problem shared is a problem halved', can become a truism. They may well feel immensely relieved to have shared their plight, particularly to a designated staff member of the HEI who 'they feel should know' how to intervene in circumstances such as these.

The staff member now has the problem of how to respond, to possibly disentangle the caller's anxieties from the original circumstances surrounding the person about whom concern has been expressed. There are many situations where this expression of fears has been immensely relieving to the sufferer, enabling them to continue going about their lives. By contrast, the resulting effect upon the helper – whether staff or a fellow student – can prove highly stressful. It is extremely easy for those consulted in such circumstances to considerably underestimate the positive effect they can have, just by being there, in an attentive and responsive manner. Often, this aspect remains hidden from the helper who almost inevitably gets caught up in the need to do something, a need which can quickly develop its own urgency for solution.

Who then is the client; who is complaining? This question can sometimes prove helpful to the staff member in particular, at least in the first instance, when disentangling the multiple implications of the helper's situation and the troubled student's own circumstances. There can be considerable danger in taking an absolutely literal view of the student's circumstances or mental state, rather than seeing these as a perception of the supporter now seeking help. Reports about third parties inevitably carry some elements of the referrer's own perceptions and concerns. Humphrey and Lago (1998) point out the very real dangers of inappropriately labelling students who seem to be unusual in some way.

At their most critical, the management of crises may vicariously traumatise staff members themselves, especially if they are already stressed from the demands of their everyday work. Though it is not of direct concern in this chapter, systems need also to be in place within HEIs to ensure staff can access relevant help and support if and when they become burnt out or stressed. There have been occasions where staff anxious to help have inappropriately set in train actions that have led to heavy-handed, ill-considered institutional responses; for example, sending university security or the police to a student's accommodation to check up on them, only to find that they are getting on with their lives and are shocked to realise that so much concern has been generated about them. In addition, some have also complained about invasion of privacy.

Concerns communicated by others therefore require considerable thought, although the above in no way implies that any actions to ascertain the state of, or to help a troubled student are invalid. But care and thought must be given by the staff member and the original helper to consider both who is to do what, and who else needs to be involved. Beyond this interpersonal interaction, there must be institutional consideration of the establishment of sets of policies and procedures that may act as guides in such situations. Appropriate policies and procedures can assist thoughtful intervention at times when levels of anxiety may be high and therefore not conducive to full consideration. This recommendation is forcibly made in the CVCP guidelines:

There are a number of areas in which universities may potentially owe a duty of care to students and to staff whose work brings them into contact with students. Much of the legal environment in this area is still evolving and is subject to amendment. (CVCP Guidelines 2000, p.12)

The legal framework surrounding the 'duty of care' as it relates to students with mental health difficulties is a complex one and potentially links to various legislation affecting all organisations. Disconcertingly and unfortunately, these different laws do not always dovetail coherently and institutions need to be mindful of this when drawing up their policies of good practice:

- Breach of Contract
- Liability for Negligence
- Health and Safety at Work
- Occupier's Liability Act
- Sex Discrimination Act
- Race Relations Act
- Disability Discrimination Act
- Human Rights Act
- Data Protection Act.

(CVCP Guidelines 2000, pp.12–15)

The individual institution's own statements and procedures must reflect the national legal framework in addition to that organisation's own structures, policy statements and procedural guidelines. Examples of these should include:

- disability statement
- admissions procedures
- confidentiality and disclosure policies
- emergency procedures

- procedures for suspension of/withdrawal from studies

- course assessment policies and practice.

(CVCP Guidelines 2000, pp.16–18)

It is interesting to note the very different ways in which the guidelines are being translated into practice by different institutions. What is clear, however, is that the organisations themselves are charged with responsibility for their implementation. At the time of writing, there seem to be a range of different approaches: some led individually by key figures developing policies, others being developed by specifically appointed committees. In some organisations there is still no development. Therefore, the answer to the questions – 'How can all these policy documents be pulled together, and who makes the connections?' – spans a wide range of approaches and inevitably reflects local conditions in each HEI. The need for supportive policies and procedures at such times is evident, for cases like the aforementioned may, if not handled thoughtfully, contravene the moral, philosophical and legal context within which higher education operates.

Students who harm themselves, who have eating or personality disorders, or high anxiety states, who suffer considerably from depression or are affected seriously by a whole range of other conditions, cause immense apprehension to those around them, sometimes seriously affecting the academic achievements of others. Advisory and supportive responses have to take into account both those who support and the troubled person in trying to identify strategies to help both parties. In general, the more supportive one can be to the troubled student's own support group, the better they are able to aid their friend's search for help and health. Sometimes listening to a friend can show them what they need to do. It might also help to draw the friend's attention to their own needs, to help them create boundaries so that the distress of the troubled student does not weigh so heavily. An example of this approach is provided in Chapter 9. Sometimes, groups of friends have drawn up a schedule to ensure one of them is present for the troubled student, allowing the others to pursue their own activities. Advising them of the emergency numbers of the HEI and local health services is essential, as is informing them of a staff member's own availability should circumstances change.

Where troubled students have eventually alienated their previously supportive friends, difficult confrontations may have to take place. Wardens and senior residents in halls experience cases each year in which they encounter difficult scenarios that eventually lead to the troubled student being requested to leave. Such steps are not normally taken until many other interventions have been tried: urging the student to seek appropriate help, trying to involve him/her in drawing up strategies to help themselves, and building in regular reviews of progress.

In the most extreme of scenarios, supporters of the troubled student may have to call for medical help and doctors, in their turn, may have to invoke compulsory hospital admission of the student under the provisions of the Mental Health Act 1983. Gemma's account in Chapter 3 provides an example of a student who recognised this need herself. It is at moments such as these that the relationships between the HEI and the helping agencies of the surrounding community are fully tested.

The capacity to offer support both to troubled students and to those who care for them is manifestly an increasing need in HEIs. Carefully and sensitively managed, it will contribute to an enhanced atmosphere amongst the group or family concerned, and ensure that academic careers are not damaged too drastically.

Conclusion

Concerns about student mental health have come increasingly to the attention of institutions of higher education in recent years, as evidenced throughout this book. The research emphasis has focused, perhaps inevitably, upon the early detection of mental illness where 'most research appears descriptive, adopting either a symptoms approach (i.e. identifying prevalence of psychological disorder), or a stressors approach (i.e. identifying factors, such as accommodation, which students report as causing difficulties)' (Fox *et al.* 2001).

This chapter has explored some of the challenges and difficulties that student mental health problems can create, not only for the students who suffer, but also for the various support and treatment services required, both within the HEI and in the surrounding community. Changes of policy and consistent under-resourcing of psychological services in the NHS over the last decade (particularly in relation to young people) have posed great challenges to staff seeking appropriate support and treatment for students. Relationships between the HEIs and the great variety of statutory and voluntary agencies are of utmost importance within the field of student mental health. Goodwill, speed of referral and skilled intervention are all necessary to ensure the student is helped towards health with as little time as possible lost to study, otherwise it may become too expensive to return, leaving both the student and society poorer.

Legislation is currently extremely complex and still developing. In some instances, policies and practices are evolving in light of the legislation, but in the absence of precedent. The wide variety of student behaviour, psychological dysfunction and mental health problems means that many factors have to be taken into account to optimise help for students, to support those around them and to ensure that all this is done within practices that are sensitive, humane and legal.

References

Association for University and College Counselling (1996–) *Annual Surveys of Counselling Services*. Rugby: British Association for Counselling and Psychotherapy.

Association for University Teachers (1994) 'Long Hours, Little Thanks.' *Bulletin 198* pp.13–15. London: AUT.

Bradley, G. (2000) 'Responding effectively to the mental health needs of international students', *Higher Education 39*, pp.417–433.

Currie, J. (2000) 'Not All in the Mind.' *Times Higher Educational Supplement*. 28 April, p.6.

CVCP (Committee of Vice Chancellors and Principals) (2000) *Guidelines on Student Mental Health Policies and Procedures for Higher Education*. London: CVCP.

Daines, D., Gask, L. and Usherwood. T. (1997) *Medical and Psychiatric Issues for Counsellors*. London: Sage.

Department of Health (1999) *Saving Lives: Our Healthier Nation*. London: Stationery Office.

Fisher, S. (1994) *Stress in Academic Life: The Mental Assembly Line*. Buckingham, Society for Research into Higher Education: Open University Press.

Fox, P., Caraher, M. and Baker, H. (2001) 'Promoting Student Mental Health' (an update paper). Wolfson Institute of Health Sciences: Thames Valley University.

Harrington, M.J. (1996) 'University acts on stress survey.' *The Bulletin 4 Novermber* Birmingham: Birmingham University.

Howe, G. (1998) *Getting into the System: Living with Serious Mental Illness.* London: Jessica Kingsley Publishers.

Humphrey, N. and Lago, C. (1998) 'Issues of difference in educational settings.' *Clinical Counselling in Further and Higher Education, 103–124.* London: Routledge.

Keeling, R. (2000) 'Psychological diversity and the mission of student affairs.' *Net Results: NASPA's E-Zine for Student Affairs Professionals,* 11 December www.naspa.org/netresults/index.cfm

Lago, C.O. and Shipton, G. (1994) *On Listening and Learning: Student Counselling in Further and Higher Education.* London: Central Book Publishing.

Leicester University (1999) *Supporting Students with Mental Health Difficulties: A Whole Institutional Approach.* Leicester: Leicester University.

Linklater, M. (2001) 'A Tale of Ordinary Madness.' *The Observer Review,* 25 February p.1.

Lodge. K. (Chair) (1996) 'Staff Survey.' Conducted by the Group for Staff Support and Fellowship. Norwich: University of East Anglia.

Matheou, D. (2000) 'Local Hero.' *The Observer Magazine* 7 Jan. p.14.

Mental Health Foundation (1999a) *The Fundamental Facts: All the Latest Facts and Figures on Mental Illness.* London: Mental Health Foundation.

Mental Health Foundation (1999b) *Bright Futures: Promoting Children and Young People's Mental Health.* London: Mental Health Foundation.

Rana, R., Smith, E. and Walkling, J. (1999) *Degrees of Disturbance: The New Agenda.* Rugby: British Association for Counselling.

Rutter, M. and Smith, D.J. (eds) (1995) *Psycho-Social Disorders in Young People: Time Trends and their Causes.* London: John Wiley and Son.

Stanley, N. and Manthorpe, J. (2001) 'Reading mental health inquiries: messages for social work.' *Journal of Social Work 1,* 1, pp.79–99.

Stewart, W. (1997) *An A-Z of Counselling Theory and Practice,* (2nd edition.) Cheltenham: Stanley Thornes.

Stewart-Brown, S., Evans, J., Patterson, J., Petersen, S., Doll, H., Balding, J. and Regis, D. (2000) 'The health of students in institutes of higher education: an important and neglected public health problem?' *Journal of Public Health Medicine 22,* 4, pp.492–499.

Surtees, P., Wainwright, N. and Pharoah, P. (2000) *Student Mental Health, Use of Services and Academic Attainment: A Report to the Review Committee of the University of Cambridge Counselling Service.* Cambridge: Cambridge University.

Woolfson, M. (1997) In R. Rana *et al.* (1999) *Degrees of Disturbance: The New Agenda.* Rugby: British Association for Counselling.

Wojtas, O. (2000) 'Suicide Rate Suggests Rise in Problem Student Intake.' *Times Higher Education Supplement,* 12 May, p.64.

PART THREE

Identifying Effective Responses

Chapter 9

A Model for Supportive Services in Higher Education

Barbara Rickinson and Jean Turner

Introduction

The model for supportive services outlined in this chapter has been developed to meet the needs of a research-led university, established in 1900, with a current population of approximately 20,000 students (2000/2001). This model reflects the high quality medical and psychological counselling support established in the older UK universities. This developed in response to the mental health needs of a predominantly 18–25 year old undergraduate population attending universities away from their home base and those of international students. The traditional student profile is now changing. The government higher education widening participation policy is resulting in an increasingly diverse student population nationally. However, in the older research-led universities the profile is only changing slowly. In this university the majority of the student population are still in the 18–25 age group and drawn from traditional academic backgrounds. The University is focusing on widening access to able students from disadvantaged and non-traditional academic backgrounds.

This model also reflects the support strategies being adopted by universities to meet the mental health requirements of a changing student profile. The Association of University and College Counsellors (AUCC) provides a framework for higher education professionals to share ideas and gain from the student support strengths of different sectors of higher education. For example, the newer universities and higher education colleges are able to contribute experience and expertise in aspects of supporting a more diverse student population (see Chapter 10 this volume). The Heads of University Counselling Services (HUCS) and the Association of Managers of Student Services in Higher Education (AMOSSHE) are valuable forums for addressing the mental health requirements of higher education and influencing policy development in the area of appropriate mental health provision. Recent examples include the publications *Degrees of Disturbance: The New Agenda* (Rana *et al.* 1999) for HUCS and *Guidelines on student mental health policies and procedures for higher education* (CVCP 2000) jointly commissioned by the Committee of Vice-Chancellors and Principals (CVCP), the Standing Conference of Principals (SCOP) and AMOSSHE with HUCS. These guidelines highlight the need for higher education institutions to review their mental health policies and procedures and to develop effective strategies to support students experiencing mental health difficulties. The model for supportive services described here was cited in these guidelines as an example of good practice.

The first part of this chapter describes the institutional policies and procedures developed by this University to support students with mental health difficulty/disability to participate fully in higher education and express their individual potential. The second part of the chapter discusses the role and experience of the Mental Health Co-ordinator. This post, established in 1998, was one of the new initiatives to support widening participation.

Support and guidance

A coherent and structured institutional approach to student support and guidance is maintained through a Student Welfare Forum chaired by the Pro-Vice Chancellor with responsibility for student affairs. All relevant student support and guidance staff from academic schools/departments, residences, the central services and the student body are represented on this Forum. The Forum provides opportunity for debate, identification of institutional pressure points, review of current support and guidance structures and presentation of recommendations for improvement. The Forum also provides a valuable channel, through the Pro-Vice Chancellor, for influencing institutional strategic planning, resourcing and policy making.

Staff development

Mental health awareness is built into the University's overall staff development programme. Staff are provided with training in recognising and managing stress within themselves, their students, and the general academic environment. This training is compulsory for all staff as part of the University's health and safety requirements. Further consultative support and training in responding to students with mental health issues are provided for tutors by the central Student Support and Counselling Service (SSCS) in liaison with the Staff Development Unit (SDU). The SSCS inputs this training into the SDU post-graduate certificate in learning and teaching for academic staff. This course is compulsory for all newly appointed academic staff and an increasing number of earlier appointed staff are also signing up for the course. Academic staff also receive training in the implementation of the University's Learning and Teaching Strategy. This strategy encourages a more flexible approach to course structures and assessment procedures while maintaining required academic standards. This flexibility, together with variety in teaching modes, is designed to better accommodate the learning support needs of students from non-traditional academic backgrounds and those with specific difficulties.

School/department support and guidance systems

All students have an allocated personal tutor who is expected to work within the University's codes of practice, which outline their responsibilities (see Figure 9.1). Increasing student numbers and academic demands have placed pressure on the personal tutoring system and of course, the quality of individual tutoring is variable. However, a research study (Rickinson and Rutherford 1995, 1996) highlighted the importance of the personal tutoring system in facilitating students' initial adjustment to higher education and their subsequent progress and achievement. It also demonstrated that, if the personal tutoring system is to be effective, tutors need training for their role and the support of an effective counselling service. This study was instrumental in the University's decision to retain and strengthen its personal tutoring system. The central SSCS supports the personal tutoring system with a consultation facility for tutors, staff development workshops and seminars, relevant booklets and web-based personal health and safety information for staff and students.

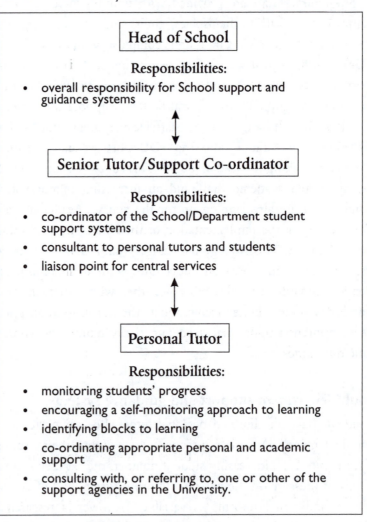

Figure 9.1. Structure of school/department systems

The student support and counselling service (SSCS)

The central SSCS complements the support and guidance systems operating in the schools/departments. Students whose progress is inhibited by practical welfare, learning or emotional/psychological difficulties, and those with specific needs such as a disability, can expect to access appropriate professional support or counselling by consulting the SSCS. A total of 1238 students used the service in 1999/2000. The service also supports staff in their tutorial, supervisory and welfare roles.

Philosophy

The approach of the service is based on the underlying belief that people are integral to the systems in which they function. Any individual student is likely to function within several social networks in addition to the large academic institution. The individual, the social groups, and the institution are dynamically interdependent. Counsellors therefore use system-oriented models of intervention as well as intrapsychic ones. Conceptualising intervention in a system-oriented way lends itself to the integration of preventive strategies with traditional therapeutic models, such as cognitive-behavioural, psychodynamic or person-centred models.

Developmental theory also underpins the work of the service. Young adults who are undergoing developmental transitions and straining to master new age-related tasks can be particularly vulnerable to the general stresses of academic demands and competition (Rickinson 1998). On the other hand, students can be resourceful and emotionally resilient. While some may react to heavy academic stress by developing prolonged emotional problems, strengthening cognitive, emotional, or behavioural coping skills often helps young adults to reorganise their lives or their identities, in the process of getting through a developmental crisis. In this way, a period of serious emotional upheaval can be transformed into a growth experience, which in turn can lead to a higher level of functioning both personally and academically. Based on this philosophy, the essential aim of the service is to support student learning and development and thus maximise students' potential to benefit from their university experience.

Confidentiality

The service operates within the code of ethics of the British Association of Counselling (BAC 1998). Students consulting the service can rely on a professional standard of confidentiality which protects their identity, communication and records. Information is only disclosed to a third party with the student's permission except, when necessary, for a student assessed 'at risk' either to themselves or to others. Permission is routinely obtained from students for liaison with their GP or academic tutors on relevant issues. Students are also encouraged to consult with their GPs or their tutors about difficulties which may impact on their academic progress. The service aims to maintain appropriate communication with GPs and academic tutors while respecting the boundaries of confidentiality. This can be difficult at times, but if policies are clear and understood by both students and staff, trust and communication can be maintained. In the event of a student being thought to be 'at risk' to themselves or to others, they are usually persuaded to accept appropriate help such as medical assessment. In the rare event that a student 'at risk' is unwilling, or unable, to accept appropriate help the service would assume responsibility for acting to ensure the health and safety of an individual or others.

Services to students

Personal and academic effectiveness

Students need to develop a broad range of personal skills in order to succeed at university and in their future careers. The opportunity for this development is best provided within the framework of normal academic courses. The SSCS supplements this process by providing specialist groups/workshops such as:

- Introductory Group Programme for first year students which facilitates students' personal and academic adjustment to university
- Specific Learning Support Programme which assists students requiring additional support in developing effective study skills and learning strategies

- Programme for Postgraduate Research Students which supports students with the process of embarking on and completing their PhD

- Examination Support Programme which focuses on improving exam performance and coping with the stress of exams.

Specialist learning support

An educational counsellor/psychologist provides a service to students with learning difficulty or disability and a consultation service to academic staff. The service offers a well-stocked educational resource centre with self-help literature on learning skills and personal health and safety issues. This resource is self-funding; many of the publications are produced by SSCS staff and sold at a small price to cover printing costs. External publications are also purchased and sold to students at cost price, and a wide range of information leaflets is available free of charge. This resource is often used as a reference point for students and staff. A web-based programme of research information on personal health and safety issues such as *Facts About Illicit Drugs, Stress and Eating* and *Understanding Depression* has recently been developed and we have now begun to monitor its use by staff and students.

Support for students with specific welfare needs

A team of 2.6 FTE support co-ordinators based in the SSCS complement the practical welfare advice provided for students by the Student Union. In addition, they provide specialist assistance to students with specific needs or disabilities. One of the team acts as mental health co-ordinator for students with diagnosed mental health problems/disability.

Support for international students

The University's international students (3200, 1999/2000) are provided with language support and study skills support by the English for International Students Unit. A full-time International Student Adviser based in the International Unit provides general welfare support to students and works with the Student Union and academic departments to raise awareness and support for international students to become academically and socially integrated into the University. International students are sometimes vulnerable to mental health crisis during cultural transition. Integrated support systems can foster early identification of difficulty and appropriate management, thus reducing the incidence of crisis.

Counselling

Professional psychologists or counsellors provide confidential counselling (individual or group) to students in therapeutic, developmental and preventative areas. The service is accessible to all registered students of the University. The majority of students self refer, but the service also receives referrals from local GPs and from academic and welfare staff. The service is open two evenings a week to improve availability. Currently, a service level agreement with the University's registrar and secretary guarantees students an initial routine appointment within 7–14 days of referral. Obviously, this agreement is dependent on the equation between staff resources and student demand remaining stable. In 1999/2000 the counselling team consisted of 3.7 FTE counsellors or clinical psychologists (including input from the Director of Service) and 0.5 FTE sessional counsellors. In addition, the counselling team provide a same day 'urgent' brief appointment facility. This is a valuable strategy for containing anxiety within the institution and ensuring a responsive service to students in crisis. Students referring via the routine referral route are offered an initial assessment appointment of 50 minutes, which includes a risk assessment (Core System Group 1998). Following this, they are offered a counselling contract based on their assessed needs. Brief interventions are the mode of choice for the majority of students and have been shown to be effective in reducing levels of psychological distress and blocks to potential academic progress (see Rickinson 1997, 1999). In 1999/2000 only 5 per cent of the 831 students seen by the counselling team required longer intervention because of the severity of their psychological profile.

Services to academic staff

The main facilitators of student learning are the academic staff. The SSCS aims to support tutors in their task by offering a consultation service. This enables staff who are concerned about the academic progress, or psychological state of individual students to receive prompt professional advice. A rota system ensures that there is a counsellor on 'consultation' duty each day. In 1999/2000 a total of 1710 calls was recorded. The majority of these callers discussed appropriate management of tutees with difficulties, particularly those reluctant to seek help. This facility supports tutors and maintains appropriate management and referral procedures. In addition the service also contributes to the staff development programme by offering workshops for senior tutors/welfare co-ordinators, personal tutors and university residence staff. These workshops aim to assist staff in recognising factors which inhibit student learning and development, managing difficult or distressing situations, and ensuring appropriate referral.

Academic staff are provided with a free confidential personal counselling facility through an arrangement between the University and the University Hospital Trust's independent staff support unit. Academic staff may be referred through the University's occupational health or refer themselves directly to the unit. This arrangement was chosen because of its perceived economic advantages (cheaper than in-house provision) and the benefit of staff having access to a confidential service outside the University. For a full debate on the advantages/disadvantages of providing staff counselling internally or externally, see Ross (1999).

Medical support

The University no longer funds a health centre, but an NHS general practice rents accommodation on campus and is known as the University medical practice. All students are expected to register with a local GP practice and many still register with the University, particularly those based in university residences (80 % of first-years and the majority of international students). The University retains a contract with the head of the practice who, in the role of University medical officer, provides advice on student issues: assessment for students in crisis and those needing aegrotat degrees or leave of absence from courses. This role is supported by a senior consultant psychiatrist whom the University employs on a consultancy basis, while maintaining links with the liaison psychiatry service.

On several occasions each year the University needs to obtain an urgent general psychiatric opinion on students whose mental illness is causing significant concern or disruption to others. These students are often living in university residences where the University owes a duty of care to other residents. The greatest difficulty arises when students are ill enough to be beyond the care that can be provided by their GP, and before a compulsory admission is possible. The senior consultant psychiatrist is able to offer an urgent assessment and formulate a management plan. The University also employs an occupational health physician (0.2 % FTE) to support the 1.6 per cent FTE occupational health nurses. This unit is administered by the Director of Health and Safety.

There are clear procedures in place for supporting students with mental health crises. Students often respond to counselling support in association with tutorial support. In more severe cases, or when temporary withdrawal from the University is indicated, a medical/psychiatric assessment is arranged by the University medical officer and, based on this assessment, the medical officer will make recommendations regarding health care and academic adjustments. It is in these crisis situations that the benefit of an on-site medical facility which has easy access to specialist services becomes evident. The University also has clear guidelines in place for the consideration of mitigating circumstances (with appropriate evidence) in relation to course/degree assessment policies and practices.

The counselling service is supported by a consultant psychiatrist/psychotherapist (one session per week). This consultant works closely with the SSCS team and, in addition to providing assessments for students whom counsellors are concerned about, provides clinical supervision and support to the team. This facility is invaluable to both students and counselling staff. Students in the 18–25 year old age range often present with dangerously high levels of psychological distress. It is important to ascertain if this psychological distress is due to developmental issues or the onset of more severe psychopathology (see Johnson 1989 and Rickinson

1997). The counsellors are supported in this assessment and management process by their internal medical consultant. Students requiring general psychiatric assessment or treatment are referred via their GP or, in an emergency, via the University medical officer for general NHS psychiatric care.

Duty of care

The University accepts a reasonable 'duty of care' to all its students, in particular those who are more vulnerable. As the case studies included in this chapter show, complex crisis situations can develop on occasion when an individual student with mental health problems behaves in a way which adversely affects other students. Often the individual student is not responsive to the appropriate support or medical help offered. This can be understood as a symptom of their mental health condition. However, other students adversely affected also need the University's duty of care. In these cases a consultation process takes place involving the University discipline officer, the medical officer and relevant university personnel. The Director of the SSCS is involved where appropriate. There are university procedures in place which make continued registration as a student dependant on a medical/psychiatric consultation. These procedures are only invoked when all other measures have been exhausted, and only on the recommendation of the medical officer. The University employs a qualified legal advisor who is consulted on the development of all policies and procedures.

Supporting access, progress and achievement

Students compete for places at the University on the criterion of academic merit. If a student being offered a place on academic merit has declared a disability on their UCAS application form, they are referred to the central SSCS for comprehensive pre-sessional information on the University's support systems and an assessment of their disability or specific needs in relation to their chosen programme of study. For students declaring a mental illness or disability this would include relevant medical/psychiatric reports, any risk assessment, recommendations for required medical support and any appropriate academic accommodations. For example, the need to sit examinations in a sheltered environment where nursing and medical support is available (the University provides this facility on campus). It is of benefit both to the student and the University that this assessment is done pre-admission, particularly for course programmes with professional requirements, such as medicine or health sciences.

Students are sometimes reluctant to declare a mental illness or disability, but through better pre-sessional information and clear confidentiality and disclosure polices, students are becoming more aware of the advantages of early disclosure. These advantages included eligibility for DfEE awards, and appropriate academic and personal support for their specific difficulties. The disadvantage of not declaring a mental health disability before being accepted on to a professional course is that at a later date the student might be assessed as not fit to continue the course because of professional requirements.

Learning support agreements

Following assessment, a learning support agreement is completed. This agreement between the student, their school/department and the University outlines academic and personal support needs, details how these will be met (such as centrally, or by the school or department), clarifies any limits on support available from the University, identifies source of financial support (e.g. DfEE award) and states any agreed academic accommodations. The agreement is signed, with acceptance of the university place, by the student, the school/department admission tutor and the disability co-ordinator.

Students who do not disclose a disability or specific need at admission complete the relevant parts of the pre-admission process at time of disclosure. Though the University has no legal requirement to meet needs not declared at admission, all efforts are made to accommodate the student. This also applies to students who develop, or recognise, a disability or specific need following admission. If a student does not want their disability disclosed to their department it is explained to them that they have the choice not to disclose, provided they are willing to forfeit extra academic support, eligibility for DfEE awards and so on. In a case where the undisclosed disability or mental health problems are considered to have implications for the chosen course (professional requirements), the decision to disclose comes under 'the risk to self or others' procedures.

The learning support agreement forms an effective base for monitoring students' academic progress and achievement within the school/department and ensuring that adequate support is in place. The SSCS also evaluates the effectiveness of its pre-admission support systems by conducting review interviews with students and collecting student feedback on their experiences of university.

The work of the mental health co-ordinator

The work of the mental health co-ordinator will be discussed within three significant areas:

- co-ordination of support for students with diagnosed mental health needs

- crisis work

- preventative work.

Co-ordination of support

The role involves the co-ordination of support for students who have, or develop, a mental health illness. A considerable percentage of time is spent interviewing students who present themselves, or are referred to the service, with a range of practical, welfare and/or emotional problems. An assessment is made in each case followed by a referral to appropriate sources, whether these be contained within the SSCS and other University departments, or to external agencies. Effective liaison with other services – student counselling, welfare services, financial support office, medical practice, community mental health agencies, accommodation and social services – will in part depend upon developing and maintaining those relationships. The developmental nature of the post has enabled much of that work to take place in the early stages and very strong links have emerged with key providers.

All students using this service are offered regular follow-up appointments to review progress or changes and to ensure that, wherever possible, support systems are in place to facilitate successful degree completion. In order to co-ordinate effective support, early detection of problems is paramount. This is reflected in pre-admission procedures relating to disability in general and is continued through the provision of a 'drop in' service to all first-year students during the start of term, where students are able to discuss any concerns they may have without waiting for an appointment. Throughout the year we also run a series of workshops and group work programmes, such as the 'anxiety management' group. This joint working initiative involves a counsellor and co-ordinator working together to combine a cognitive behavioural approach with practical, solution focused strategies.

Records maintained by the counselling service from student registration forms indicate that anxiety is one of the major concerns presented by students and that this is often related to academic difficulties and other mood disorders, such as depression. Due to the numbers presenting with anxiety difficulties, and because of the positive effects of peer group support, group programmes are seen as a feasible method of intervention. Anxiety management groups are run during term time for four weekly sessions for a maximum of six students and are well attended. Students are referred to the group by support co-ordinators and counsellors. In addition to the anxiety group, specific exam anxiety workshops are offered during the summer term, supported by a walk-in service during the actual examination period to contain high levels of stress.

The following case studies serve to illustrate how the several strands of support can work together to assist a student, and that the need for co-ordination is vital to ensure that the support systems all work together. While the students' names have been changed, the following scenarios are based upon incidents that have occurred in the University.

Alan

Alan was a first-year student living in university self-catering accommodation and had registered with the service early in the first term when he came in for some practical financial advice. Alan was a mature student

returning to education after several years working and having successfully completed an access course. There was no other contact until
mid-way through the second term when the mental health co-ordinator
received a phone call from one of Alan's flatmates expressing concern
regarding Alan's 'bizarre' behaviour. He had apparently been experiencing extreme mood swings and was very agitated. The flatmate described
Alan's speech as occasionally 'delusional'. At this point there were clearly
very real concerns, and the co-ordinator suggested to the flatmate that
Alan should come into the service for an appointment. Alan seemed very
willing to seek out help, as he came in the following day. Although he
felt he was coping, Alan was aware that he had found the whole experience of coming away to university very stressful, and at times this trig-
gered episodes of panic and confusion. Alan was referred to the counselling team and an appointment made to see the University medical
practice. Alan was reluctant to accept counselling help, but did keep his
medical appointment where he was prescribed medication.

Although in the short term this seemed to contain the situation, it
soon became clear that Alan's problems were much more deeply rooted.
Within a couple of weeks of the medical appointment, the co-ordinator
received a further phone call from the Hall Warden who was extremely
concerned about Alan's personal safety and also that of other residents, as
Alan's behaviour had deteriorated. Although his behaviour was
described as 'aggressive', there was no actual violence towards anyone,
but his flatmates were very concerned that this could become a real possibility given his unpredictable state. Alan was estranged from his family
and therefore had no parental support or family home to return to.

Following a case discussion with Alan, the Hall Warden and the
co-ordinator, it was felt that Alan would benefit from some time away
from the University. Through contacts with local services, the
co-ordinator arranged emergency accommodation in a YMCA hostel
where Alan would have a 'key worker' linked with the local psychiatric
social work department. As he was a full-time student, Alan had no entitlement to benefits to pay for the cost of accommodation at the YMCA,
and was already paying Hall fees to the University. An emergency application was made on behalf of Alan to the University's access fund to meet
the additional costs, and this enabled him to stay at the YMCA to review
and make further plans. The mental health co-ordinator visited Alan at
the YMCA and provided a valuable link with the University. Alan then
made the decision to withdraw temporarily from the University on
health grounds and to restart his course the following September. Prior

to resuming his studies, he was seen by the co-ordinator to assess his support needs and to look at ways of dealing with stress in the future. At the time of writing, Alan has nearly completed his first year and there have been no further crises.

Jane

Jane first came to the attention of the service through her flatmates who, as in Alan's case, were very concerned about her behaviour. Jane had an eating disorder and was quite severely anorexic. Although her three flatmates were very concerned about her health, they were also finding it very difficult to live with Jane's constant obsession with food. They also reported that they were becoming overly conscious of what they ate in front of her and had started to eat alone in their rooms. In addition to this, Jane was also self-harming by cutting herself and this was, understandably, causing considerable distress to her flatmates.

Jane was initially reluctant to come in to the service for help so the mental health co-ordinator visited the flatmates and offered mediation sessions. The three were very worried about Jane's reaction when they told her that they could not live with her continued behaviour the following year and they wanted her to find alternative accommodation and also to seek help. During the two sessions held with all four students, they were each able to express their feelings and concerns in a safe environment. They agreed to continue to live together for the remainder of the academic year, and Jane agreed to look for alternative accommodation as well as registering with the counselling service. Although it could be seen that in many ways Jane was the student with the mental health needs, the key issue seemed to be to contain and manage the other students' concerns and anxieties in dealing with a very distressing situation. Jane continued with counselling and was referred to an eating disorder group, while her former flatmates moved into private accommodation and had no other contact with the counselling service.

As the account of work with Jane demonstrates, innovative approaches to case work have led to mediation sessions where there have been interpersonal problems between groups of students (flatmates). Although this could be seen as co-ordinating support for the student concerned, it clearly has a preventative element. In many cases, this situation would have been seen as part of the normal transitional difficulties associated with learning to live with other people, but in some, the problems seem to be much deeper and require a greater level of professional help.

Crisis work

Inevitably, there will be occasions when crises occur and the ability to respond in an appropriate manner depends to an extent upon the strength of support systems already in place. The training workshops, such as those for post-graduate supervisors and Hall tutors, include sessions on managing crisis situations. Although they are rare, a knowledge of available support systems can often contain panic and anxiety in the short term to allow immediate appropriate responses to the situation. The following are all examples of potentially crisis situations requiring 'management' which the support service has dealt with in recent times:

- Assisting a tutor to break the news to a parent that her son had attempted to commit suicide and was dangerously ill in hospital (this was an international student who had been reluctant to seek help and whose difficulties only came to light in a crisis). The situation was managed following the University's crisis procedures and the student concerned was taken to hospital and later flown home.

- Co-ordinating support to deal with a situation when a member of staff alerted the emergency services to avert an attempted suicide.

- Advising a personal tutor on how to break the news to a student that her father had died suddenly.

- Addressing concern for a student in a hall of residence who would not leave his room because of severe obsessional compulsive disorder, managed through visits to the hall and liaison with his GP.

As we have already seen, students are likely to function within many different networks; these examples all clearly demonstrate the need for the work of individual services to be co-ordinated by a designated person.

Preventative work

The developmental nature of this new post meant that a certain percentage of time was given over to setting up preventative strategies and systems to meet the needs of a more diverse student population. In many instances, the fundamental nature of the work remained the same, but it was important to recognise that for any organisation going through a period of change this can produce a certain level of anxiety for people within that organisation.

It was largely recognised that staff working in the University's self-catering accommodation were quite often dealing with 'front line' incidents with very little training or support. Typically this would include matters such as homesickness and distress, as well as more severe issues such as suicide or suicide threats. These can be extremely alarming for anyone to deal with, especially so for staff who feel isolated and ill-equipped. As part of the preventative work, post-graduate students are appointed in self-catering accommodation to a pastoral role, and consequently encounter a wide range of issues within the student population, and not only among first years. Whilst they have the back-up of hall wardens and the University's support systems, in many situations they are the first point of contact with a distressed student or incident, and are expected to contain these situations or make immediate assessments.

Training is offered to all post-graduate supervisors and is located within the context of a wider support system. To achieve this, the mental health co-ordinator is part of the selection and interview panel which convenes prior to the start of the new academic year. Early links are thus established with these students. Their training includes a basic introduction to listening skills and an awareness of dealing with students in distress. It covers practical strategies to assist with the social integration of students as well as looking at crisis reduction and overall support systems. It employs a combination of active involvement, such as role play, with small group discussions. Following this, all post-graduate supervisors are made aware of the support available to them, particularly in the form of a consultancy service to discuss any concerns or difficulties they may experience. Additional seminars and presentations on specific issues such as drug and alcohol awareness are provided to staff working in halls of residence.

The mental health co-ordinator also offers mental health awareness training to residence staff covering referral procedures to sources of support, as well as developing an awareness of the possible signs and symptoms of mental health problems.

Another aspect of preventative work has been the production of advice and information including a leaflet entitled: *Going away to University – A Survival Guide for Parents.* This was the result of a growing demand upon the service to respond to enquiries from concerned parents about the welfare and/or the emotional well being of their children. (See Figure 9.2)

Parents can play an important role however in helping their sons and daughters through this transitional stage:

- come along to open days and find out what it is all about
- encourage your son/daughter to handle finances and prepare budgets prior to starting university.

Advance financial planning:

Your Local Education Authority is responsible for assessing eligibility and entitlement to tuition fee support and student loans, and also for assessing the levels of parental contribution. For further information, contact Dfee free information line on: 0800 731 9133.

Be prepared to listen:

Adolescents are more likely to confide and trust in you if they feel you will respond to their worries and not automatically criticise them. Remember that sensible rules can be the basis for security and agreement.

Find support for yourself:

Many parents can feel rejected when their children leave home. If you are concerned, then speak to one of the Student Support Co-ordinators at the Counselling Service. We offer a confidential telephone service BUT are unable to divulge personal information about students.

Figure 9.2. Extract from Going Away to University – A Survival Guide for Parents, *Student Support and Counselling Service.*

This has proved to be very popular with academic departments when they talk to parents, and at Open Days. The leaflet outlines the transitional experiences for students coming away to university and gives practical advice for preparing for university life, as well as listing support services for students and useful contact numbers for parents. A similar information leaflet has been designed for school leavers to give practical advice and information on university life. Both leaflets provide information about external agencies which can give support to individuals, their friends and families. These agencies may be local or national, and include telephone helplines, websites and voluntary bodies in addition to statutory services.

Conclusion

The opportunity to engage in higher education can make a positive contribution to mental well-being. However, some students, among them some of the most academically gifted, are vulnerable to the stresses of higher education. In relation to mental health, a preventative, developmental approach needs to be adopted by higher education institutions (HEIs). This is best achieved by the establishment and maintenance of university-wide student support and guidance systems, actively supported by an effective central counselling service with appropriate medical links. It is important to note that the establishment of institutional support and guidance systems is a developmental process in itself. In response to the recent Mental Health Guidelines (CVCP 2000) HEIs are reviewing and developing written policies and procedures. The formulation of appropriate policies, procedures and codes of practice is an essential first step.

The implementation of university-wide support systems is a more complex process. Staff in academic schools/departments are working under increased pressure with limited resources; in order to engage them in the process, they need to be made aware of the benefits of establishing preventative systems. These include reducing the number of academic or personal crisis incidents, and increasing student retention and successful completion rates. Factors which have aided the process of establishing student support and guidance systems at this University include:

- the commitment of the Director of Student Support and Counselling to a systemic institutional approach

- learning from research at this University, which demonstrated the effectiveness of appropriate support in relation to student retention and successful completion

- an active staff development programme

- encouraging Heads of school/departments to appoint an appropriate member of academic staff to the role of support and guidance co-ordinator and then working with these co-ordinators to establish systems relevant to their school/department and that incorporate the essence of the central guidelines

- inclusion of 'support and guidance' as an aspect of subject assessment by the QAA, which provided an external impetus to the process; schools/departments preparing for assessment were keen to ensure their arrangements met QAA standards, providing an opportunity for the development and implementation of improved systems

- encouraging schools/departments to evaluate the effectiveness of their support and guidance systems in relation to student progress and achievement.

Institutions also need to ensure that they have appropriate professional structures in place to support students with mental health problems and maintain appropriate links with NHS services. Overall institutional involvement, through effective systems, assists students to make the most of their higher education experience.

References

British Association of Counselling (BAC) (1998) *Codes of Practice.* Rugby: BAC Publications.

Committee of Vice Chancellors and Principals (CVCP) (2000) *Guidelines on Student Mental Health Policies and Procedures for Higher Education.* London: CVCP.

Core System Group (1998) *Clinical Outcomes in Routine Evaluation (CORE).* Leeds: The Psychological Therapies Research Centre, University of Leeds.

Johnson R.W. *et al.* (1989) 'Psychological symptoms of counselling centre clients.' *Journal of Counselling Psychology 36*, 1, 110–114.

Rana, R., Smith, E. and Walkling, J. (1999) *Degrees of Disturbance: The New Agenda* Rugby: British Association of Counselling.

Rickinson, B. and Rutherford, D. (1995) 'Increasing undergraduate student retention rates.' *British Journal of Guidance and Counselling 23*, 2, 161–172.

Rickinson, B. and Rutherford, D. (1996) 'Systematic monitoring of the adjustment to university of undergraduates: A strategy for reducing withdrawal rates.' *British Journal of Guidance and Counselling 24*, 2, 23–225.

Rickinson, B. (1997) 'Evaluating the effectiveness of counselling intervention with final year undergraduates.' *Counselling Psychology Quarterly 10*, 3, 271–285.

Rickinson, B. (1998) 'The relationship between undergraduate student counselling and successful degree completion.' *Studies in Higher Education 23*, 1, 95–102.

Rickinson, B. (1999) 'Increasing undergraduate students' capacity to complete their degree programme successfully.' *Psychodynamic Counselling 5*, 3, 319–337.

Ross, P. (1999) *Dealing with Stress in Higher Education.* London: Universities and Colleges Employers Association.

Chapter 10

A Model of Supportive Services in Further Education

Kathryn James

Equity dictates that all should have the opportunity to succeed

(FEFC 1997)

In September 1993 Clarendon College (now part of New College Nottingham) set up the Mental Health Education Project and appointed a mental health guidance worker on a part-time basis to work closely with the Directorate of Rehabilitation and Community Care of Nottingham NHS Mental Health Care Trust. The purpose of the project was to see whether mental health service users could or would want to access further education.

The initial success of the project enabled us to extend the remit to include referrals of service users from the General Psychiatry and Psychotherapy Directorate, and later from the Addiction and Forensic Directorate. Referrals also came from the voluntary sector, user groups, homelessness and learning disability services. The guidance worker became full time and another part-time guidance worker was employed. By 1996, the project had become a support service within the college and was receiving approximately four referrals per week. It was providing learning opportunities, guidance and support to over 300 students each year who were referred from mental health services.

This chapter is both a description and a personal reflection on setting up the Mental Health Support Service at Clarendon College. As such it describes one model of support for mental health service users in further education, charts some of the developments of that service and offers ideas as to how other education providers may develop their services or approach certain issues. In the further education sector there are many examples of good work supporting access to learning for people with mental health problems and readers may wish to look at other models of support in other areas around the country, such as: Lancashire, Birmingham, Wolverhampton and Barnet. Other examples of good practice may be found in *Images of Possibility* (Wertheimer 1997).

The unifying experience of stigma?

The challenge for colleges is to develop their capacity to respond to different approaches to learning and to identify individual learning goals. (FEFC 1996)

Colleges of further education attract a wide variety of people who choose to take up learning for diverse reasons. Students who also happen to have mental health problems are no exception. The age-range of students accessing guidance and learning opportunities through the Mental Health Support Service is from 16 to 65 years plus. Their levels of academic achievement also vary; some students have basic skills needs, others have first degrees, while some have further degrees. Some students have never worked, many have encountered long-term unemployment, while others have, until they became ill, held skilled or professional jobs. Their previous experiences of education and time away from education differ greatly. The range and age of onset of mental health problems also vary enormously. A significant proportion of the students have other factors in addition to their mental health needs, such as: learning problems, drug or alcohol misuse, or homelessness. There is no typical student with mental health difficulties. Therefore, responses to the learning needs of this group of students will never be simple or straightforward.

If there is any defining feature of this group of individuals it is that each will have experienced the stigma of mental health and the resulting sense of exclusion, although the degree of this will also vary. The effects of this stigma and exclusion can shatter self-esteem and confidence, with a resulting increase in emotional vulnerability. It makes it less easy to participate in learning, to make decisions or take risks; it may be harder to take the knocks of everyday life. Any individual wishing to enter education wants to be treated with dignity and respect. If we encourage people to participate in learning then we have a responsibility to respect the efforts that they have made to do this – we need to be even more conscious of this responsibility for students with mental health problems. If we can get it right for them, then we will get it right for all students.

Collaboration and partnership

> Partnership works best when the players have a shared picture of what it is they are working towards. (Wertheimer 1997, p.74)

When the Mental Health Support Service was first set up, the guidance worker was based within a day centre located in the grounds of a psychiatric hospital which was shortly to close. This location proved to be important in making the links between health professionals and the education system. Getting your face known, developing an understanding of the various roles in mental health services, and seeing the type of environment potential students might be coming from proved valuable. Mental health services and further education are complex systems, each with their own ways of working, their own expectations. For individuals from one service to access another, there needs to be a shared understanding and joint ways of working.

Early on, a steering group was established comprising the guidance worker, managers from the college, and managers and practitioners from rehabilitation and community care services. This proved a useful forum for agreeing realistic targets, identifying the boundaries between each service and allocating responsibility. The group also provided valuable support for the guidance workers. The need for mental health awareness raising for college staff became clear, and it was decided that mental health professionals and users could contribute to this awareness raising. It was also apparent that most mental health service professionals needed information about further education and what it could offer. Some had not been in education for many years, or had gone from A levels to university, and had little experience of what further education had to offer. If they were to make referrals and support service users through the learning process, then they needed to develop an awareness of what was on offer. Therefore, an open day for mental health staff was organised.

The project secured long-term funding and became a service, and the steering group evolved into an advisory group. This included support service staff, managers from the college, health practitioners from each directorate the service worked with, and some students who used the support service. The advisory group has been a critical force in ensuring that the support service has developed professional and ethical ways of working. These focused on meeting the needs of students and on ensuring that good practice became embedded in the college. The advisory group now meets termly or more often if required. The staff of the support service provide the group with a report on their work; an effective way of monitoring the source of referrals and the size of the workload. The group also identifies successes and achievements, which help in ensuring credibility with college management and mental health services.

At each meeting there is opportunity for students to report back on what is helpful and what is not. This is a powerful lever in securing resources, and also highlights for the college the simple but effective ways in which it can support students with mental health problems and create a more accepting and welcoming environment. An example of this was the importance of clear signage around the campus and the allocation of good teaching rooms. However, students sometimes ask for support which, from discussion in the advisory group, is seen as inappropriate for the college to provide, for example: the same level of support as would be provided by mental health services, or a mini-bus to bring students to college. Such proposals are always discussed in the advisory group and a way forward agreed, and students have been appreciative when their suggestions have been acted upon.

The advisory group works to an agreed understanding of the value of learning to mental health service users. This is not only about an individual's right to be in college or to access learning in a way that feels comfortable – it is also about ensuring that the learning experience is a positive experience that enhances mental well-being. From this position, agreement on issues can be achieved. The advisory group has proved a learning experience for all its members,who feel they have gained as much from being a part of it as they have contributed.

The advisory group has further been a useful means of obtaining the resources needed for the support service to function effectively; one of these was the securing of support for the guidance workers. Students and mental health practitioners argued that professional supervision was necessary for the guidance workers, to ensure good practice in working with individuals and to support them. Clinical supervision is the norm in mental health services, and is seen as important in supporting staff and ensuring good working practice; its applicability and appropriateness were therefore easy to argue, and eventually the college agreed to pay for an external professional supervisor. This support was later provided at no charge by the local mental health service in recognition of the benefits their users gained from the Mental Health Support Service. Supervision, or 'mentoring', is essential to maintain ethical and professional boundaries. It also provided a safe and confidential forum in which guidance workers could discuss issues relating to individual students that were not appropriate to raise in the advisory group. Project work, especially that which is innovative, can be very lonely work. The advisory group and the supervision provided lessen that sense of isolation, and have been extremely supportive for the guidance workers. Students also felt very strongly that if a college had provided a Mental Health Support Service, then it had a responsibility to ensure the well-being of its staff.

With the development of the support service, it became appropriate for the guidance workers to be based within the college, but to maintain links with the mental health service. This contact can take many forms: attendance at team meetings, invitations to speak, attending and facilitating joint training events. The support service has become part of the range of resources with which new mental health staff have to familiarise themselves as part of their induction. Furthermore, when educational courses are set up in mental health service premises, there is agreement that their tutors receive support from a designated member of staff within the centre, and that service users attending those sessions have student status. Each of these small measures ensures good practice and a heightened awareness of the role of learning. It also helps in the dovetailing of one service into another.

Collaboration and partnership with students have been important, and their representation on the advisory group has been hugely beneficial. Students have also been involved in staff development sessions, and were remarkably patient while the college sought to find a way of paying them for their contribution. A student forum was established because it was recognised that many students did not have the confidence or the opportunity to participate in the advisory group. The student representatives on the group agreed to facilitate the development of the forum with the support of the guidance worker.

The student forum has fulfilled three functions. First, concerns from other students can be fed to the advisory group through the student representatives. Second, when students from diverse learning programmes in the college meet and share experiences, they can support each other and tackle some of the issues that are of mutual concern. This relieves the guidance worker of some of the responsibility for support, and enables students to acknowledge that they have the resources and coping skills within themselves to be independent learners with an important contribution to make. The college and the students gain from collaboration at this level. Last, and no less important, the forum also performs a social function. Some students, particularly those on mainstream courses, have valued the opportunity to meet and talk to other students with mental health problems. It has increased the number of 'friendly faces' they know at college.

Guidance

> ...(inclusiveness) concentrates on the idea of 'the match', that is, the degree of fit or correspondence between the learner's individual requirements and the components of the learning environment. In order to bring the match about, some learners might have more time or resources allocated to certain components than other learners. (FEFC 1996)

Guidance is the focal activity of the Mental Health Support Service and the role and skills of the guidance worker are crucial. Mental health service professionals refer individuals for a guidance interview or individuals can self refer. An appointment, at a time and place to suit the individual, will be arranged. Initially, this may involve meeting somebody in his or her home. The guidance process is very individualised and flexible. The focus is on what individuals want to do, what they enjoy doing and want to learn. This process helps individuals explore how their mental health needs may affect them in their learning, and helps them identify what learning opportunities and environments would be most appropriate. Time spent at this stage is important; helping individuals to identify their learning goals and needs enables them to access appropriate opportunities with the minimum amount of support, and to sustain their learning and attendance. Students may need more support at certain times than at others, and so are encouraged to seek it out as necessary. Opportunities for independence and success are maximised without any assumptions about levels of support. Confidence and self-esteem grow from a sense of coping and achieving. With positive learning experiences, students are more likely to progress to other courses by building on their initial successes.

For many students, perhaps particularly for adults returning to learning after a long break, guidance can be a learning process in itself. It is not time limited and may require several meetings between the guidance worker and the individual. These are not restricted only to meetings within an office to discuss choices, but may involve visits to various parts of the college, meeting tutors or sitting in on teaching sessions to observe the level of work and other students. This practical process, followed by discussion, can help students to make informed decisions about the kind of learning opportunities they want.

After the first meeting with the guidance worker, individuals are given an information sheet about guidance: what they can expect and the role guidance can play after enrolment. Students requested that information be provided in this form because, although these issues are explained during the first meeting, it can be hard to take everything in, particularly when students are already anxious about the outcome of the guidance process. Students were also aware that support existed, but many lacked the confidence to ask what was available for fear of seeming uninformed or demanding. It is, in a sense, a 'service level agreement' that reassures the student about seeking support, while also defining the boundaries to the support available. Each meeting is also documented in guidance notes that define the contract with the student – who will do what in the next stage of the process – these also serve as a reminder and written evidence if necessary for the guidance worker.

The guidance process does not stop when the student has enrolled, but is available as ongoing support to the student; this has been termed a 'choose, get, keep' model of guidance. The guidance worker helps the student *choose* a course by talking about learning goals and needs and matching them to available opportunities. The guidance worker then helps a student to *get* a course by supporting any application and enrolment process, and assists them to *keep* their place on a course by providing support. This is not tutor support in how to tackle an assignment, but is rather about learning to ask for help in producing an assignment. Many students with mental health difficulties believe they are the only ones who feel anxious and nervous about being in college, they are the only ones who are struggling, who don't know how to start their work or plan revision. Encouraging students to assert themselves or to advocate on their own behalf is important, and offers a very inclusive model: it not only enables individuals to participate, but also empowers them. As one student said, when talking about his expectations of support at college:

> That is when I first became aware that it was unrealistic to expect the same level of mental health support within the college as I had been used to at the Day Centre; nor could the college be so immediately responsive to my views and requests. At first I felt resentful and let down. Gradually however, I discovered and developed my own coping skills. Surprisingly, some problems could be resolved without professional help. It was a period of conflict and confusion, but one that led to a growing sense of independence, empowerment and freedom of choice.

The *choose, get, keep* model of guidance is also a cyclical process: by working with students in this way, the guidance worker builds a relationship with them. At the end of a course, the guidance worker and student can reflect on the current learning opportunity and decide whether further learning is desired. So the *choose* part of the process starts again. This time, however, the student will be more knowledgeable about the learning opportunities and environments that are appropriate, and therefore will be more able perhaps to make a decision about the next step. Hopefully, confidence will have increased and so the student will be more ready to be more independent and more willing to take risks.

There are benefits for both the guidance worker and the college in this way of working. A typical guidance worker formulates an action plan that the student takes away and, we hope, puts into action. But very rarely does the student go back to the guidance worker to report on success or otherwise. The guidance worker therefore does not receive feedback on the effectiveness of their guidance skills. In the *choose, get, keep* model the guidance worker maintains a dialogue with the individual student allowing feedback and a chance to reflect on the effectiveness of their input. At New College the guidance worker is supported by a supervisor in order that issues such as boundaries and dependency can be discussed and dealt with.

The other main beneficiaries are the tutors and the college. The guidance worker helps students during the *keep* stage to articulate their support needs or advocates on the student's behalf, if appropriate. The guidance worker thus fulfils a crucial role in enabling students to describe, and tutors to understand, their individual support needs. This helps to break down many of the barriers concerning the teaching and learning of students with mental health difficulties. Time spent with the student discussing their mental health needs (who needs to know and what they need to know), particularly in the assessment of risk, has done much to demystify mental health and allay anxieties. This is an informal way of undertaking staff development work with tutors. It could also be argued that support to *keep* a student on a course helps to improve retention and achievement.

Discrete provision

It has also meant that if you are having a bad day and just burst into tears no one is going to ostracise you. I have also noticed how much it has brought us together outside of our centres in being able to share our problems, generally giving us more confidence, so to speak, in the outside world. (Student at Clarendon College)

The guidance process provides a means of identifying whether an individual wants to move on to a mainstream course. However, many learners choose courses that are set up specifically for mental health service users, often because they want to study in a setting where mental health is an open and acknowledged issue. For many students their first experience of learning as a mental health service user, or indeed as an adult, is as a student on a course set up in a mental health centre. These courses are established by discussing what a group of individuals would like to study, and have included: conversational French, craft subjects, organising and participating in meetings, African-Caribbean cookery, line dancing and local history. Learning undertaken in mental health settings or in community venues is important in that it allows people access to education in an environment in which they feel comfortable and valued, and with the support of mental health professionals and other service users whom they know and trust.

However, in running these courses there is always a fine line between offering a learning opportunity which is supportive and at the right pace and level for the group, but is different from the activities that are offered by staff within the centre. It rests upon the need to define the difference between therapy, and learning that is therapeutic. It is also important to clarify the aim of setting up the course. One centre recognised that the further education courses delivered within their centre were working counter to its aim of rehabilitating users. The courses gave people a chance to learn new skills and therefore enhanced their confidence, but they also greatly increased the richness and variety of the activities within the centre. When users could have such a rewarding experience at the centre, why would they move on to a non-mental health setting? This is not an argument against setting up the courses, but indicates more time should have been spent discussing the expected outcomes and how to avoid conflicting with the long-term aims of the host organisation.

Another centre chose to set up a singing course. At the outset, however, staff were clear that this course would only be based at the centre temporarily and if successful, would move to college premises. The course was set up for ten weeks and, towards completion, the established group of students together with the tutor went to visit the college where the course was to continue. The students were initially anxious but, by ensuring that everybody was settled in the group and carefully planning the transition, a successful move to the college was achieved. Such was the success of this group that it has performed publicly in many venues. It is also useful for course tutors and development workers who set up courses to be aware of the role of the guidance worker. They can encourage students completing courses to make use of the support service to discuss further opportunities, or invite the guidance worker to meet the group.

Courses intended for mental health services users have also been set up in the college. Initially, these were in subjects such as computing, painting and drawing, and music, but it became apparent that a significant number of users were identifying a need for assertiveness and confidence-building courses. In partnership with the Mental Health Employment Co-ordinator appointed by social services, courses focusing on career decisions and job searches were introduced. This resulted in a range of short courses that individuals could access, and from which they could build their own learning packages. These courses are advertised in the booklet *A Mind To Learn* sent to all mental health services. The booklet contains details of times, dates and content of courses, in addition to location maps and details of bus services. Students in the advisory group made a significant contribution to the development of the booklet.

Initially, these courses were set up by the support service as part of the Additional Support Team, which managed and co-ordinated learning support for students. The guidance worker advertised the courses, recruited the students, appointed tutors (part-time) and found venues for the courses. A major step towards the full integration of the support service and the college occurred when it was decided that courses for mental health services users should not be the responsibility of the support team, but of the curriculum team teaching that subject. Therefore, computing for mental health service users came within the remit of the information technology and administration team. Work was done with the team to highlight good practice in teaching and learning for mental health service users. The guidance worker continued to market the courses, recruit the students and provide ongoing support, but the curriculum team now had responsibility for staffing the courses and arranging venues. The benefits were immediate: tutors who wanted to extend their experience were allocated to these groups; better classrooms were allocated, and curriculum expertise was enhanced. However, the greatest benefit came from the removal of many of the barriers around mental health.

It became apparent that teaching this group of students did not require any special skills or knowledge, but only good teaching. Immediately, these students were no longer seen as somebody else's problem, but became 'our' students. Tutors recognised their responsibility for their students' learning and for meeting their needs. Furthermore, tutors would often encourage students to consider other courses; knowing the tutor, the students found it much easier to progress to other courses taught by the same member of staff. Many students overcame those hurdles encountered in moving from discrete to mainstream provision. There is a risk of discrete provision becoming 'ghettos' for students with nowhere else to go, but this development seemed to avoid this. It also freed places on discrete courses for other students new to the support service and the college.

One of the concerns voiced by curriculum teams and tutors was of what might happen if a crisis occurred or a student became ill while in class. When such situations do arise (although not as frequently as people suppose) the guidance worker does not rush in to take over. Instead, they work alongside the tutor to resolve the situation. The guidance worker may have completed a risk assessment with the student prior to starting at college – a procedure agreeing disclosure, so tutors will have been informed of any risk, if it is appropriate. This procedure provides an opportunity to raise awareness with individual tutors, helping them to recognise they already have the skills to support students with mental health problems.

The decision to locate courses for mental health service users in the curriculum teams accomplished more than any awareness-raising events or staff development in breaking down the barriers and stigma surrounding mental health issues. It helped to embed the Mental Health Support Service within the organisation as a whole.

Mainstream learning

Some individuals referred to the support service choose not to join any of the discrete provision that is available. The learning they want may not be available in discrete classes, or they may not want to bring the label of mental health service user into college. Through the guidance process, appropriate mainstream provision can be identified. Support needs, if any, can be identified and arrangements made as to how they can be best met. The skills of the guidance worker are very important at this stage in ensuring the student finds the right course to achieve their learning goals, receive support, but also be as independent in their studies as possible.

It is also important to spend time discussing and clarifying how much to disclose to a tutor regarding the student as a mental health service user. A useful starting point is the question, 'How will your mental health affect your learning?' Often the answer will be very simple: 'I will be so nervous for the first six weeks that I won't take anything in', or 'My medication makes me very thirsty so I need to have a drink with me'. With this information, the guidance worker and student will decide whether they want to let the tutor know this, and if so, how. Some students have chosen to write a confidential letter to the tutor outlining their learning needs. Using everyday language, rather than giving a diagnosis or details of medication is helpful to tutors and also breaks down barriers about mental health. Students are always encouraged to see the guidance worker again to review their learning, or if they are experiencing difficulties. If they discover that they have other learning needs, then these can be met before they become a problem. Some students follow individual learning programmes that are a mixture of mainstream and discrete provision, and may move between these depending on their learning needs. Time spent at the initial guidance stage is time well spent. Front-loading of support maximises success and minimises the risk of crisis. This can be a great confidence booster for the student and the guidance worker.

Final thoughts

> I would like to tell you how good I feel since I have been going to college. (Student)

> All that I have gained from this experience has touched and enriched every aspect of my life, has given me a *new* life, a new sense of personal identity and many new exciting opportunities for my future. Perhaps that is a true measurement of the real gain – two years ago I felt I had no future and now – who knows? (Student)

Perhaps these comments above summarise why education providers should consider how they enable access to learning for mental health service users. This area of work is about equality of access but, done well, it should also be about confidence, self-esteem, independence, health, hope and a better quality of life. Students with mental health problems do not want to be treated differently or in any special way, but they want to be treated well. Students want to be welcomed into an environment in which they can feel comfortable. They want to know where they will study, and to have a name or a face they can turn to. They want to be valued as learners, gently challenged and encouraged, and given opportunities for growth and development. They want to be treated politely and respectfully as adults. Tutors and support staff do not need a different expertise or set of skills to work with this group of students. Tutors and learning providers need to listen to what individual students require, to try to meet those learning needs and to be honest where they cannot. It is about recognising the human and emotional aspect to the learning experience. This is an important area of work for individuals, organisations and society: mental health is not about them and us – it is about all of us. The more we strive to break down the barriers to learning for this group, the easier we will make it for all to participate in learning.

References

Further Education Funding Council (FEFC) (1996) *Inclusive Learning. Report of the Learning Difficulties and/or Disabilities Committee.* Coventry: FEFC.

Further Education Funding Council (FEFC) (1997) *Learning Works. Report of the Committee on Widening Participation.* Coventry: FEFC.

Wertheimer, A. (1997) *Images of Possibility.* Leicester: NIACE.

Chapter 11

Using Structured Self-help Materials

Graeme Whitfield and Chris Williams

The use of self-help approaches offers one possible means of providing access to effective psychosocial treatments in a way that is popular and acceptable to a student population. This chapter will review the rationale for self help, and discuss how it may be used in practice. Depression is a common condition that is associated with marked distress for the sufferer, and has a significant impact on social functioning. Since concentration problems are so prominent in depression, and the ability to concentrate so crucial to studying, it might be predicted that depression would be more damaging to students than to many other social groups. In the US, depression is the most common mental health-related reason for withdrawal from college, as well as a strong predictor of poor academic outcome (Meilman *et al.* 1992). Issues of stigma commonly influence access to treatment of mental health problems. In a survey of attitudes to student mental health services in all 126 US and Canadian medical schools, Plaut *et al.* (1993) found that students showed most concern with issues of privacy and confidentiality. Examples of concern included confidentiality of records, location of the mental health service and availability of therapists who would not be in a position to evaluate the student academically at some point after the therapy. Students fear that acknowledging and seeking assistance for mental health problems may endanger their position in education and might prevent them from taking up a preferred career such as law or medicine. This may result in low or delayed uptake of services to support students experiencing such difficulties.

What is self-help?

The term self-help has been applied to many different approaches, ranging from groups and voluntary agencies, to self-care – where a person takes steps to change his or her current experience. In the context of mental health, this last approach is associated with the concept of using self-help resources to improve how you feel:

> the patient receives a standardised treatment method with which he can help himself without major help from the therapist. In (the approach) it is necessary that treatment is described in sufficient detail, so that the patient can work it through independently. Books, in which only information about depression is given to patients and their families, cannot be used. (Cuijpers 1997)

A second definition used by Marrs (1995) is:

> the use of written materials or computer programmes or the listening/viewing of audio/video tapes for the purpose of gaining understanding or solving problems relevant to a person's developmental or therapeutic needs. The goals of the (therapy) should be relevant to the fields of counselling and clinical psychology.

Although information-provision is a component of self-help approaches, it is important to differentiate these approaches from materials that aim only at education. The goals of self-help and education are very different, and this should be borne in mind when considering self-help. In this chapter, the term self-help is used to describe the delivery of materials that employ a media-based format to treatment (such as book, audio or video tape or computer-based formats), and that is used by an individual for self-treatment. This may be provided without practitioner support (*unsupported* self-help), or in conjunction with sessions with a health care practitioner (*supported* self-help: Williams 2001a).

Formats of self-help delivery

People prefer to learn in different ways and have different likes and dislikes; this influences which self-help formats they prefer. Self-help materials may be delivered using:

- audiotape

- videotape

- written materials (handouts, workbooks or books delivered in paper format or via the internet, i.e. as downloadable files); this is the most frequently used format of self-help and is sometimes described as *bibliotherapy*

- computer-based delivery methods: the advantage is that interactive materials may be offered where questions may be asked, and depending on the responses, specific information or interventions provided.

Rationale for self-help approaches

Considering heavy caseloads and long waiting times, the potential benefits of self-help are substantial for both practitioners and clients. However, it is clear that they are not for everyone. Some may prefer not to use such approaches, and for others self-help techniques may be useful, but only during phases of their illness when they are able to concentrate and motivate themselves. Overall, these approaches seem popular with the general public, as evidenced by the sizeable self-help sections found in most bookshops. A recent UK survey has confirmed that self-help materials are also widely recommended by psychotherapists (Keeley *et al.* 2002). Another recent study by Jorm *et al.* (1997) investigated the beliefs of the Australian public, as well as those of psychiatrists and GPs, regarding their views of different interventions for mental health disorders. A population of over 2000 nationally representative adults responded.

Compared to professionals, the public gave much higher ratings for the potential usefulness of self-help books, and lower ratings for both medication and psychotherapy in the treatment of mental illness. This may be related to what Marrs (1995) describes as our 'increasing self-help orientated society', and is further support for the potential growth of such materials in the future. At the same time, there has been increasing suspicion and hostility towards traditional medicine (Robinson 1985). Perhaps the most important advantage of self-help approaches is the increased sense of empowerment and control that comes from helping yourself rather than being given assistance by someone else.

Who gains the most from self-help?

When it comes to considering who gains the most from self-help, Mahalik and Kivlighan (1988) studied 52 mildly depressed psychology under-graduates in the US. Thirty five students completed the seven-week recommended course of self-help and overall, their levels of depression fell significantly. In terms of personality type, the authors found that students who had 'internal loci of control' (Rotter 1966), that is, those who see themselves as responsible for their own outcomes, achieved better results with self-help. People with high 'self-efficacy' (Bandura 1977) have general expectations that they will be able to perform competently across a broad range of challenging situations. Students who exhibited this characteristic also achieved better results with self-help. Mahalik and Kivlighan (1988) suggest that this group desire less attention from others and are therefore better suited to helping themselves. Those students who succeeded with the self-help materials believed that privacy was of paramount importance. In contrast, those students characterised as 'artistic, social and enterprising' found self-help 'a chore'. This appeared to be because self-help failed to provide the opportunity for the student to interact with others in some way. Mahalik and Kivlighan (1988) conclude that there is a 'goodness of fit' between people who have certain personality characteristics and the form of therapy with which they are most likely to succeed.

The effectiveness of self-help

Four meta-analyses of the combined results of other studies draw general conclusions about the usefulness and acceptability of the self-help approach. The meta-analysis by Gould and Clum (1993) is based on 40 self-help studies, identified as three groups by the type of problem they targeted. Interestingly, the depression and anxiety related studies were much more successful than those aiming to reduce or eradicate problem behaviours or habits such as smoking. Marrs (1995), in a second meta-analysis, combined 70 studies, 30 of which made direct comparisons between equivalent patients treated by therapists and self-help patients. The meta-analysis by Scogin *et al.* (1990) incorporated 40 studies, while that of Cuijpers (1997) incorporated six. As Gould and Clum (1993) had, Marrs (1995) found that self-help was more effective with diagnosable problems than with habitual behaviours. Those meta-analyses that contained studies comparing the outcomes of patients treated by self-help compared to face-to-face therapy observed no significant difference in outcome between the two forms of treatment (Cuijpers 1997; Gould and Clum 1993; Marrs 1995; Scogin *et al.* 1990). Significantly greater improvements were observed, however, in the self-help group when compared to those who received neither face-to-face therapy nor self-help. Similarly, those studies that analysed the effect of adding some therapist input to the clients while they worked through the self-help materials did not appear to improve outcomes (Gould and Clum 1993; Marrs 1995; Scogin *et al.* 1990). Marrs (1995) observed one notable exception to this: anxious patients appeared to respond better when they had some therapist contact. Such suggestions fly in the face of the beliefs of many therapists and counsellors that supported self-help approaches are more likely to be effective than unsupported approaches.

One of the major problems in many of the studies is that most of the above research has been carried out on US-based non-clinical populations. Many of the participants were recruited by advertising in the media to the general public. Participants who have taken part in a programme after replying to a newspaper advertisement may be much keener to comply with treatment as a result. Some US-based researchers even offered financial rewards to those participants who completed their studies (Brown and Lewinson 1984; Gould and Clum 1993; Lidren *et al.* 1994). In many studies, participants were excluded from participating if they had certain major physical or mental illnesses, or a drug and alcohol problem (Gould and Clum 1993; Jamison and Scogin 1995; Lidren *et al.* 1994). Therefore, they used specialised populations with relatively minor psychological problems, who are probably not representative of British students. Consequently, it is not surprising that these same studies show much lower dropout rates than are experienced in UK studies of self-help, such as those by Donnan *et al.* (1990), and Holdsworth *et al.* (1996) where the dropout rates approached 50 per cent.

Using self-help approaches effectively

If, after an initial assessment of an individual by a mental health practitioner, it is thought that self-help approaches may be beneficial, the role of self-help materials can be discussed as part of the treatment plan and attitudes concerning the use of such materials evaluated. Useful assessment questions to explore attitudes include:

> 'What is your initial reaction to the idea of using self-help.'
> 'Have you used any self-help materials before? Were they useful to you?'
> 'Has anyone else you know used this approach?'

Doubts and concerns about the use of self-help materials need to be addressed. It is important to emphasise that the use of self-help materials is only one potential part of the whole approach. Sometimes the person may choose not to take up the offer of self-help materials, or it may be more appropriate to consider their use at a later time.

Setting up a self-help room

Self-help materials can be used in different parts of the support and treatment services. For example, self-help may be offered:

- to those on waiting lists (supported or unsupported by limited access to a practitioner)

- as an adjunct to support individual work with a practitioner: a student counsellor, psychologist, psychiatrist, community psychiatric nurse, occupational therapist or social worker

- in support of group treatments.

The self-help approach has a role not only within clinical services. Some of the issues addressed in self-help materials, such as low mood and coping strategies, would have potential in a range of non-clinical applications, such as student counselling, or disability services.

One way that self-help delivery can be encouraged within a service is to introduce a focus for it. One such approach has been developed at Malham House Day Hospital in Leeds, located very close to two universities. Here, a specific self-help room was designated within an adult acute day hospital setting. This provided a central resource for use by day hospital staff, outpatients (including waiting list patients) and also patients seen by members of the multi-disciplinary sector psychiatric service. Self-help approaches can be with treatments already offered within different clinical settings (e.g. at the day hospital or resource centre, and to both inpatients and outpatients). This has the advantage to the team and the user of allowing consistent management across these different settings.

In developing a self-help room, several issues should be addressed: which materials to offer; how to support the room (e.g. the practicality of providing photocopied worksheets used by patients and original copies of the materials); and how to create an atmosphere that encourages self-help approaches. In the Malham House self-help room, only two written sets of materials – *Mind over Mood* (Greenberger and Padesky 1995) and *Overcoming Depression: A Five Areas Approach* (Williams 2001b) – are used. This ensures that all staff are aware of and familiar with, the content of each set of material.

Plants, rugs and attractive pictures ensure a relaxing atmosphere; a desk, pens and paper maintain a central focus on the materials. Only one person uses the room at a time to ensure privacy, and a booking system allows users sessions of up to one hour. Users are encouraged to use the room once or twice a week, and to keep all their own completed workbooks and worksheets to create a personalised treatment pack. The room is kept neat and tidy, and one of the secretaries has a role in ensuring that pens, paper and photocopied workbooks/worksheets are available during all times the room is open.

Staff training sessions were offered on a weekly basis prior to the opening of the room. Everyone in the team had the task to read the next components of the materials, and sessions allowed discussion of how the materials might be best used, aided familiarity with content (a crucial component for effective use), and included role-play practice of how to respond to difficulties in treatment. Ongoing training and clinical supervision were offered to support staff in their use of the materials that were offered when appropriate and acceptable to the clients themselves. In addition, the self-help room was made available to selected clients on the waiting list for treatment by the community team, and a study of the effectiveness of this approach is described next.

Using Mind over Mood

This Leeds-based study considered whether students referred from the local medical practice to a community mental health team with symptoms of anxiety and depression would elect to use the self-help manual *Mind over Mood* (Greenberger and Padesky 1995). This was part of a larger research project investigating both students and non-students (see Whitfield *et al.* 2001).

Mind over Mood is a structured manual based on the Cognitive Behavioural Therapy (CBT) model of the treatment of anxiety and depression (Beck 1976). It has sold over one hundred thousand copies worldwide in English and Spanish. Although it is just over 200 pages in length, much of this is made up of 37 worksheets to be completed by the reader. The manual introduces readers to the difference between thoughts, feelings and moods, and behaviours, and illustrates how each of these influence each other, and can therefore influence their symptoms of anxiety and depression. Key beliefs held by the reader are questioned as well as any recurring 'automatic thoughts'. Readers are encouraged to explore and challenge these thoughts and beliefs by completing the exercises, and by looking for evidence from their day-to-day lives to support or refute them.

The students who participated in the study were 20 consecutive non-urgent GP student referrals to a Community Mental Health Team (CMHT); 13 of these were from GPs based at the Leeds Student Health Centre. All 20 students were invited by post to attend an introductory session on how to use the book. During this session, students were advised to use the self-help room and manual for each of the subsequent six weeks when they were due to have their initial appointment with a mental health team practitioner. The study provided access only to *Mind over Mood* as well as photocopies of all of the worksheets contained within it. These photocopies were available to the students to complete both in-session and at home. No other written materials or professional input were provided to those using the room after their initial 20 minute introduction. Questionnaires were given to those students who attended the self-help room, both at the initial introductory interview (baseline questionnaire), and just before their mental health worker assessment six weeks later. Those who failed to attend at all were posted their questionnaires, but because of the low response rate these were not analysed.

One of the measures included in both questionnaires (baseline and six-weeks) was the General Health Questionnaire (GHQ-28: Goldberg and Hillier 1979), a widely-used scale measuring 'psychological morbidity'. It is made up of 28 questions measuring levels of anxiety and insomnia, severe depression, impaired social functioning and bodily symptoms. The Beck Hopelessness Scale (BHS, Beck and Steer 1993) was also used at both times. This comprises 20 questions that clients answer as applying or not to their lives, which reflect the levels of hopelessness they are experiencing. Hopelessness has been shown to be a powerful predictor of suicide risk (Beck *et al.* 1985) and was included as an outcome measure. The students also assessed their own subjective knowledge of issues relating to anxiety and depression at baseline and six weeks, while the students' satisfaction with the room and manual was measured at six weeks.

Of the 20 students included in the study, 12 (60 %) attended the introductory session to the room. All 12 completed the baseline questionnaire, but one student moved and could not be traced, so that only 11 completed the six-week questionnaire. It is noteworthy that 16 of the 20 student referrals were female, of whom 11 (69 %) attended the self-help room. Only one of the four men invited to attend the self-help room actually did so. The number of sessions attended by the 12 students who came to the self-help room ranged between one and six, with a mean of three and a half. The proportion of student health centre GP referrals who attended the self-help room (7 of 13 or 54 %), was slightly lower than the proportion of other student referrals (5 of 7 or 71 %), but the difference was not statistically significant.

Responding to the questionnaire after 6 weeks, six of the 11 students (55 %), stated that *Mind over Mood* had taught them new skills that they intended to use in the future. All but one (10 or 83 %) stated that they would recommend the use of the book to others, and seven (58 %) intended to use the book again themselves in the future. When asked to choose between the 'written text', 'stopping and reflecting' and 'answering questions' as the most important element of the intervention, six (55 %) identified the 'stopping and reflecting' option.

The students were asked to allocate on a scale (between 1 and 7) a score that they believed reflected their knowledge and abilities in five areas. They did not have access to the scores that they had allocated themselves at the baseline sessions when they allocated a further score for themselves six weeks later. All the students' subjective levels of their own knowledge on each of the five items improved significantly over the six weeks ($p < 0.05$ for each item using Wilcoxon Signed Ranks Tests: see Table 11.1).

Table 11.1. The development of knowledge/ability over six weeks

Test item	Mean score at baseline	Mean score at 6 weeks
Overall knowledge about anxiety and depression	3.8	4.8
Knowledge of the causes of anxiety and depression	3.4	5.0
Ability to describe how anxiety and depression affects their thinking, behaviour, and bodily responses	3.8	4.9
Ability to notice negative thoughts	3.4	5.0
Ability to challenge negative thoughts and seek more moderate thoughts instead	2.3	3.9

The levels of psychological ill health as rated on the GHQ scale fell significantly over the six-week periods that the students were visiting the self-help room. The students' mean GHQ-28 score fell from 44.8 at their introduction sessions to the room, to a significantly lower score of 31.3 six weeks later (Wilcoxon Signed Ranks Test, $Z = -2.347$, $p < 0.05$). The 11 students also appeared less hopeless at the end of the six-week period. The BHS scores fell from a mean of 8.58 to 6.45; however, this change was not statistically significant (Z=-1.757, p<0.079) since this may well have been due to the small numbers involved, which restricted the power of the study.

When the 11 students were asked to comment on the three best aspects of *Mind over Mood*, five responded by praising the simplicity and ease of understanding of the manual. A further five specifically recommended the case examples of actual patients included in the book. Two felt that the worksheets were one of the best features, and two praised the fact that the self-help intervention allowed them to work at their own pace. When asked to comment on the three worst aspects of the manual, four answered that they would have preferred someone to talk to rather than the manual alone, and three found it too impersonal or patronising.

In this study, 60 per cent of student referrals from primary care chose to try self-help in an allocated room when it was offered during a six-week waiting list period. This is lower than the uptake found in some other UK-based studies that also offered self-help as a treatment option (Donnan *et al.* 1990; Holdsworth *et al.* 1996; Sorby *et al.* 1991). However, these three studies all incorporated additional face-to-face contact with health practitioners, and this may have increased the participants' motivation. In our study more women than men chose to attend the self-help room. The difference in take-up was not statistically different (probably because of the small numbers involved) and therefore it would be unwise to ascribe a general trend here. Most of the aforementioned research in the area of self-help provision for mental health issues has not found a difference between men and women in terms of their likelihood of using self-help.

All of the students who attended the self-help room spoke English as their first language; we do not have data on the first language of the students who failed to attend. It might be necessary in a multicultural environment where students have a wide variety of national and linguistic backgrounds to develop and advertise a range of self-help materials. These may be in different languages, and may even differ to some extent in content, to concentrate on issues that are more commonly encountered by different groups in society. This may make the materials more relevant and may therefore encourage more people to attempt to use the materials.

Of the 12 who did attend the room, only two came for the recommended six sessions. Despite this, the majority of these students stated that they had benefited. They believed that they had learned new information and skills and, at the end of the six weeks, they judged that they were better able to identify their negative automatic thoughts and challenge them, one of the main targets of CBT. The feedback did not suggest that they found the content of the book difficult to understand. The levels of distress exhibited by the students also appears to have reduced over the study period as indicated by the falls in the GHQ and the BHS scores. However, in view of the absence of a control group, these falls cannot necessarily be ascribed only to the effect of *Mind over Mood.*

Unfortunately, we do not know why 8 of the 20 referred students chose not to take up the offer of using self-help. However, only 1 of the 12 self-help room students subsequently failed to keep their appointment with a team mental health worker, compared with four (50 %) of the eight referrals who did not attend the room. This may indicate differing levels of motivation to use mental health services, but may also suggest that the use of self-help materials encourages the use of other services.

Rather than providing a room for the self-help manual and worksheets, the students could have been given their own copies to take away with them. However, over half of the students in this study observed that the most important element of the intervention was not the book itself, but the space and time to stop and reflect on the contents of the manual. It appears likely that the self-help room acted as a refuge for many of the participants, away from the stresses of student life. The physical characteristics of the room, quiet and pleasantly furnished, may have encouraged this.

Cognitive Behaviour Therapy (CBT) and self-help

Cognitive Behaviour Therapy (CBT) has a proven effectiveness in the treatment of depression and anxiety (Andrews 1996). Interestingly, most studies evaluating self-help have used a CBT format. CBT has several other advantages as a model for use in self-help treatment. It is an educational form of psychotherapy, has a clear underlying structure and theoretical model, and focuses clearly on current problems. Finally, it encourages the patient to work on changing how they feel by completing various specific tasks. It is noteworthy that, in reviews of self-help, CBT materials are amongst the group of materials with the strongest evidence for effectiveness. Table 11.2 summarises several self-help materials used by CBT practitioners (based upon Williams 2001a).

Table 11.2. Examples of CBT self-help materials

Examples of structured written self-help materials that use a CBT format	*Description*
Feeling Good (Burns 1998)	Developed in the US. Details are available at www.feelinggood.com
'Managing anxiety and depression' (Holdsworth and Paxton 1999)	Short booklet, recently revised. Produced by the Mental Health Foundation. UK developed. Aimed at milder levels of distress rather than for moderate or severe depression. Details are available via www.mentalhealth.org.uk
Mind over Mood (Greenberger and Padesky 1995)	Aimed at anxiety and depression, this US developed book has been very successful. Allows photocopying of worksheets for use with patients. Details are available at www.padesky.com
Overcoming Depression: A Five Areas Approach (Williams 2001b)	Series of 10 workbooks, some of which can be downloaded free of charge from www.calipso.co.uk Licence provided for unlimited photocopying for use with patients and in teaching. Includes accompanying notes for health care practitioners.

Overcoming depression: a UK-developed self-help approach

The second set of self-help materials used within the Malham House self-help room – *Overcoming Depression: A Five Areas Approach* – was originally commissioned by Calderdale and Kirklees Health Authority, and has been widely tested by a range of health care practitioners. It comprises ten structured CBT workbooks that address common problems experienced in depression. Feedback from users and representatives of these different professional groups has led to changes and improvements in the content over the last two years. Training is offered to health care practitioners to help familiarise them with the content of the materials and local 'experts' have been trained in Calderdale and Kirklees to offer sustainability of the training. Some of the materials can be downloaded free of charge from www.calipso.co.uk

Although the workbooks are sometimes used alone (unsupported), they have been designed to support sessions with the health care practitioner (supported self-help). Workbook 1 is designed to help the user identify their current problem areas and which of Workbooks 2–9 they may benefit from using. Finally, Workbook 10 helps to summarise what the reader has learned, and to plan how to respond to any future feelings of depression. This aims to offer relapse prevention work. An outline of the workbook content corresponding to those areas of functioning affected by depression, is included below.

Overcoming depression course: overview

Regular reviews between student and practitioner allow materials to be used by the student between sessions and then discussed within a treatment session that is offered once a fortnight or so. At its shortest, a seven or eight minute review will allow a discussion of areas that are going well, identify areas the student is having problems with, and allow receipt of the next set of materials to work on at home. Sometimes more time is available for the review sessions. When additional time is offered, specific components of the content can be discussed in greater detail:

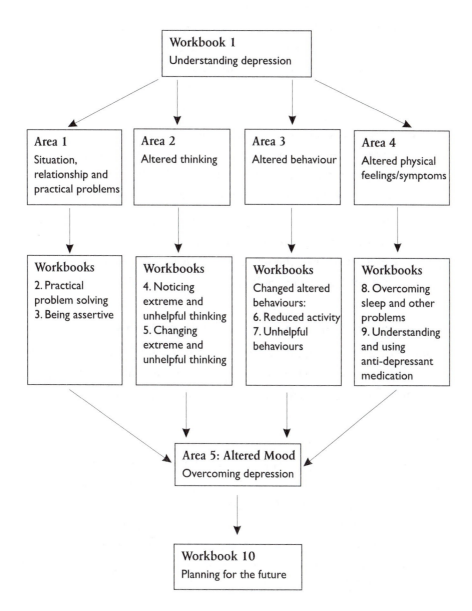

Figure 11.1 Structure and Content of the Overcoming Depression Course. Source: Williams 2001b.

- Encouraging the student to stop, think and reflect on the materials as they are used helps them to interact with the materials. Evidence suggests that students who interact with written worksheets and complete any homework suggested do better than those who do not. Answering all the questions that are asked aids this.

- This process can be encouraged by asking students to write down notes in the margins or at the back of the materials to help them remember information that has been helpful. They can be encouraged to review these notes each week.

- Once each chapter has been completed, it is best to put it on one side and then read it again a few days later. It may be that different parts of the text become clearer, or seem more relevant on second reading.

Common difficulties in using self-help materials

Sometimes students run into difficulties in using self-help materials. The following summarises some common problems encountered, and suggests strategies that have proved effective in overcoming these difficulties.

'I didn't have time to do it'

Breaking old habits and starting new ones take practice. The student has the right to set aside time to change. It may be that they think they have too many external pressures (e.g. a partner, coursework or additional job) to look after their own needs, but getting better should be a priority. It is therefore important for the person and for those around them, that they allow time to get better. A problem-solving or time management approach may be helpful for discussion here.

'I didn't understand what I had to do'

If the student feels stuck, they can be encouraged to read the materials again and discuss any particular difficulties they may have with under-standing what to do. If symptoms of depression are interfering with their use of the materials, an anti-depressant may be helpful; this can be discussed with their doctor. If problems continue, it may be that other self-help materials are more appropriate, or that a change to other treatment options is indicated.

'I tried but it didn't seem to make any difference'

Change takes time. The person may have been depressed for quite some time and it will take time to begin to change. The first steps are often the most difficult, and encouragement to stick at it is required. Using self-help approaches involves new knowledge and gaining new skills to overcome problems. Although it may take time to learn these, those using such an approach can change one step at a time.

Conclusion

A review of the research assessing self-help methods has shown that it can be particularly effective for anxiety and depression. These also appear to be the two most common disorders addressed by the self-help materials currently available. Other clinical problems for which self-help materials exist include: alcohol and substance misuse, chronic fatigue, eating disorders, post-traumatic stress disorder, and sexual and relationship problems. Self-help materials are also available for non-clinical issues such as financial planning, study skills, and interview skills, which may have particular relevance to students, and could be offered alongside clinical materials.

Students may be particularly suitable for self-help approaches in that they are usually literate, intelligent, and well motivated. The approach also uses a 'study method' familiar to students. The Leeds study described here describes how a sizeable proportion of students with symptoms of anxiety and depression may use and gain benefit from self-help materials, and such treatments may be offered in supported or unsupported ways as best suits the individual. Offering access to self-help facilities, possibly as a self-help room where students may self-refer and access informally, may reach some who would not otherwise be willing to seek formal help. A quiet room in which to reflect may serve as a potential refuge from the numerous stresses of student life, some of which are described in other chapters of this book.

There appears to be a range of other situations where self-help could effectively supplement the care given to students, including student counselling and dedicated services dealing with non-clinical issues. It has been suggested that the very high rates of distress and illness in first-year students in particular, could be addressed by some form of preventative 'pre-counselling service' that they would attend before starting their courses (Monk and Mahmood 1999). This could, at least partially, be presented as self-help materials. The same authors, in their study of Glasgow University students, point out that students need more assistance to help them cope with high levels of stress. Undoubtedly, some students would benefit from counselling or other forms of support, although some may also benefit from a self-help approach. Educating themselves about stress would be only one part of this approach. More importantly, self-help aims to increase individuals' knowledge and also teach new self-management skills. Self-help may be used as the sole treatment, or as an adjunct to traditional face-to-face counselling or non-clinical appointments, and thus may reduce the number of sessions required.

Acknowledgements

Information and the structure and content of the Overcoming Depression course, and information on overcoming blocks to using self-help materials, are reproduced with the permission of Dr C.J. Williams and the University of Leeds Innovations Limited (ULIS).

References

Andrews, G. (1996) 'Talk that works: The rise of cognitive behaviour therapy.' *British Medical Journal 313*, 1501–2.

Bandura, A. (1977) 'Self-efficacy: toward a unifying theory of behavior change.' *Psychological Review 84*, 199–215.

Beck, A.T. (1976) *Cognitive Therapy and the Emotional Disorders.* New York: International Universities Press.

Beck, A.T., Steer, R.A., Kovacs, M. and Garrison, B. (1985) 'Hopelessness and eventual suicide: a ten-year prospective study of patients hospitalised with suicidal ideation.' *American Journal of Psychiatry 145*, 559–563.

Beck, A.T. and Steer, R.A. (1993) *Beck Hopelessness Scale Manual.* San Antonio: The Psychological Corporation, Harcourt Brace and Company.

Brown, R.A. and Lewinsohn, P.M. (1984) 'A psycho-educational approach to the treatment of depression: comparison of a group, individual and minimal contact procedures.' *Journal of Consulting and Clinical Psychology 52*, 774–783.

Burns, D. (1998) *Feeling Good.* New York: Avon Books.

Cuijpers, P. (1997) 'Bibliotherapy in unipolar depression: a meta-analysis.' *Journal of Behavioural Therapy and Experimental Psychiatry 28*, 2, 139–147.

Donnan, P., Hutchinson, A., Paxton, R., Grant, B. and Firth, M. (1990) 'Self-help materials for anxiety: a randomised controlled trial in general practice.' *British Journal of General Practice 40*, 498–501.

Goldberg, D.P. and Hillier, V.F. (1979) 'A scaled version of the GHQ.' *Psychological Medicine 9*, 1, February, 139–145.

Goldberg, D.P. and Huxley, P. (1980) *Mental Illness in the Community: The Pathways to Psychiatric Care.* London: Tavistock.

Goldberg, D. and Huxley, P. (1992) *Common Mental Disorders; a Biosocial Model.* London: Tavistock/Routledge.

Gould, R.A. and Clum, A.A. (1993) 'Meta-analysis of self-help treatment approaches.' *Clinical Psychology Review 13*, 169–186.

Greenberger, D. and Padesky, C.A. (1995) *Mind Over Mood: Change how you feel by changing the way you think.* New York: Guilford.

Holdsworth, N. and Paxton, R. (1999) *Managing Anxiety and Depression.* London: Mental Health Foundation.

Holdsworth, N., Paxton, R., Seidel, S., Thomson, D. and Shrubb, S. (1996) 'Parallel evaluations of new guidance materials for anxiety and primary care.' *Journal of Mental Health 5*, 2, 195–207.

Jamison, C. and Scogin, F. (1995) 'The outcome of cognitive bibliotherapy with depressed adults.' *Journal of Consulting and Clinical Psychology 63*, 4, 644–650.

Jorm, A.F., Korten, A.E., Jacomb, P.A., Rodgers, B., Pollitt, P., Christensen, H. and Henderson, S. (1997) 'Helpfulness of interventions for mental disorders: beliefs of health professionals compared with the general public.' *British Journal of Psychiatry 171*, 233–237.

Keeley, H., Williams, C.J., and Shapiro, D.A. (2002) 'A United Kingdom survey of BABCP accredited cognitive behaviour therapists' attitudes towards and use of structured self-help materials.' *Behavioural and Cognitive Psychotherapy 30*, 105–115.

Lidren, D.M., Watkins, P.L., Gould, R.A., Clum, G.A., Astorino, M. and Tulloch, H.L. (1994) 'A comparison of bibliotherapy and group therapy in the treatment of panic disorder.' *Journal of Consulting and Clinical Psychology 62*, 4, 865–869.

Mahalik, J.R. and Kivlighan, D.M. (1988) 'Self help treatment for depression: who succeeds?' *Journal of Counselling Psychology 35*, 3, 237–242.

Marrs, R. (1995) 'A meta-analysis of bibliotherapy studies.' *American Journal of Community Psychology 23*, 6, 843–870.

Meilman, P.W., Manley, C., Gaylor, M.S. and Turco, J.H. (1992) 'Medical withdrawals from college and their relation to academic performance.' *Journal of American College Health 40*, 217–223.

Monk, E.M. and Mahmood, Z. (1999) 'Student mental health: a pilot study.' *Counselling Psychology Quarterly 12*, 2, 199–210.

Plaut, S.M., Maxwell, S.A., Seng, L., O'Brian, J.J. and Fairclough, G.F. (1993) 'Mental health services for medical students, student affairs deans, and mental health providers.' *Academic Medicine 68,* 5, 360–365.

Robinson, D. (1985) 'Self-help groups.' *British Journal of Hospital Medicine,* August.

Rotter, J.B. (1966) 'Generalized expectancies for internal versus external control of reinforcement.' *Psychological Monographs 80,* (1, Whole No.609).

Scogin, F., Bynum, J., Stephens, G. and Calhoon, S. (1990) 'Efficacy of self-administered programs: meta-analytic review.' *Professional Psychology: Research and Practice 21,* 1, 42–47.

Sorby, N.G.D., Reavley, W. and Huber, J.W. (1991) 'Self help programme for anxiety in general practice: controlled trial of an anxiety management booklet.' *British Journal of General Practice 41,* 417–420.

Whitfield, G., Williams, C. J., and Shapiro, D. (2001) 'An evaluation of a self-help room in a general adult psychiatry service.' *Behavioural and Cognitive Psychotherapy 29,* 333–343.

Williams, C. J. (2001a) 'Ready access to proven psychosocial interventions? The use of written CBT self-help materials to treat depression.' (In Press) *Advances in Psychiatric Treatment 7,* 233–240.

Williams, C. J. (2001b) *Overcoming Depression: A Five Areas Approach.* London: Arnold Publishers.

Chapter 12

Faith and Spirituality in Students' Mental Health

Angela Bailey

University life at its best opens up a whole new world of ideas, brings new perspectives, and calls students beyond their past experience. Not least, in the UK, for most undergraduates going to university involves moving home and living independently for the first time. This chapter reflects on some aspects of the influence of belief and spirituality on students' mental well-being and illness. The contribution of university chaplaincy to helping students manage their mental health and to recover from illness is discussed from the author's perspective of Anglican chaplaincy at the University of Hull.

Chaplaincy services vary from one Higher Education Institute (HEI) to another, according to the nature of the institution (some universities are secular by statute, others are Christian in foundation) and the local history of chaplaincy. Chaplaincy may be part of the student services department, seen primarily as a welfare service. It may be focused on the student union and be viewed as mainly for students. Although this chapter is about students, the model adopted at Hull was that chaplains were a resource for the whole institution, available to all in the university: staff, students and non-academic staff alike. We were well staffed with full-time Anglican and Catholic chaplains, and part-time chaplains from other denominations. Chaplaincy was integrated into University structures through the Religious Activities Committee which dealt with all matters of religion and spirituality. This was the forum to which the needs of different faith groups were brought, and in which ways of meeting needs were identified. There were, during my time at Hull, active Islamic, Jewish and Buddhist groups with named representatives on the Religious Activities Committee.

The University has a modern chapel which is used only for worship and recitals. Although technically available for use by any faith group, the chapel was only used by Christians, the design being obviously Christian (a large pipe organ, fixed altar, pew style seating). Both the Anglican and Catholic chaplaincies had houses near to the campus with meeting rooms, cooking and eating facilities, resident students and the chaplain's office. The Catholic chaplaincy also had a chapel. Although a lot of our work was done on campus (in departments and in the student union) these chaplaincy houses were a focus for our work and shaped some of what we did. Chaplaincy in HEIs where there is neither chapel nor chaplaincy buildings would have a different look from the Hull model, which is fairly typical of non-collegiate nineteenth and twentieth century institutions.

There are many aspects of religious belief and spirituality which can contribute to mental health or distress. The first part of this chapter will consider the role of religious belief in contributing to the sense of personal identity, the place of guilt in mental distress, and students' experience of maintaining rigid belief systems and religious practice. Whatever else goes on for students, those who engage with university life academically and socially are bound to meet new situations which necessitate rethinking their understanding of the way the world is. Religious belief is one of the ways in which people make sense of the world and construct meaning in their lives. Whatever the religion, whatever its claims to hold truth exclusively or its openness to other revelations of truth, there are different ways of believing which for most people change in the course of life. As we mature, so our ways of believing and practising spirituality mature. Beginning higher education is one of the life changes that can precipitate a different approach to belief and religious practice. It was my experience that for most students this process was managed in a healthy way, often with a great deal of commitment to really thinking through the hard questions and to developing a spiritual life of deep integrity. For some, a period away from faith and the practice of faith ensued: for now, at least, sense could be made of life without religious faith. Many return to faith during their studies or later, others give up the faith of their childhood. Some will return much later in life.

Modes of belief

One way of understanding different stages in belief is described by Michael Jacobs and summarised by him in his contribution to *The Spiritual Challenge of Health Care* (1998). Jacobs' psychology of belief and his analysis of ways of believing are described in the context of understanding how people with mental illness approach and view their own ill health. Some of the modes of believing he describes are more conducive to mental well-being than others. How faith affects a student's mental health during the challenging life event of being at university depends partly on their mode of believing and stage of maturity in faith. Jacobs' ideas on modes of believing are summarised below:

Faith as trust and dependency

This mode is characterised by unquestioning trust that God is good, that God provides, that whatever happens is part of God's purpose and, whether we understand it or not, God is working out his purpose. Those who believe this do not need logical explanations for apparent contradictions between articles of faith and experience of the world as it is. One classic contradiction arises when belief in a God of love who is in control of his creation meets the suffering evident in the world. A painful crisis such as the sudden death of a fellow student may cause a student in this mode of believing to question their faith, perhaps for the first time. Because it seems that an absolute belief is called into question, considerable mental distress can be felt, beyond the normal range of feelings in bereavement. More has been lost than is immediately apparent, even to the believer.

Faith as authority or autonomy

This mode is characterised by an awareness of the contradictions that cannot be reconciled within the simple trust of the first mode. This second mode parallels a stage in psychological development where the need is for external authority to give order and meaning to an individual's experience. An external authority can provide safety on the way to autonomy in belief, as in other aspects of personal development. The positive aspects of the mode are reflected in the role of chaplaincy as a 'place of familiarity' described below. The potentially negative aspect is that the external authority can be belief in a rigid set of rules, or membership of a student group with strict rules of membership and a strong culture of conformity, which at its most extreme becomes cult-like. The rules are often assumed in the culture of the group and not made explicit, with the result that students would only know they had contravened them when it was too late and they were excluded from the group. For some this is liberating but others find the experience extremely distressing, especially if they feel they have contravened a religious ideal with ultimate authority. This is not by any means confined to religious groups: political or other groups may exhibit similar traits. As Jacobs says, 'Many of those whose beliefs are either anti-religious or apparently non religious often demonstrate just as great a conformity to cultural norms as many of their counterparts in churches, synagogues, mosques and temples' (p.65).

Competitive and co-operative faith

This mode entails a striving towards autonomy through the mode of belief in which the individual breaks away from conformity to the group. Initially in this stage of the journey, the believer's search for self-determination may mean setting up in opposition to established beliefs. The process of thinking through faith and moving towards autonomy in religious practice can be a lonely time, expressed in the spiritual metaphors of wilderness and pilgrimage, central to the Judaeo-Christian tradition among others. With the security and maturity that the process brings may come a willingness to co-operate with others on the same sort of journey regardless of content of belief or spiritual practice. For students encountering all sorts of new ideas this can be a very exciting time of openness to others' thoughts and understandings without having to defend one's own belief in which there is now more security.

The 'letting go' expression of faith

This mode is characterised by renunciation, by moving beyond our own self-preoccupation, and is experienced as a letting go of the anxiety surrounding belief and spirituality. In my own university work I met few undergraduates at this stage of faith development. I would associate it more with the wisdom of years and variety of experience. In fact, one of the challenges of working with young students is to help them to a realistic perspective of life and faith when they are living in the 'hothouse' environment of student halls and houses, where things take on a very immediate and sometimes disproportionate significance.

These modes of believing offer one useful tool for understanding the sense of personal identity for students with faith or exploring spirituality and questions of faith. Jacobs' analysis offers a context for looking at challenges to identity which some students experience in higher education. Two common responses to challenge that I found were guilt, and a hardening of religious practice as a personal defence. I will look briefly at these before looking at the practical ways in which the chaplaincy sought to help people stay well.

The experience of guilt in spiritual life

It is important to acknowledge at the outset that guilt has a useful part to play in keeping people well and happy in their lives. The guilt arising from doing something we believe to be wrong, from causing hurt or harm to others, from going against the standards and ideals we set ourselves, is a useful and healthy experience, albeit an uncomfortable one. It reminds us of our integrity and the way we should live in order to be true to ourselves. Living a life with which we fundamentally disagree causes great dissonance and something has to be done with those feelings psychologically. If not resolved, such feelings may result in at least a sense of restlessness and unease, and possibly a deeper experience of depression, use of alcohol or drugs to manage or anaesthetise the feelings, and so on. Although there may be illness as a result, this guilt is not pathological in origin. There are other guilt experiences which are unhealthy in origin.

Some of those who came to university as Christians, in the first of Jacobs' modes of believing, active in their home churches and enthusiastic recruits to student Christian groups, found that their complete trust and dependency on God could lead to a sense of guilt arising from an imagined idea of letting God down. Arriving at university may have been the first time that a student had mixed socially – let alone lived with people of other beliefs or indeed no religious faith. For the small minority brought up in a clear Christian tradition there could be guilt about departing from the specific received tradition to which the student belonged. Someone from a more Bible-based tradition might take literally texts about mixing with unbelievers. Some will only choose friends with the same type of faith. Some will find it difficult in a mixed house or hall, especially if sharing a room as many do in the first-year, to find privacy to say their prayers or read their Bibles. Ironically, it is often assumed that members of other faiths will need this privacy and facility but that Christians are mainly non-practising! There may be truth in this but it does not help the first-year Christian student to live as he or she believes God wants them to live.

In some ways this is just one example of cultural and personal differences that all people living communally experience. The difficulty arises only if students place an ultimate significance on their feelings and treat the experience as qualitatively different from the other adjustments they and their fellow students are making. It often feels different, as the context is one of faith and life's biggest questions. Another example of this in my experience arose in helping Roman Catholic students to fulfil their religious duties when travelling in a group without a Catholic priest. Faith and spirituality take on a great significance in personal identity; anything that threatens the way faith is held or practised threatens identity and can cause mental distress in extreme cases. In my experience, most people resolved their feelings in a rational and healthy way and as a chaplain, I would be wanting to strike the balance between respecting a student's faith and helping them to be realistic about what God might want of them. Sometimes this was not possible because my understanding of the locus of authority was different from the student's.

In one case I worked with a student who felt that her lifestyle was disapproved of by God, on the basis of a reading of the teaching of St Paul that I did not share. The student was very distressed by the conflict she felt and I was unable to help her because in my faith perspective there was not such a conflict. After many weeks' work I offered to find her another chaplain to help whose views of the authority of scripture were closer to hers, which offer she accepted. If a student were already under stress, his or her distress might manifest itself around belief and faith, even though religious practice was not the main cause.

The sense of competition among belief systems and the need to defend the integrity of a faith could also lead to guilt. People with a clear idea of who is on the inside and who on the outside of the faith group can feel a deep sense of personal responsibility for getting their peers to join too, and great guilt if they fail to convert them. Some students will want to move into another way of believing and experience some conflict in leaving behind an old way. Although this can be distressing at the time, I found most people quickly accepted this as part of their maturing in faith, unless they were harassed by members of groups to which they had previously belonged (again this applies not only to religious groups, but also to some political groups).

Many young people at university and away from home for the first time experience tensions in becoming independent but the great majority work through them in a healthy way. The potential difficulty for people with religious beliefs is that everything takes on an eternal significance. It can be very difficult to maintain a realistic perspective on these healthy processes when God is involved and God's laws disobeyed, or whatever the student perceives to be happening. Similarly, when academic coursework raises questions about truth, about human nature, questions of ultimate significance, it may seem that it is God who is being attacked. This can be distressing to people of faith. If a student has a philosophical or political belief challenged in the course of study it seems a natural part of the educational process. In contrast, challenging religious belief is sometimes experienced as a much more personal threat, to the believer and also to God.

Most students manage these questions and tensions well enough. Difficulties in a person's state of mind and mental health often presented in a religious faith context when they were not at all connected with faith; in my experience people often knew this. For example, a small number of students I knew who lived with a clinical diagnosis of obsessive compulsive disorder had behaviour which was manifested in the practice of their faith. However, they recognised that faith was not connected with their distress – it was simply the arena where their symptoms presented. It could equally well have been in their studies, or in sport, that obsessive and perfectionist traits were evident, but for them it was religion. For some, obsessive beliefs and behaviours (by which I mean those that interrupted the chosen normal course of a person's daily life) were a sort of refuge to keep them in a familiar though difficult framework. It felt safer than living without the framework. For others, obsessions lived out in a faith or spirituality environment were experienced as a sort of prison: limiting and restricting the student from normal student life. This rigidity of practice, providing protection from the pace and change in student life, is not uncommon in first-year students, and most become more relaxed with experience. One part of our work in chaplaincy is to provide a place, a context for a variety of experiences to help students grow healthily in their faith. The second part of this chapter describes some of the ways this might be accomplished.

Chaplaincy as a place of familiarity

For those who have grown up in a faith community the chaplaincy can offer a place of continuity. This is true in all denominations; if the chaplaincy uses the same sort of liturgy and music as the home church there will be a familiar culture. Some students never go near chaplaincy events for that reason – they are making a break from the things belonging to home and want a complete change, including either a break from church altogether, or to sample a different tradition. It was my experience that for some students, both home and international, being at university presented something of a culture shock. At first excitement might carry people through the change but towards the end of a semester, with deadlines looming, some students would go through typical culture shock reactions: an inability to make simple decisions, losing things, or a difficulty in remembering appointments. For some this was very distressing and such reactions were sometimes taken to be symptoms of a deeper unease or illness, in extreme cases might lead a student to feel he or she simply could not cope with the course. This happens much less as students are more likely to be at university nearer home if not in their home city, and as they are becoming more mobile. The student who arrives in September and does not visit home, family or friends until mid-December is the exception rather than the rule. For those who do feel uprooted, the familiar culture of the chaplaincy can provide a sense of belonging, and contact with other students who have had similar experiences earlier in their university career. This is less in the *content of belief* and more in *the culture* of eating together, meeting in small groups for fellowship: Bible study, pizza parties, or afternoons out. In Hull, the different denominational chaplaincies had links with local churches which welcomed students and again provided a cultural anchoring place.

Chaplaincy as a context for maturing faith

The challenge for us in chaplaincy was to help students feel familiar and comfortable in the environment we provided and to help them to mature in their faith as they were maturing in other areas of life. In this students learned much from each other: first-year students were supported by others who had already gone through a similar maturing process, and all could call on the support of adult members of local churches, many of whom worked in the university. Staff and students might attend weekday services in the university chapel and then be together in a local church on Sundays. We always sought to help students move towards an adult approach to faith, integrating them with other adults rather than extending the church youth group experience from which they had come. It was a common misconception amongst church people who did not have contact with students that chaplains were running a sort of youth group, but we did not do this in my time. To have encouraged students to stay with the Sunday School or youth group way of being Christians would have done nothing to help them move through the sort of process Jacobs describes. Maturing in faith helped people to develop the mental and emotional robustness they needed to enjoy the challenges, decisions and new relationships they were experiencing. The students themselves ran denominational societies which were affiliated to the student union and to national networks of Christian student societies. To these groups we chaplains acted as a resource.

During my time at Hull the nature of these groups changed. Religious groups, like other student societies, became much more fluid in membership, reflecting the national social trend away from organisations. In the mid-eighties Christian societies, like political groups, had a clear culture and identity that would be easily understood by people in other universities. Angsoc, Cathsoc, Methsoc (the Anglican, Catholic and Methodist Societies) shared a culture and ethos with their equivalent groups in student unions throughout the country – in the same way that the Socialist Worker Student Society, Labour Club, Third World First and other groups did. By the late nineties, students were less likely to belong to groups and be committed to everything that the group did, and were more likely to opt in and out of different events. This called for some changes in the way we resourced student-led activity, and meant that sometimes there was little continuity among students in the chaplaincy from one year to the next. What were our resources on offer to these groups?

Chaplaincy as a resource centre
Offering a wider perspective on life

One resource, links with local churches and adults with faith, I have already mentioned. For those exploring questions of faith for the first time at university, the chaplaincy had much to offer. Above all, we were a constant reminder that there is more to life than what we can see and know, that there is a focus beyond ourselves which can help us to keep a healthy perspective on our own lives. Developing a mature faith to support an adult life was one of our main goals. In taking seriously students' concerns and anxieties, and in bringing to these a faith perspective, we offered some basic training in looking after mental and spiritual health.

An example of this was the 'How to survive Christmas' workshop we used to run in early December. For some students going home at Christmas was stressful: financially, work-wise (in terms of finding space and time to revise), and socially (missing university friends). For students who enjoyed sharing faith with others, the prospect of Christmas with families who had a different perspective, who might not celebrate the religious feast at all, was depressing. For those away from home for the first time there was also the temporary surrender of newly-found independence. Some enjoyed going home to be pampered – others struggled to be seen as adults in their families. In the workshop we looked at these issues, worked with students to see things from their parents' point of view as well as their own, and helped them to identify pressure points and coping strategies. Those who had come to university straight from school might have good study skills with the ability to manage work effectively, and yet have few skills in making personal choices and managing emotionally difficult situations.

We offered a similar service in the weeks before exams, encouraging people to keep a healthy balance of sleep and exercise, offering space away from revision, and time for quiet prayer. Later in my time at Hull we stopped doing this and encouraged people to attend the revision work-shops and relaxation sessions put on by the student union and counselling service. In theological terms we tried to put even exams and dissertations in perspective! In the stress of revising and completing coursework, people often became isolated, which could lead to their anxiety getting out of pro-portion. Some students put themselves under unbearable pressure to achieve, and our task was to remind them of their value and worth aside from the class of degree they were hoping to gain. In my own ministry this was very significant.

Much of this side of the work was teaching lifeskills and helping people to develop their own mental and spiritual resources. Often we worked in a similar way to other provision from the student union and the counselling service. Where other agencies might have different philoso-phies about human value and a higher purpose from our Christian belief, we did share a respect for individuals and a desire to empower people in living healthy lives.

The value of spiritual practice

Much of our work involved helping students to grow and sustain a spiritual life, drawing upon the rich heritage of Christian prayer and worship. The discipline of regular private prayer gives many people a focus in the day and a means of rooting and centring the rest of their life. Morning prayer was said most weekdays in the university chapel and a small number of students made this their practice. We did not advocate any one pattern or method of prayer but we were always keen to teach the spiritual traditions of the different Christian denominations. Again, this made us more conservative than some people's image of chaplaincy. Some thought that with younger students we would be encouraging a radical departure from the traditions of the churches, into new ways of ritual and spiritual expression. We found, however, that to be doing new things all the time was unsettling and ultimately unhelpful – people needed to have some grounding in the basics of the traditions before they were free to experiment. Of course, students were all at different phases in their own development and were able to learn much from each other. We encouraged students to attend worship in traditions different from their own, or from what they were familiar with already, not least because different styles suit different personalities, as well as the varied modes of belief.

Public worship was offered in the university chapel using the forms of service provided by the denominations. Students organised less formal worship in the chapel and in other places: halls of residence, chaplaincy buildings, local churches and church halls. There was a stability and predictability about these rituals that again offered familiarity. It is a function of ritual (and worship in this context is ritual) to hold and contain some experience of life. Regular Sunday and weekday worship held the day-to-day aspects of life, and brought them before God. Occasional services and celebrations held and contained some of the less routine aspects of life.

In churches generally, the pattern of the Christian year provides the seasons of waiting, of celebration, of penitence, and so on. Since the major Christian festivals (Christmas, Easter, Pentecost) all fall outside university teaching time, we brought some smaller festivals into greater focus in order to give ritual expression and containment to some of the big human questions. One example of this was our 'Saints and Sinners' celebration. On 1 November the Church celebrates All Saints, and 2 November is celebrated as the feast of All Souls, both remembering those who have gone before in faith and have died, the famous and the not so famous. We had a celebration at this time, with a meal and worship, giving people a chance to look back over their lives at the people who had been influential. If any had died, this was a ritual context for grieving as well as thanksgiving. Another example was the Shrove Tuesday event, which began as a simple pancake party and grew to include a worship element with opportunity for penitence, celebrating forgiveness and a new beginning. All of these aspects of life are important to the students with whom we worked – deciding on a lifestyle, admitting mistakes, dealing with guilt, grieving friends, grandparents or others who had died. We tried to help students deal with these issues in a healthy way, using the resources of the spiritual traditions in Christianity.

Another context for both teaching the tradition and departing from it, developing new ways of using what was familiar and building on it, was our time on pilgrimage and retreat. Every year there were short three/four day retreats and fellowship weekends, with longer pilgrimages in the vacations. We went to places where the local community was working to reinterpret historic Christian resources for this generation: Lindisfarne, Iona and Taize. These were times of great learning and growth, high points for all of us and pivotal experiences for many of the students.

Community building as a function of chaplaincy

Pilgrimages and retreats were a good way of building community and a sense of belonging. At one national gathering of chaplains, the 'hothouse' metaphor was suggested as a model for chaplaincy; so much of students' experience was heightened in the concentrated span of a term or a semester that keeping a sense of perspective was crucial. One way of getting out of the 'hothouse' was in a commitment to service beyond the confines of the university. Many students offered service through HUSSO, the student-run volunteer organisation, and this we supported. At their chaplain's suggestion we also developed a link with the chaplaincy at a local prison. Again, this was a highly significant piece of work in that it opened to our students a whole new world and a different perspective on life. Students were constantly impressed by how much they had in common with the men in prison, and yet how different were the opportunities given to them. Educationally, financially, socially – so much was open to the students. Regular prison visits brought all sorts of questions about the way our common life is organised: about justice and rehabilitation, and sharing faith with others whose circumstances are so different from our own. In terms of helping students to a realistic perspective on the challenges, opportunities and problems of their own lives, this was one of the best pieces of work we did.

Support during intellectual challenge

As noted above, intellectual challenge to faith can, and probably should arise in the course of study. Students may find themselves forced to a place of growth, moving from one mode of belief to another as a result. Typically, the move would be from faith as authority/autonomy towards the co-operative/competitive mode, which sees the believer becoming self-confident in faith and willing to break from a need to conform.

There is a paradox for Christians in that, although this individual growth is a positive and beneficial development, Christianity is very much a communal religion, both in the present and in the belief in continuing revelation throughout the history of the Church. It is not possible to be an isolationist Christian: faith requires common worship, the sharing of bread and wine in the celebration of the Eucharist and shared Bible study and prayer. Neither is it possible to break from the history of the Church. Christianity cannot be reinvented in our own day; it relies on God's revelation of God's own self throughout history and uniquely in the life, death and resurrection of Jesus. It was central to the work of the chaplaincy to hold people through this process. In practice they were breaking away from dependency on the belief and faith of a group and yet, theologically speaking, were maturing as part of a community of faith. There are metaphors within the Christian texts for this process. In the accounts of the life of the early Church in the Acts of the Apostles and in early Church writings, we read of dissent, of factions of believers choosing to follow this or that preacher, just beginning the process of making faith their own. In the Bible there are stories which reflect this process in the lives of those who encountered Jesus. One of our tasks was to make these stories available in ways that helped students to use the resources of their faith to grow in faith.

One example is the Samaritan woman at the well in Chapter 4 of St John's Gospel. The conversation between Jesus and the woman begins simply enough with him asking her for water. She immediately moves into the territory of theological debate, challenging Jesus with her questions: 'How is it that you, a Jew, ask a drink of me, a woman of Samaria?'; 'Where do you get that living water? Are you greater than our father Jacob?'; 'Sir, give me this water, that I may not thirst, nor come here to draw'. Once she has moved from intellectual questioning into this position of faith, Jesus responds with an insight into her own personal life regarding her marital status. In this she sees the true nature of Jesus: 'Sir, I perceive that you are a prophet'.

In this short dialogue she has already moved to a personal statement of faith and immediately realises she needs to rethink what her own community of faith believes: 'Our fathers worshipped on this mountain; and you say that in Jerusalem is the place where men ought to worship'. She came with faith, but it changes throughout the encounter as she challenges Jesus and questions the beliefs of her community. In her willingness to mature, Jesus reveals himself to her. John ends the account with Jesus saying to the woman, 'I who speak to you am he [the Christ]'.

Another example is the story of the prodigal son and the forgiving father in Chapter 15 of St Luke's Gospel. The story as Jesus tells it is rich in metaphor. Central to it is a man who chooses to make his own way in the world and then comes home to his father's love. For students who felt that they had betrayed an earlier faith by moving from faith as trust and dependency into autonomy and, possibly, into a way of believing that opposed the earlier belief, this parable offers a useful metaphor: the father is always looking out for his son. (It may be a coincidence that he is looking out on the very day the son does come home, or we can assume he looks out every day.) God is greater than any of our ideas about God, and there is always the possibility of a new and deeper way of believing. It is not necessary to be consumed with guilt because we have rebelled and enjoyed challenge and independence (as the son did before his poverty and the famine). The debilitating contrition that could stop people maturing in faith is simply not a part of the story Jesus tells. The encouraging irony for those who have broken with faith, challenged the community of faith and maybe swung to extremes in opposing the earlier belief system, is that it is the older brother (who has stuck to the rules, lived and worked on the farm and challenged nothing) who is consumed with jealousy and unable to trust his father's love. In stories like this, Jesus encourages the move towards maturity in faith, moving beyond an over-anxious desire to please and to conform. He encourages risk-taking as a context for growth in faith and trust in God.

These are just two examples of using the Bible as a resource for developing faith; there are countless other stories with similar potential. For some the authority of the Bible becomes in itself one of the articles of faith that comes under question. We did not support one view of Biblical authority over another, except to maintain that the Bible is the definitive text for the church. Using the texts in different ways helped us to respond to the students' own varied interpretations and to teach them creative ways of engaging with the Bible. This chapter has offered just one way of looking at the process of maturing faith and promoting mental health, in one faith context, and has given a number of examples of the role of chaplaincy in facilitating these processes. There are other models and other appropriate responses – this has what is worked for us.

References

The Bible, revised Standard Edition (1993) London: Collins.
Jacobs, M. (1998) In M. Cobb and V. Robshaw (eds) *The Spiritual Challenge of Health Care.* Edinburgh: Churchill Livingston.

Chapter 13

Responding to Student Suicide

Nicky Stanley and Jill Manthorpe

The phenomenon of student suicide has attracted increasing public concern, sustained in recent years by media coverage of a number of tragic cases. This chapter concludes the final section of this book by examining ways in which higher education institutions (HEIs) can respond to student suicide through developing a focus both on individual students who may be vulnerable and on the needs of staff and students following a suicide. Having considered the extent of suicide and some of the research in this area, we will report the findings of a small-scale study, which offer some indications as to the directions further research and policy developments might take. This study was the fruit of the earlier research project on students' mental health needs described briefly in Chapter 1 (see also, Stanley *et al.* 2000; Stanley and Manthorpe 2001).

When undertaking this research, we were struck by the very vivid accounts of some academics who had supervised students who had taken their own lives. These accounts, often describing events many years distant, left us with the impression that HEIs had not, in the past, offered those affected by student suicides much in the way of support or even debriefing. The study was designed therefore to explore two aspects of student suicide: first, whether it was possible to distinguish factors which contributed to individual students' vulnerability to suicide and which HEIs could feasibly be expected to identify and act upon; second, the response of the institution to the event of a student suicide.

Suicide is a relatively rare event with profound consequences. Research into suicide frequently aims to improve the identification of those who are more likely to take their own lives, in order that preventive interventions can be appropriately targeted at this group. There is considerable interest in using research findings to construct lists of risk factors which can inform preventive strategies (Williams and Pollock 1993; Williams and Morgan 1994). However, in the context of higher education, it is necessary to acknowledge that institutions may be more able to act on some risk factors than others. We would not, for instance, advocate that HEIs should exclude certain groups of people on the grounds that they are more vulnerable to suicide, nor can the majority of HEI staff be expected to have access to individuals' inner thoughts or family histories. Therefore, in exploring what we have described as 'vulnerability factors', we have focused on those that are both known and susceptible to the influence of HEIs.

Research which examines the impact of suicide on those who are involved with the event, either personally or professionally, is less common although there have been several powerful personal accounts published (Wertheimer 1991). Margaret Harvey's chapter in the first section of this book brings together a number of such narratives. However, developing strategies for limiting the damage that a suicide leaves in its wake may be the area in which research has most to offer HEIs. This task should not be seen as secondary to that of preventing individual deaths; it is the other side of the coin, but one that is frequently undervalued. Redfield Jamison (2000) quotes Toynbee's (1968) view that those who live through the suicide of a family member or close friend carry the brunt of suffering and describes the experience of those who are left behind thus:

> They are left with the shock and unending 'what if's'. They are left with anger and guilt and, now and again, a terrible sense of relief. They are left to a bank of questions from others, both asked and unasked, about Why; they are left to the silence of others who are horrified, embarrassed or unable to cobble together a note of condolence, an embrace or a comment; and they are left with the assumption by others - and themselves - that more could have been done.

(Redfield Jamison 2000, p.292)

The evidence concerning suicide clusters lends particular urgency to the need for HEIs to focus on the impact of student suicide within the institution. Suicide clusters involve a series of suicides in an area or institution over a limited period of time. They are more likely to occur among young people and there have been some well-documented examples of this phenomenon on university campuses, including six suicides within three months at Michigan State University (Redfield Jamison 2000) and several between 1992 and 1994 at Oxford University (Bell 1996). Such clusters may be partly explained by a susceptibility to imitative behaviour among young people and the removal of some of the inhibitions that normally surround suicide when it occurs close at hand, but a failure to address the feelings evoked by suicide may also be relevant.

The extent of student suicide

As with community studies of suicide, there are considerable difficulties in establishing reliable figures for student suicide. These difficulties may be explained by a reluctance on the part of coroners to identify suicide in the case of young people, the mobility of the student population and its changing age-profile, which includes increasing numbers of older students. Figures for full-time students in the UK starting their first degree in the year 1999/2000 show that 30 per cent of this cohort of 318,050 was over 20, and the vast majority of the 51,060 first-year post-graduates commencing their studies in the same year were, not surprisingly, also aged over 20 (Higher Education Statistics Agency, 2001). Despite this distribution, the larger part of the student population remains in the under-21 age group.

The student population will therefore reflect the very rapid increase in the suicide rate of young men, which rose by 60 per cent in England and Wales between the periods 1976–1981 and 1986–1991 (Williams and Morgan 1994). McClure's (2001) study showing that the steep rise in suicide rates among 15 to 19 year old males between 1970 and 1990 remained at a high level in the 1990s, is particularly relevant for the student population. Foster's (1995) report on student suicide offered a national picture which suggested increasing rates of student suicide, although the methodology used was somewhat haphazard, as it relied heavily on information supplied by vice-chancellors' offices. Hawton *et al.* (1995) found that, when deaths with open verdicts were taken into account, the suicide rates for students at Oxford University from 1976 to 1990 were no higher than the rates for the same age group in the general population. Moreover, the figures represented a drop when measured against the rates for the 1940s and 1950s at Oxford and Cambridge universities. However, this study was confined to the University of Oxford which may not be representative of the wider student population. With the exception of this study and Bell's account (1996), which is also Oxford-based, there has been very little published work in the UK which has explored either suicide prevention in HEIs, or the institutional response following a student suicide.

Research undertaken in the US suggests that rates of suicidal thinking amongst students may be high. The 1995 National College Health Risk Behavior Survey found that 10 per cent of the 4,600 undergraduates surveyed had seriously considered attempting suicide during the previous 12 months, and 7 per cent had drawn up a plan (Centers for Disease Control and Prevention: Redfield Jamison 2000). Similarly in the UK, the Head of the Counselling and Advisory Service at Westminster University reported that over a third of the students seen in 1995/1996 had discussed suicide (Heyno 1997 in Rana *et al.* 1999). Mental illness (particularly depression), self-harm, and alcohol and substance misuse are significantly associated with suicide in young people (Williams and Morgan 1994). This book has provided a substantial amount of evidence concerning levels of mental health problems in the student population. Deliberate self-harm is more prevalent among young people, particularly females (Pritchard 1995), and Chapters 5 and 6 in this volume have examined the high levels of alcohol consumption amongst HEI students. We can therefore conclude that a number of the risk factors for suicide are present in the student population and are likely to be associated with high rates.

The CVCPs' (2000) guidelines have little to say about the institutional response to suicide, noting only that it may be appropriate to lift restrictions on students' rights to confidentiality following an attempted suicide. There is increasing interest in applying risk assessment procedures in the

HEI setting in order to be able to identify particularly vulnerable students; the service described in Chapter 9 of this book provides an example of the application of one such approach. However, it is not always clear with whom such procedures should be used, or what interventions should follow such an assessment. HEIs generally are at an early stage in recognising and thinking through the need for guidance in this area. The findings outlined below are based on a limited number of cases, but offer some directions for further investigation and future policy development.

The study described

The approach used in the study drew on the methodology used in psychological autopsy (Beskow *et al.* 1990) and the critical incident approach (Redpath *et al.* 1997). Two cases of student suicides which had occurred within the last 12 months were selected from two HEIs whose staff had expressed interest in the authors' earlier work on students' mental health needs. Data concerning both the students' behaviour and circumstances and the HEIs' responses to the deaths, was gathered through a series of taped interviews: with HEI staff, including personal tutors and relevant support staff; student union staff; and former students who had known those who died. Details of the two cases are given below, although we have taken care to give anonymity to the institutions and the individuals concerned.

Analysis of the transcripts yields some interesting findings concerning both vulnerability factors, and the elements of what could constitute a positive institutional response in the aftermath of suicide. However, this approach has its limitations. Two cases can do no more than offer pointers for further research; hindsight may have a distorting effect on individuals' recollections of events, and our data draws only on evidence supplied by those who knew the students concerned in the setting of higher education. However, this study does aim to focus on the HEI rather than the community or family response. The research used a number of informants, which allowed for cross-checking of information and for an analysis of the ways in which systems, rather than individuals operated. Staff and former students from both HEIs commented that it had been helpful to reflect on a distressing experience, and to think constructively about the institutional response to death.

Case A: Laura

Laura, aged 20, was studying at a small HEI where a personal approach was possible and evident. She took her own life on campus during a period when most other students were away. She had taken some time out of her programme of study due to mental health problems, but had returned to the course and was managing the academic demands well. In retrospect, it emerged that her history of mental health problems dated back over a number of years.

Case B: Andrew

Andrew was a post-graduate student in his thirties who had turned to study after a period of employment. The HEI was a large institution where students were well-known within their departments but not beyond. He died in the period leading up to examinations in his privately rented accommodation where he lived on his own. The university staff did not know of any mental health problems in respect of Andrew, and none emerged in the enquiries leading up to the inquest or afterwards.

Identifying vulnerability

Caution is necessary in identifying vulnerability factors from just these two cases. It is also essential to recognise that an HEI can only implement preventive approaches for students considered to be at risk of suicide either by offering services to the student population as a whole or to clearly identified groups within that population, or by providing additional support for individual students who request help. However, the two cases discussed here do provide examples of how such approaches might be developed.

Laura had taken time away from her course with the agreement of her tutors. On her return to the HEI, she provided as required, a medical certificate from her doctor stating that she was fit to resume her studies. In retrospect, the staff felt that they might have treated this note as an indication that all was now well, and that her problems had been overcome. One tutor acknowledged a limited awareness of her mental health problems: 'I don't think that I saw the medical certificate... She might have had severe depression.' Although arrangements were made for Laura to have additional contact with the HEI support staff whose services she had used earlier in the year, there was clearly little information available to them concerning the nature of her depressive illness and the risks this might entail for the future. Laura herself communicated to staff the view that her problems were behind her.

A history of depression is clearly associated with the risk of suicide (Williams and Morgan 1994). Maris (1991) has estimated that two-thirds of all those who commit suicide have a depressive illness. Students who take time away from programmes on the grounds of severe depression could be identified as constituting a group vulnerable to suicide. Regular ongoing contact with a mental health professional who could monitor their health might be appropriate; and could perhaps be stipulated as a condition of their return to study. This would naturally need to be negotiated between the HEI and the community mental health services, and would require an established framework of communication within which such arrangements could be constructed. Some of the issues which impinge on the development of such an approach are identified in Colin Lago's chapter in this book.

On resuming her programme of study, Laura moved into a hall of residence with students whom she did not know. She had requested such a room, although they were generally allocated to first-year students. This meant that her timetable was out of step with that of the other hall residents. At the time of her death, according to the student counsellor, the university accommodation was 'very, very deserted and empty'. Laura's death occurred at a weekend when hall staff were also not so evident, and she had told some students that she was going away for the weekend.

In contrast to Laura, Andrew did not emerge from the research as a student about whom there was a history of concern. He had, at the time of his death, been at the HEI for less than a year. He was therefore known to fewer staff, particularly as he had not made use of any support services. As a post-graduate student on a small course, Andrew was not part of a large student grouping. Living on his own, he had no contact with student housing services or flatmates, but was not seen as isolated. A fellow student described him thus:

> ...he was somebody on campus that when I saw him I would have a drink with him in the coffee bar.... It wasn't a terribly close group but it was a very friendly group...it was a nice group to work with.

Andrew died in the period before examinations when there were no regular seminars or lectures. His tutor noted that he was:

> probably a bit isolated over that period when a lot of the other students went away and he was kind of left here, he had decided to stay here and revise for exams...

In both cases, the students' isolation at the times of their deaths was self-imposed. Eglé Laufer's (1995) small study of attempted suicide among adolescents using a specialist support service identifies 'fear of abandonment' (p.111) as the most common factor predisposing young people towards suicide. It is easy to acknowledge how the psychological experience of abandonment might be intensified by the real experience of isolation. HEIs have already recognised the need for additional support for students, particularly international students, who are often alone in student accommodation over the Christmas period, and many provide a range of services targeted on this group. More evidence for the significance of the timing of suicide might suggest that students who remain in student accommodation at any time when the majority of residents are away are vulnerable. Information concerning support and services could be offered to those in university-owned accommodation at such times.

The other factor common to both Andrew and Laura was a high level of need for reassurance. Andrew's tutor provided an account of the student's uncertainty about his academic ability and performance:

> He had decided not to take the exams and really he had sort of given up on revision so when the exams loomed he knew he wouldn't be able to take them and do himself justice. He had already put in one or two essays I believe and they'd been marked with extremely good marks you know - sort of first class sort of ones - and I think he was a bit shocked by this because he found out all of his essays had been marked so highly and I think his expression was 'well this has put a spanner in the works'...I think he had more or less made up this mind and had taken what he

thought were irreversible steps to leave and then he's told: 'you're actually doing very well, you have a future here'...

Similarly, Laura's tutor described her unwarranted anxiety about her academic performance: '...she was doing fine, there was no difficulty about that at all but she would not take it... She wanted to find things that weren't right about it.'

O'Connor and Sheehy (2000) posit an association between perfectionism and suicidal ideation, but this vulnerability factor is hard to detect in the academic setting where all students are encouraged to set themselves high standards. Further investigation of the significance of perfectionism is required, but it is a clear example of a vulnerability factor whose meaning in the HEI context can only be appreciated if it is identified either in combination with other causes for concern, or in a student who is already expressing distress and seeking help.

Co-ordinating the response

Small size and integrated provision in the HEI where Laura was a student may help to explain the high level of co-ordinated response from the institution to her death. The response was managed and appeared to have been sensitive and reflective. These characteristics continued after the immediate events following the death: the funeral and the inquest. The co-ordination involved the student community, and relationships between the college and its external environment. Separate interviews identified a chain of communication which included staff at all levels and students. In this case, the student union was involved as a channel of communication and of support. Three individuals, at senior level, provided the focus and took a co-ordinating role. The welfare head explained:

> We called it the Incident Team and...we met very frequently and made decisions on who was going to do what next... I was involved in informing anybody and everybody...we did it collectively, so for example, informing the students, putting up notices, informing the staff on email, all those kind of things we did jointly, we read wording jointly...the actions were collective...no one person ever took an important decision about a letter...we found it extremely helpful...because these things are very sensitive. One can't afford to get anything wrong.

This team approach – centralised and proactive – was highly valued by those we interviewed. The staff involved saw their role as managing the environment, and illustrated the extent of the work involved: liaison with the police and coroner's office, handling the press, arranging support for students who attended the funeral, and communication with Laura's family.

Not only was this approach viewed as efficient and a way of minimising further distress, it also provided support for the staff involved. For one member of the team, the 'unthinkable was now not unthinkable'. Reflecting on the work of the incident team, he acknowledged that the death had had a 'major effect' on him, and that it had been helpful to talk about it:

> ...we sort of went over things. Probably at the end of the second day to some extent...about 9.30 in the evening, because both were very long days. Sounds awful if that's the case but suddenly there's so much to do and it seems to take so long...we went for a drink away from the place in the evening.

For another member of the team, the impact hit home at the funeral: '...all that weighed very heavily on me and I was very upset. I was never upset in public but privately for a while after that experience.'

This highly co-ordinated response appeared to be mirrored in that of the student union. While the HEI saw itself as offering a range of support – with nurses, chaplains and counsellors available to the students almost instantly – it was some time before these were used. The student union reported a more informal response which coped with the students' immediate distress and practical issues. One union sabbatical officer reported:

> The students came to get me because they knew something was wrong. They had all been told to stay (in a particular place) and knew something was wrong... I had to keep the girls there and shut the door... I went and sat with them.

The union officers then kept in contact with the students:

> I sat up with them most nights...they seemed to use me more than they used services the college put on, like the counsellors and the nurse and that... I think the first night we all slept in one bedroom, just moved all the furniture out...

This union officer was also able to draw on her own support system, describing how she had talked to another officer: '...Dave was as deeply involved as I was. He stepped back so when things were bad I could go and talk to him. And my mum.' The HEI also appeared to have recognised that help was necessary for those providing support:

> (it) sent myself and Dave to the student counsellor a couple of days afterwards when they found out that the students were using us instead of the counsellors. They sent us so that (the counsellors) could put a lot of things straight in our heads. And she kind of conned us really into talking to her. We started off talking about the students and in the end she turned it round to talking about us... I wasn't going to go at first but I came out a lot happier... And she helped us, she put a lot of things straight... We felt we should have spotted it... and she put a lot of things straight there for us, explaining that we wouldn't have spotted it and couldn't have done anything.

The short and long term

Both the staff and the student union identified a range of short- and long-term impacts on the college and students. The death took place in a hall of residence on a relatively small site; this meant that many individuals knew Laura and were soon aware of her death. The co-ordinating approach adopted was able to respond to the need for rapid communication and responses. In the long-term, other predictable issues could be planned and handled sensitively. These included the planting of a commemorative tree in an appropriate location and thinking about the use of the room Laura occupied. The death of another student some months later however, was thought to have affected some students unexpectedly: 'One cried quite openly. He didn't cry at Laura. It was the second one' (student). The union officer referred to a very protective atmosphere among the students which endured throughout their time in higher education and acknowledged that the student union could have been seen as 'smothering' in its concern about their well-being and sociability.

The incident team, some months after the event, took the opportunity to review its response and the institution's relationship with Laura. It realised that there had been a 'dramatic increase' in the numbers of students using the counselling service in the time leading up to the next period of assessment: 'there was very much a heightened awareness of, feeling that perhaps we had major difficulties...' (counsellor). The review also prompted a more formal setting out of policies and procedures: 'We've learnt from the experience, and hopefully, I mean we're very close to what we actually did, so I think organisationally, it's had quite an impact' (Head of Welfare). We have characterised this institution's response as co-ordinated and considered. It took a whole system perspective, encouraging mutual support and aimed to minimise harm. The next case, however, provides an account of another approach.

An ad-hoc approach

Andrew's death was described as a 'tremendous shock' for the academic staff and the students who knew him. However, his personal tutor reported that the impact was limited, as the news was very much confined to the small number of staff and students involved in the course. Other members of the department had not known Andrew, as they were not teaching on his course. The response was an individual one and was very much confined to the personal tutor; some students were informed, but others were not until the start of the teaching session. There was little communication between the academic staff and their colleagues working within the student support or administrative sections of the HEI.

No-one offered the academic staff opportunities to discuss what had happened. The secretaries were told of Andrew's death but, similarly, no support was offered. One academic discussed the death with his wife, who 'had some experience of that kind of thing'. The departure of his colleague soon after the death, removed the opportunity to talk with the only other member of staff who had been closely involved in the discussions with Andrew around his academic progress. Two academic members of staff attended the funeral, which they described as a harrowing experience. A telephone call from the press asking for a photograph of Andrew was seen as particularly insensitive.

This lack of communication continued after the funeral: the personal tutor went on his own to the inquest, with no support or briefing before the event or afterwards. He had felt uncertain about his role:

> I think I was there, I mean I was the only person there from the (HEI), so I did kind of feel I was representing (it) you know when I got there. So that was a little bit uncomfortable in a way.

He described how giving evidence at the inquest had been difficult for him. To his relief however, Andrew's parents had come up to him after the inquest to say that they 'didn't see us as being in any part responsible'.

The research interviews appeared to be the first opportunity for staff in this HEI to reflect on Andrew's death, and the sense of shock was still evident:

> for (my colleague) and myself it was a great, great shock and I don't know how you kind of build this into your job, how you sort of approach your job in the future…

In respect of the students who knew Andrew, the HEI left it to the course leader to think about who to contact and how: one student we interviewed had been telephoned at home and asked to 'pass it on'. She had informed some students and mentioned it to others on the first day back after the assessment period. This had not been easy: '…it's horrible really in a way because it's very difficult to know what to do… Death is not nice for people who are left you know.' She had been able to talk to a family member about it but reflected: 'I think that had I been on my own, it would have been worse in a way you know. I felt that I would want to talk to somebody just really.'

The student had not been advised to make use of the counselling service nor offered any support. The newspaper report of Andrew's death could have been seen by others on the course who had not been contacted. As a group, the students were informed of his death on their return from the break, but there was no opportunity for them to mark this. One academic's observations about the presumed maturity of some students may have been relevant: 'I think post-graduate students are more, there's more of a problem with post-graduates because they are and expect themselves to be more self-sufficient.' At the time, this HEI was one that was heavily reliant on individual staff to provide a response to the death of the student. The staff involved were highly experienced and senior. This might in part account for the fact that they did not receive offers of support, and did not draw on the institution's systems. The risk of further problems or a ripple effect was not considered. For the staff and for the students, a process of self-doubt and questioning emerged as both worried about whether they should have been more alert. It appeared that the student's parents had been able to offer some reassurance concerning this to the tutor who attended the inquest, but this might not have transpired.

This case was not widely known within the institution and no inquiry resulted; there was thus little opportunity to learn from the event. Nonetheless, a series of other incidents and service reconfigurations have resulted in a number of changes within this institution in connection with such incidents. We have returned to this HEI since this research, and have cause for confidence that this ad hoc response would not be replicated in the future. It provided a sobering example, however, of the potential for long-term harm resulting from systems which do not seek to minimise the damage to others from such incidents.

Conclusion

The methodology used in this small study suggests an approach to identifying vulnerability factors which may provide a basis for the development of preventive strategies for HEIs. Such strategies need to be realistic and to address those areas where HEIs can either offer broad interventions which reach vulnerable groups, such as support for students on their own in university accommodation during vacation periods, or target students who are known to support services and can be identified as 'at risk' through evidence of significant numbers and levels of risk factors. These might include a history of depression, self-harm or severe problems of alcohol misuse, or these factors in combination. Further work is needed to identify such factors clearly in the context of HEIs. However, the HEI is likely to require specialist input from external agencies in monitoring and responding to such problems. The CVCP (2000) guidelines encourage HEIs to develop partnerships with such external organisations.

The cases described here give an indication of the need for HEIs to develop policies and guidance on student suicide that embrace all aspects of the institution's work. Such guidelines should define the respective roles of staff following a student suicide and identify the communication channels between them. It may be helpful to designate key individuals as members of a rapid response team in the event of suicide and to specify how such a team would co-ordinate their work. A wide range of staff can be drawn into the tasks of both identifying and supporting vulnerable students and responding appropriately after an individual death. Such staff will include domestic and security staff, academics, accommodation staff, student support staff, chaplains and administrators. Moreover, there is a need to consider the role of the student population and its representatives in developing such guidance. The 'whole institution approach' advocated in Chapter 5 and elsewhere in this book, is relevant to the issue of student suicide, as well as to student mental health problems.

In considering the aftermath of student suicide, the mental health needs of HEI staff come into focus. This volume has, for the most part, confined itself to discussion of students' mental health, although some authors, such as Kathryn James in Chapter 10, have stressed the need for those who support others to receive appropriate professional supervision. The staff and students involved in Andrew's case were clearly left with the long-term emotional consequences, which make it impossible to define suicide as a one-off event (Pritchard 1995). Most HEIs now have support systems in place for staff but, like the student union officers at Laura's university, staff who are actively engaged in helping others may find it hard to seek assistance for themselves. Such support needs to be offered proactively and on an ongoing basis, as the need for professional input may not be felt immediately.

The methodology of the study described here is one which stresses the importance of learning from the tragedies that have occurred. Learning is integral to the task of higher education, therefore the approach is uniquely suited to this sector. It is an approach which can be adapted for use by the individual institution as well as being used in larger scale research studies, and its value lies in offering a voice to a wide range of participants in an event. We were unable to interview parents or relatives for this small-scale study, but their perspectives would provide a useful balance to the views of those within the HEI. A focus on learning avoids allocating blame, and achieves an emphasis on future change and responsiveness rather than past mistakes (Alaszewski and Manthorpe 1998).

The relationship of suicide to mental health problems is a complex one. Although mental health problems are strongly associated with suicidal behaviour (Williams and Pollock 1993), not all those who commit suicide will evince symptoms of mental illness. Laufer (1995), however, argues that the suicidal act always involves a loss of contact with reality for adolescents, and is a sign of acute mental disturbance. In seeking to define the relationship between suicide and mental health problems in sociological, rather than clinical terms, suicide can be seen as the most extreme manifestation of distress in the student population: the 'tip of the iceberg'. The public response to individual suicides mirrors the responses evoked by student mental health problems, with attempts to examine the issue hampered by stigma, shame and sensationalism. O'Connor and Sheehy (2000) emphasise that suicide needs to be normalised and destigmatised, in order that those who are most at risk can access services and support more readily. This plea has echoed throughout this volume with regard to student mental health problems generally.

If mental health problems among students are to be destigmatised, support services need to be available at an early stage and through a wide variety of access points. The 'whole institution' approach emphasised throughout this book aims to provide students in distress with a range of help: other students, teaching and non-academic staff, student support services, primary care and mental health services. However, such a network relies on good communication and co-ordination if it is to be effective. These have often proved elusive, both within HEIs and at the interface between HEIs and community services, but they are increasingly recognised by institutions as essential cornerstones of a mental health strategy.

The pressures on the higher education sector to provide an integrated response to students' mental health needs are profilerating. The chapters in this book have identified multiple external imperatives, including disability legislation, quality assurance processes, social inclusion policies and a move to more consumer-focused services. Many HEIs are already responding to these agendas, but the sector has not as yet become widely involved in the design and provision of mental health services at local or national levels. Further incentives in the form of national guidance or funding opportunities might serve to promote co-ordination at the level of service planning.

Service development needs evidence to inform and shape its growth. This volume has brought together a range of illustrations and research that can be used by HEIs seeking to respond to the pressures described above. The book provides a model of the way in which those in higher education can apply their skills in research and learning to develop their sensitivity to student need. HEIs are organisations dedicated to learning, but the gaze of academia is usually turned outward in study. Learning is increasingly conceived as a life-long process that involves much more than the acquisition of knowledge about the external world: a reflective focus on the internal world of HEIs embodies the self-critical and analytic approach that higher education aims to inculcate.

References

Alaszewski, A. and Manthorpe, J. (1998) 'Welfare agencies and risk: formal structures and strategies.' In A. Alaszewski, L. Harrison and J. Manthorpe (eds) *Risk, Health and Welfare.* Buckingham: Open University Press.

Bell, E. (1996) *Counselling in Further and Higher Education.* Buckingham: Open University Press.

Beskow, J., Runeson, B. and Asgard, U. (1990) 'Psychological autopsies: methods and ethics.' *Suicide and Life-Threatening Behavior 20,* 307–323.

CVCP (Committee of Vice-Chancellors and Principals) (2000) *Guidelines on Student Mental Health Policies and Procedures for Higher Education.* London: CVCP.

Eglé Laufer, M. (1995) 'A research study into attempted suicide in adolescence.' In M. Laufer (ed) *The Suicidal Adolescent.* London: Karnac Books.

Foster, D. (1995) *A Report on the Level of Student Stress and Suicide Rates.* London: House of Commons.

Higher Education Statistics Agency (HESA) (2001) *Students in Higher Education Institutions 1999/2000.* Cheltenham: HESA.

Laufer, M. (1995) 'Understanding suicide: does it have a special meaning in adolescence?' In M. Laufer (ed) *The Suicidal Adolescent.* London: Karnac Books.

Hawton, K., Simkin, S., Fagg, J. and Hawkins, M. (1995) 'Suicide in Oxford University students, 1976–1990.' *British Journal of Psychiatry 166,* 44–50.

Maris, R.F.W. (1991) 'Introduction to a special issue: assessment and prediction of suicide.' *Suicide and Life-threatening Behavior 21,* 1–17.

McClure, G. M. G. (2001) 'Suicide in children and adolescents in England and Wales 1970–1998.' *British Journal of Psychiatry 178*, 469–474.

O'Connor, R. and Sheehy, N. (2000) *Understanding Suicidal Behaviour.* Leicester: BPS Books.

Pritchard, C. (1995) *Suicide – The Ultimate Rejection? A Psycho-Social Study.* Buckingham: Open University Press.

Rana, R., Smith, E. and Walkling, J. (1999) *Degrees of Disturbance: The New Agenda.* Rugby: British Association of Counselling.

Redfield Jamison, K. (2000) *Night Falls Fast.* London: Picador.

Redpath, L., Stacey, A., Pugh, E. and Holmes, E. (1997) 'Use of the critical incident technique in primary care in the audit of deaths by suicide.' *Quality in Health Care 6,*1, 25–8.

Stanley, N., Manthorpe, J. and Bradley, G. (2000) *Responding Effectively to Student Problems: Project Report.* Hull: University of Hull.

Stanley, N. and Manthorpe, J. (2001) 'Responding to students' mental health needs: impermeable systems and diverse users.' *Journal of Mental Health 10*, 1, 41–52.

Wertheimer, A. (1991) *A Special Scar: The Experiences of People Bereaved by Suicide.* London: Routledge.

Williams, R. and Morgan, G. (eds) (1994) *Suicide Prevention: The Challenge Confronted.* London: HMSO.

Williams, J.M.G. and Pollock, L.R. (1993) 'Factors mediating suicidal behaviour: Their utility in primary and secondary prevention.' *Journal of Mental Health 2*, 3–26.

Contributors

Angela Bailey was a full-time chaplain at Hull University for over nine years. An Anglican priest, she now works in two village parishes west of Hull, and as a mental health chaplain in Hull and East Riding Community NHS Trust.

David Brandon trained and worked as a social worker for many years in London and the South-East, particularly in the area of homelessness. He also worked for MIND. Moving to academic life, he was Professor in Community Care at Anglia Polytechnic University, and published widely. He was a former Chair of the British Association of Social Workers and a Zen Buddhist monk.

Annie Grant is Director of the Educational Development and Support Centre at the University of Leicester. She directed a major HEFCE-funded project designed to address student psychological health and promote student well-being. She is a member of the editorial group of CONNECT, the journal of the Association of Managers of Student Services, and has recently been elected to the AMOSSHE Steering Group.

Margaret Harvey is a retired head teacher and a founder member of Papyrus (Parents' Association for the Prevention of Young Suicide). Since the death of her son in 1994, she has been involved with The Compassionate Friends, working on the publications committee to write leaflets and other materials to support bereaved parents and their families.

Lionel Jacobson is a part-time GP and an honorary lecturer at University of Wales College of Medicine in Cardiff. In the latter post he has had a long interest in the health of young people, and has conducted many research projects into the health of teenagers in relation to primary care. He also teaches undergraduate medical students.

Kathryn James set up the Mental Health Support Service at Clarendon City College, New College Nottingham in 1993, and is a regular contributor to debates in further education on the subject of student support. She is currently working as a development officer for the National Organisation for Adult Learning (NIACE).

Colin Lago is Director of the counselling service at the University of Sheffield. He was chair and executive committee member of the Association for Student Counselling, and a founder member and co-chair of the RACE Committee of the British Association for Counselling. He is an accredited counsellor and Fellow of BACP, a registered practitioner with UKRC, and has published widely on counselling, particularly around transcultural concerns.

Jill Manthorpe is Reader in Community Care at the University of Hull. She worked on the HEFCE-funded student mental health project with Nicky Stanley, and has a long-standing interest in student progress matters. She is the author of a number of texts on community care and articles on services and professional education.

Jo Payne is a researcher, consultant and practitioner in the field of mental health. She has worked on developing strategies for carers and is interested in comparative European perspectives on mental health care. She is currently a part-time postgraduate student.

Barbara Rickinson has been Director of student support and counselling at the University of Birmingham since 1990 and has also retained a clinical input to the psychological counselling service. Her main focus during this time has been the facilitation of student learning and development at both an individual and an institutional level.

Ron Roberts is a lecturer in the Social, Genetic and Development Psychiatry Research Centre at the Institute of Psychiatry, London. He has held previous posts at the University of Westminster, University College London, St Bartholomew's Hospital, King's College and the Tavistock Institute. He is the author of a number of articles and books on health psychology and parapsychology.

Nicky Stanley has worked in mental health services and is now a senior lecturer in social work. She managed the project Responding Effectively to Students' Mental Health Needs and has contributed to the development of disability and mental health policies at the University of Hull. She teaches and researches on issues concerning mental health, children and young people.

Jean Turner is Senior Student Support Co-ordinator at the University of Birmingham. She qualified as a social worker in 1989, and worked for six years in the criminal justice system as a probation officer before moving into higher education, initially as a counsellor, and then to the University of Birmingham in 1998 to expand the role of student support. Her current remit includes co-ordination of support for students with mental health needs.

James Wade is Young People's Officer for the National Schizophrenia Fellowship. His work has included mental health promotion in the student community, a national conference examining suicide issues and students' vulnerability, and development of @ease – a website resource for young people. He has worked in the voluntary sector for three years since graduating in his late twenties.

Graeme Whitfield is a Specialist Registrar in CBT at the University of Glasgow. He is a member of the Royal College of Psychiatrists and holds a post-graduate diploma in cognitive behaviour therapy. He is a national committee member of the British Association for Behavioural and Cognitive Psychotherapies. He has a particular interest in mental health services for university populations.

Chris Williams is Senior Lecturer in Psychiatry at the University of Glasgow. His main clinical and research interest lies in the area of cognitive behaviour therapy. He was Chair of the Behavioural and Cognitive section of UKCP 1997–2000 and is President of the British Association for Behavioural and Cognitive Psychotherapies (BABCP).

Christiane Zelenyanszki is a quality assurance facilitator working in the NHS Executive, London. She has particular interests in screening behaviour in cancer services.

Subject index

Author index